PUB QUIZ 2

Collins

First published in 2008 by Collins

Collins is an imprint of HarperCollins Publishers

HarperCollins Publishers
77-85 Fulham Palace Road
London
w6 8jb

www.collins.co.uk

© 2008 HarperCollins Publishers

Created and produced by The Printer's Devil
www.theprintersdevil.co.uk

ISBN 13   978-0-00-728657-7
ISBN 10   0-00-728657-0

A catalogue record for this book is available
from the British Library.

Printed and bound in Great Britain by Clays Ltd,
St Ives plc.

Contents

Introduction

This second volume of Collins Pub Quiz is bigger and better than ever with over 4000 questions on a wide range of topics. Adverts and Art, Food and Drink, Sport and Death, Walt Disney and the Simpsons are all here. How well do you know your British icons? Find out by testing yourself against James Bond, Harry Potter, Doctor Who, Shakespeare and the Beatles. Each double-page spread contains a set of 30 questions on a theme, with a cross-reference to the answers at the back of the book.

New in this volume are the Wildcard sections where there is no single theme: instead, each question is prompted by the answer to the previous one. So for example you could start out the section with a question on Ireland and end up with one on 'Dad's Army'. Or answer a first question about Gene Hunt and a last question about Jane Fonda, working your way through football, flags, theatre, card games and celebrity on the way.

Occasionally you'll find a little bit of extra information in brackets with the answer – for example, a first name where the question only calls for the surname, or an alternative to an imperial or metric measurement. You don't need to give this information to get the answer right – it's usually just there to give you some extra detail.

There's no grading of difficulty in the questions and the span of topics means everyone should find something they're an expert in. So enjoy the quizzes, and good luck!

Quizzes

Quiz 1

1 Who were the composers of 'The Sound of Music'?

2 From what musical comes the anthem 'You'll Never Walk Alone'?

3 Who wrote the script for the Queen musical 'We Will Rock You'?

4 Who wrote the song 'Who Wants to be a Millionaire', featured in 'High Society'?

5 'Mean Green Mother from Outer Space' was specially written for the film version of which stage musical?

6 Paul Michael Glaser found fame in 'Starsky and Hutch' in the late 70s, but in 1971 he was co-star in what Oscar-winning musical?

7 '525,600 minutes, 525,000 moments so dear, 525,600 minutes, how do you measure, measure a year?' This is 'Seasons of Love', from which musical?

8 What actor, later famous for portraying Sherlock Holmes, sang 'On the Street Where You Live' in the movie 'My Fair Lady'?

9 'You're a Grand Old Flag', 'Give My Regards to Broadway' and 'Over There' came from what patriotic American Oscar-winning musical?

10 'If you could see her through my eyes, I guarantee you would fall, If you could see her through my eyes, She wouldn't look Jewish at all.' Name the musical.

11 What award-winning and long-running musical was based on a collection of poems by TS Eliot?

12 What rock opera was written by Pete Townsend and performed by the Who before being made into a movie in 1975?

13 'We'll be over, we're coming over, And we won't come back, we'll be buried over there!' Name the musical these lines come from.

14 From what musical does the song 'Over the Rainbow' come?

15 Norman Jewison's movie adaptation of what musical featured a group of hippies performing it in the desert?

16 This musical featured Ray Charles, Cab Calloway, Aretha Franklin, James Brown, John Lee Hooker and a white R&B band. What is it?

17 'Don't be stupid, Be a smarty, Come and join the Nazi Party!' – lines from 'Springtime for Hitler', in what Mel Brooks musical?

18 Fat Sam's Grand Slam speakeasy in the Prohibition era is the backdrop for this G-rated gangster movie. What is it?

19 This big audience-participation show featured, in its cinema release, Tim Curry as Dr Frank N Furter. What was it?

20 Who plays the mother of Tracy Turnblad in the 2007 movie adaptation of 'Hairspray'?

21 In what kingdom is 'The King and I' set?

22 In what musical do the T-Birds and the Pink Ladies appear?

23 Who wrote the music and lyrics for the hit show and movie 'Mamma Mia!'?

24 What New York-based retelling of 'Romeo and Juliet' won 10 Oscars, though not for its writers, Bernstein and Sondheim?

25 Another 'Romeo and Juliet' story was a massive hit for Disney Channel and proved to be the start of a popular series. What was it?

26 Dorothy followed the Yellow Brick Road with what three companions?

27 What stage show, first performed in 1960, featured child actors such as Phil Collins, Davy Jones, Tony Robinson and Steve Mariott?

28 What song from 'The Lion King' won an Oscar for Elton John and Tim Rice ?

29 He was half of Starsky and Hutch, had two UK no. 1 singles in the 70s and in 2004 starred in 'Jerry Springer: The Opera'. Who is he?

30 The lead in this famous production has been played by Stephen Gately, Philip Schofield, Jason Donovan and Donny Osmond. What is it?

Quiz 2

1 Who was the lead singer of the 70s punk band Generation X?

2 Which vampire in 'Buffy the Vampire Slayer' claimed Billy Idol stole his look?

3 What classic cartoon features a bulldog called Spike?

4 In the nursery rhyme 'Tom, Tom, the Piper's Son', what did Tom steal?

5 In what allegorical novel do the pigs Napoleon and Snowball take over power at the farm on which they live?

6 'Animal Farm' was written by George Orwell. Orwell was a pen name; what was the author's real name?

7 What year did former Prime Minister Tony Blair first become leader of the Labour Party?

8 1994 saw the inauguration of the first black leader of what African country?

9 How many colours are on the South African flag?

10 666 is the Number of the Beast, according to the Bible. What book of the Bible says this?

11 Revelations following a break-in at a Washington hotel in 1972 ultimately led to the downfall of President Nixon. What was the hotel?

12 The Water Gate into the Tower of London became better known by what name?

13 Portuguese footballer Figo was famously branded a traitor in 2000 following his move to Real Madrid from which side?

14 'Barcelona' was a hit in 1987 for operatic soprano Montserrat Caballé and which UK pop singer?

15 Mercury is the planet closest to the Sun. Which one is the next closest?

16 Botticelli's painting 'The Birth of Venus' is held in the Uffizi Gallery. In which city is the Uffizi?

17 Florence Nightingale, the famous nursing pioneer, came to prominence in which mid-19th-century war?

18 What monarch was on the throne during the Crimean War?

19 Victoria is the capital city of which Canadian province?

20 The space shuttle 'Columbia' broke up on re-entry into Earth's atmosphere in 2003, killing its crew. Which shuttle undertook the next mission?

21 'Discovery' was the first ship ever built for a scientific expedition in Britain. Whose voyage was she built for?

22 If you were promoted from the rank of captain in the army, what would your new rank be?

23 The constellation Canis Major was said by the Ancient Greeks to be the hunting dog of which nearby constellation?

24 Orion was a superhero deity who appeared in DC Comics. Who is credited with being DC Comics' first-ever superhero?

25 What was Superman's real name?

26 The foremost see of the Church of England is based in what Kent town?

27 What author wrote 'The Canterbury Tales' in the 14th century?

28 What Geoffrey played the part of Captain Barbossa in 'Pirates of the Caribbean'?

29 The last big gold rush began in 1897 at the Klondike river. What country is the Klondike in?

30 When did Canada gain full independence from the British parliament?

Quiz 3

Name the products behind these classic ad slogans.

1   Labour isn't working.

2   Your flexible friend.

3   It's fingerlickin' good!

4   All Human Life Is Here

5   Never Knowingly Undersold

6   It beats... as it sweeps... as it cleans

7   They're grrrrrreat!

8   Anytime, anyplace, anywhere, There's a wonderful world you can share, It's the bright one, the right one, it's...

9   The totally tropical taste

10 Made in Scotland from girders

11 A million housewives every day...

12 Light up the sky with...

13 Snap... Crackle... Pop!

14 Shhh – you know who

15 'Papa?'... 'Nicole?'...

16 She flies like a bird in the sky

17 Australians wouldn't give a xxxx for anything else

18 Desperation. Pacification. Expectation. Acclamation. Realisation.

19 It's frothy, man

20 I'll be your dog

21 Full of Eastern promise

22 Monsieur, with these – you are spoiling us!

23 Central heating for kids

24 They drink it in the Congo

25 Helps you work, rest and play

26 Splash it all over

27 How do you eat yours?

28 Let the juice loose!

29 Vorsprung durch technik

30 lipsmackin'thirstquenchin'acetastin'motivatin'goodbuzzin'cool-talkin'highwalkin'fastlivin'evergivin'coolfizzin'...

Quiz 4

1   What Wild West outlaw did Sheriff Pat Garrett shoot in 1881?

2   This English poet died of sepsis en route to fight in Gallipoli in 1915. Who was he?

3   Emily Wilding Davidson was the Suffragettes' first public martyr in 1913. How did she die?

4   Reputed overindulgence at a feast caused the death of which all-conquering hero in 323 BC?

5   Three pop stars died in a 1959 plane crash in Iowa. Name one of them.

6   This American outlaw was shot from behind by Robert Ford in 1882 and became the subject of a folk song. Who was he?

7   Two pop stars died in 1974 and 1978 in the same London flat which was owned by singer Harry Nilsson. Name one of them.

8   The Roman writer Pliny the Elder was killed during which famous event in AD 79?

9   What Roman leader killed himself by falling on his sword in 31 BC?

10   What English writer drowned herself in the River Ouse in Sussex in 1941?

11   How did painter Vincent van Gogh die?

12   What Latvian-born American painter died in 1970 after slashing his wrists?

13   What poet composed his own epitaph: 'Cast a cold Eye On Life, on Death. Horseman, pass by'?

14   'A wound over his right eye of the depth of 2 inches and of the width of 1 inch.' Which 16th-century poet died this way in a tavern brawl?

15   What have Star Trek creator Gene Roddenberry and actor James Doohan, who played Mr Scott in the series, had in common since 2006?

16 The last words of which British hero were, 'Thank God I have done my duty'?

17 What Argentinian doctor and revolutionary, one of the 20th century's iconic figures, was executed in Bolivia in 1967?

18 'A Soldier of the Great War Known Unto God'. Which British writer penned this epitaph for unknown soldiers?

19 'Be sure you show the mob my head. It will be a long time before they see its like.' The final words of what French revolutionary?

20 'Go tell the Spartans, stranger passing by, That here, obedient to their laws we lie.' This epitaph by Simonides commemorates what famous battle?

21 What captain's last words were reputed to have been, 'Be British!'?

22 What Ancient Greek philosopher, renowned for his wisdom, was Plato's teacher and was forced to kill himself by drinking hemlock?

23 What American writer suggested for her epitaph both, 'Excuse My Dust' and then 'This Is On Me'?

24 Ancient Greek playwright Aeschylus died in 458 BC when an eagle dropped what object on his head?

25 What seminal 50s rocker died in a taxi accident in Wiltshire 1960?

26 What top-selling rap artist was murdered in a drive-by shooting in Las Vegas in 1996?

27 Three renowned musicians, all age 27, died within a year of each other between 1970 and 1971. Who were they?

28 Whose Latin inscription in St Paul's Cathedral translates as, 'If you seek his memorial, look around you?'

29 What legendary hellraising actor said, 'I've had a hell of a lot of fun and I've enjoyed every minute of it.'

30 Whose gravestone bears the inscription, 'That's All Folks'?

Quiz 5

1   What do the letters in TARDIS stand for?

2   Which writer, who created Blake's 7, also created the Daleks?

3   Who played the sixth Doctor, from 1984 to 1986?

4   What actor played the sixth incarnation of Doctor's nemesis, the Master, on his return in 2007?

5   Which companion has been given her own spin-off series?

6   What planet does the Doctor come from?

7   Former Doctor Who Tom Baker married an actress who played one of the Doctor's companions. Who was she?

8   Up to and including David Tennant, how many Doctors have there been?

9   Brigadier Alistair Gordon Lethbridge-Stewart is head of which organisation?

10   Which former 'Blue Peter' presenter played Steven Taylor, a companion to the first Doctor?

11   Which noted British actor played Professor Yana, an alias for renegade Time Lord, The Master?

12   What writer was given the job of resurrecting the Doctor for a new audience in the 21st century?

13   Who had a no. 1 hit in 1988 with 'Doctorin' the Tardis'?

14   What is the name of the robotic dog owned by the Doctor and, later, companion Sarah Jane?

15   Which actor successfully reincarnated the Doctor in 2005 after a long absence?

16 What 51st-century conman was a companion of the Doctor and became immortal as a result of his adventures on the TARDIS?

17 What award-winning writer was named to take over from Russell T Davies as the show's executive producer for the 2010 series?

18 With which incarnation of the Doctor did his granddaughter appear?

19 With which incarnation of the Doctor did his cloned daughter appear?

20 What was the name of the companion played by comedienne Catherine Tate?

21 What is the maximum number of times that the Doctor can re-generate?

22 If the TARDIS is travelling through a red tunnel in the Time-Space Vortex, is it going forwards or backwards in time?

23 What handy tool can operate a lock, send and receive signals, weld metal, cut and burn, and work as an anti-personnel device?

24 The Fourth Doctor episode, 'City of Death', was written by what popular British comic sci-fi writer?

25 Who are the ruthless enemies of the Doctor who first made their appearance in the 2005 episode, 'Aliens of London'?

26 He created the Daleks and first appeared in the classic 1975 episode, 'Genesis of the Daleks'. What is his name?

27 What companion of the Doctor's was also a Time Lord and able to regenerate?

28 In what city is 'Doctor Who' mostly filmed?

29 The eighth incarnation of the Doctor only ever appeared on screen in Doctor Who: The Movie. Who played him?

30 It's an alien-monitoring organisation and an anagram of 'Doctor Who'. What is it?

Quiz 6

1   Which is the biggest of the Earth's continents?

2   Which of the five major circles of latitude passes through Argentina, Brazil, South Africa and Australia?

3   What mountain range runs down the west coast of South America?

4   If you travel west across the International Date Line, do you gain or lose a day?

5   What is the circumference of the Earth at the Equator? (to the nearest thousand miles)

6   What is the largest lake on Earth?

7   In which direction do tornadoes usually spin in North America – clockwise or anticlockwise?

8   What percentage of Earth's water is freshwater?

9   What is the smallest country in South America?

10 What is the astronomical symbol for Earth?

11 Earth Day is meant to focus attention on environmental issues. What date has been appointed Earth Day?

12 What is the world's most populous city?

13 What term is used when there are two full moons within the same month?

14 What is the lowest-lying body of water on Earth?

15 The deepest point on Earth is over 36,000 ft below sea level in the Pacific. What is the name of this ocean-bed feature?

16 The geological feature called Uluru is also known as what?

17 Is there more, less, or around the same amount of water on Earth now as when the planet was first formed?

18 At what speed does the Earth travel through space (to the nearest 5000 mph)?

19 What is the Earth's biggest ocean?

20 New York is on the same latitude as which European capital?

21 How many major tectonic plates are there on the surface of the Earth?

22 What is the Earth's average surface temperature?

23 What's the Earth's fastest animal?

24 What is notable about Mauna Loa on Hawaii?

25 Which desert is the world's largest?

26 When it is midday in Rio de Janiero, what time is it in Tokyo?

27 Approximately how many billion years old is the Earth?

28 One of the world's largest calderas lies underneath which US national park?

29 What on Earth was Pangea?

30 What famous fictional book described the Earth as 'mostly harmless'?

Quiz 7

1 What battle, lasting three months in 1940, secured Britain from German invasion in the Second World War?

2 What political party seized power in Russia in 1917, consolidating the Russian Revolution?

3 Who was the British Prime Minister when Britain declared war on Germany in 1939?

4 What were members of the Women's Social and Political Union a century ago better known as?

5 Ireland first issued its own stamps as an independent country in what year?

6 The former British colony of Rhodesia declared UDI from Britain in 1967. What does UDI mean?

7 In 1969 Golda Meir became only the third woman prime minister in the world. Of what country was she PM?

8 What year were East and West Germany reunited?

9 The USSR was the Communist Soviet nation. What did its initials stand for?

10 Irish leader Eamon de Valera was saved from execution by the British after the 1916 Easter Rising because of his birthplace. Where was he born?

11 Which British philosopher was a founder member of CND, the Campaign for Nuclear Disarmament, in 1958?

12 What was the Communist-inspired movement started in China in 1966, that attacked the country's traditional practices and beliefs?

13 What Boer War hero founded the Scout Movement in 1907?

14 Who was the Austrian archduke whose assassination in Sarajevo ultimately sparked the outbreak of the First World War in 1914?

15 From what countries did ANZAC troops in the First World War come?

16   What ban came into force in England on 1 July 2007?

17   What event on Oahu island on 7 December 1941 brought it to world attention?

18   What Russian city, besieged by the Germans from 1941 to 1944, was named Leningrad until 1991?

19   What was the only country to hold a referendum in 2008 on the Lisbon Treaty for handing over national powers to the EU?

20   In what year did the Falklands War begin?

21   During the Cold War, what was Checkpoint Charlie?

22   The 18th Amendment to the US Constitution banned it in 1919, and the 21st Amendment legalised it in 1933. What was it?

23   It's known as the Great Sumatra-Andaman earthquake; what natural disaster did it cause in 2004 in the Indian Ocean?

24   What happened in the US on 11th of September, 2001?

25   What two royal couples divorced in 1996?

26   What year saw the first private manned space flight in Space-ShipOne?

27   RAF 617 Squadron, famous for Operation Chastise in 1943, are better known as what?

28   In the US, what did the Warren Commission investigate in 1963–64?

29   What former Pakistani leader was assassinated on 28 December 2007 by a killer who then blew himself up?

30   In what year did Tony Blair step down as British Prime Minister?

Quiz 8

1   'Pugh, Pugh, Barney McGrew, Cuthbert, Dibble and Grub'. Where would you find this team of firefighters?

2   In what modern adults' programme can Zippy and George from 'Rainbow' be seen?

3   'Supercar' was Gerry Anderson's first venture into sci-fi. What year did it start?

4   'As if by magic, the shopkeeper appeared.' On what classic children's animation would you hear this?

5   In what African-set show did Clarence, the cross-eyed lion appear?

6   Who were Andy Pandy's two friends?

7   What creatures began recycling rubbish on Wimbledon Common in 1969?

8   In this year, BBC1 and ITV were broadcasting in colour, and new programmes on British TV were 'Wacky Races', 'The Clangers' and 'Star Trek'. What year was it?

9   This iconic children's show celebrated its 50th birthday in October 2008. What is it?

10 Who was Emily's 'saggy old, baggy old cloth cat'?

11 What did Derek Griffiths, Floella Benjamin, Johnny Ball and Brian Cant all have in common?

12 What classic children's TV character was reported to the police for alleged racism in 2008?

13 'Thunderbirds' five Tracy brothers were Scott, Virgil, Alan, Gordon and John. What distinguished group were the boys named after?

14 'It's Friday, it's five to five...' This was the catchphrase of which show?

15 In what kids' TV show did Jeremy Irons and Anita Dobson, among others, appear?

16 What was the title character in the show 'HR Pufnstuf'?

17 What very useful engine can be found on the island of Sodor?

18 What group of telepaths were called Homo Superiors and operated near an old London Underground tunnel?

19 A stable of Austrian Lippizaner horses were among the stars of what imported TV hit?

20 This glamorous British actress played The Siren on 'Batman' and guest-starred as campaigner Edith Keeler in 'Star Trek' (the original series). Who is she?

21 In what classic animation would you find The Slag Brothers, The Gruesome Twosome and Professor Pat Pending?

22 'Spooks' boss Peter Firth played the leader of a gang of kids whose clubhouse was an old London bus. Who were the gang?

23 'Monty Python' began in 1969 but its forerunner was a 1968 BBC children's show. What was it called?

24 What animated character made her wishes come true by touching the magic wishing flower on her dress?

25 What animated character lived off stolen picnic baskets in Jellystone National Park?

26 Who, according to their theme tune, were the modern Stone Age family?

27 What time-travelling wizard was amazed by 'electrickery' and the 'telling bone'?

28 British secret agents the Thompson Twins appeared in which classic animated series?

29 What was the name of the van driven by Scooby Doo's gang?

30 The creator of 'Brookside' also wrote a children's soap set in a school which ran for 30 years from 1978. What was it?

Quiz 9

1   Who has been the most successful British driver in World Rally Championship races?

2   Which sports league is the world's best attended?

3   The BBC's Sports Personality of the Year is presented annually; but who won the Sports Personality of the 20th Century?

4   In which tournament is the Jules Rimet trophy awarded?

5   Zara Phillips won BBC TV's Sports Personality of the Year in 2006. Which other member of her family was a previous winner?

6   Where are the Commonwealth Games to be held in 2010?

7   In polo, what is a chukka?

8   How many players are there in a shinty team?

9   If you were to score an albatross at a golf hole, what would you have done?

10 What racer has dominated the Tour De France winners' rostrum in this century?

11 What is the only non-English side to play in the County Cricket Championship?

12 Camogie is the women's version of which traditional game?

13 If you are a yokozuna in sumo wrestling, what are you?

14 What colour is the centre target in archery?

15 How many points does a touchdown earn in American football?

16 What name is given to the area in which a cricket ball must be bowled?

17 A black-and-white checkered flag signals the end of a motor race. What does a red flag signify?

18 What is the full name of New York's famous baseball team?

19 In what sport do competitors compete for the America's Cup?

20 Name a sport in which the competitors move backwards.

21 In show jumping, what is the puissance?

22 The backwards-flopping technique used by modern high jumpers is named after its pioneer. Who was he?

23 In ten-pin bowling, what is the maximum number of points that can be scored in a single frame?

24 In darts, what name is given to the board's wire frame?

25 If you play a roquet in croquet, what do you do?

26 What is tack in equestrianism?

27 In cricket, what is a wicket maiden?

28 What sports competitors are not allowed to wear beards?

29 What first did Susan Brown achieve in the 1981 Boat Race?

30 In what sport would you use a besom?

Quiz 10

What is the British English for the following Americanisms?

1 Scuttle butt

2 Alligator pear

3 Pan handler

4 Apple polisher

5 Realtor

6 Bodyshop

7 Broil

8 Weenie

9 Popsicle

10 Jelly

11 Divided highway

12 Tic-Tac-Toe

13 Bleachers

14 Crosswalk

15 Stroller

16 Line

17 Desk clerk

18 Jelly roll

19 Faucet

20 Streetcar

21 Pants

22 Vest

23 Billfold

24 Sedan

25 Traffic circle

26 Wrench

27 Cotton candy

28 Pacifier

29 Longshoreman

30 Overpass

Quiz 11

1   What are the names of Donald Duck's three troublesome nephews?

2   Who was the voice of oversized Southern chicken Foghorn Leghorn?

3   Who was the love rival of Popeye the Sailor Man?

4   What Oscar-winning Japanese animé follows the story of a girl called Chihiro who wanders into the spirit world?

5   What Raymond Briggs story became an Oscar-nominated movie and is shown on Channel 4 each Christmas?

6   How did Spider-Man come by his superpowers?

7   On what planet was Superman born?

8   What writer-artist took Batman back to his dark roots with the mini-series 'The Dark Knight Returns'?

9   What writer created, among others, the Hulk, the X-Men, the Fantastic Four and Spider-Man?

10 When was the Comics Code, designed to regulate the content of US comics, first introduced?

11 What comic-book company published the 'Captain America' comics?

12 What popular cartoon character made his first appearance in the 1940 short 'A Wild Hare'?

13 Whose pet beagle is Snoopy?

14 What John Lasseter-scripted Pixar short starring a toy and a baby won the Best Animated Short Film Oscar in 1989?

15 What is the name of the dinosaur in the 'Toy Story' movies?

16 What graphic novel tells the anthropomorphic story of a Holocaust survivor, with the Jews depicted as mice and the Germans cats?

17 An official report into what event in American history was turned into a bestselling comic by Sid Jacobson and Ernie Colón?

18 What was the name of the police officer in 'Boss Cat'?

19 Who is the author of the syndicated strip featuring the bespectacled engineer Dilbert?

20 What English-born writer created the 'Sandman' series?

21 What British comic magazine which ran from 1846 to 1992, first used the word 'cartoons' for its satirical art, and was famous for its political cartoons?

22 What comic actor played Popeye in a live-action 1980 movie?

23 What is the name of Mickey Mouse's dog?

24 Dennis the Menace lives there and Bash Street School is there; what is the name of this fictional town?

25 First published in 1937, it is British and is the world's longest-running comic. What is it?

26 What snickering American teenagers attend Highland High School, criticise music videos and appeared on MTV in the mid 90s?

27 What Alan Moore and Eddie Campbell novel set in the time of the Ripper murders was made into a film in 2001 starring Johnny Depp?

28 What Steven Spielberg-produced animation featured two genetically enhanced mice, one of them a megalomaniac, living in Acme Labs?

29 What small and resourceful purple dog lives in Nowhere, Kansas, with his owners Muriel and Eustace Bagge?

30 In what story, first seen in 'Scorcher', did a boy own a pair of football boots previously owned by 'Dead-Shot' Keen and which gave him super skills?

Quiz 12

1   In the Second World War, Operation Barbarossa was the codename for what invasion?

2   There are five Foot Guards regiments in the British Army; name three of them.

3   What is unusual about the Duke of Atholl Highlanders?

4   What was the last battle fought on British soil?

5   What was the original name of the RAF?

6   Its codename was Operation Overlord; what was it?

7   Which cavalry regiment do the Life Guards and the Blues and Royals make up?

8   In which conflict was the Battle of Edgehill the first battle to be fought?

9   What name is given to the American Special Forces?

10   What is the name given to the first bugle call of the day?

11   What is the highest rank in the Royal Navy?

12   At what American Civil War battle did General Lee surrender to northern commander General Grant?

13   Which two cities fought in the Punic Wars?

14   The British Army officer training college is Sandhurst; what is the RAF equivalent?

15   Who in the UK is Head of the Armed Forces?

16 The book and movie 'Beau Geste' featured a man who joined which army regiment?

17 What was the name of the British battleship that revolutionised naval warfare in the early 20th century?

18 You'll find a NAAFI services on any British forces base. What does NAAFI stand for?

19 Which English wars did the Battle of Bosworth Field bring to an end?

20 Who was the commander of the British forces during the 1991 Gulf War?

21 Who were the opposing commanders at the crucial Battle of El Alamein in 1942?

22 What name was given to the seven-month period after Britain's declaration of war in September 1939 until the spring of 1940?

23 What war lasted from 1337 to 1453?

24 Utah, Omaha, Gold, Juno and Sword were all what?

25 What name was given to the bloody Chinese nationalist campaign against Westerners and their influence in China from 1899 to 1901?

26 What war did Britain fight from 1775 to 1782?

27 What British gallantry medal bears the words 'For Valour'?

28 'Half a league, half a league, Half a league onward, All in the valley of Death Rode the six hundred.' Tennyson's poem describes which engagement?

29 At what First World War battle was poison gas first used?

30 Who was the Supreme Allied Commander in Europe at the end of the Second World War?

Quiz 13

1 The Irish state broadcaster is RTE. What do the letters RTE stand for?

2 In what year did the Berlin Wall come down?

3 Which car company had classic models called the Capri, the Zephyr and the Zodiac?

4 Which mid-western city in the US has the nickname the 'Windy City'?

5 How much was an old-fashioned farthing worth – a tenth, a quarter or a half of one penny?

6 What did British prime ministers Edward Heath, Arthur Balfour and William Pitt the Younger have in common?

7 What happened to Solomon Grundy on Wednesday?

8 What is the full name of the international organisation ICRC?

9 In the 'Times' newspaper, the clock on the Diary page is always set to the same time. What time?

10 The CND logo was widely adopted as the peace symbol. Which two semaphore letters are used to make the logo?

11 Which medieval English philosopher and Franciscan monk was called Doctor Mirabilis for his work with alchemy and science?

12 Pop star Roy Wood shares his real first name with a James Joyce novel and an Ancient Greek epic poem. What is it?

13 What country buys more newspapers than any other?

14 Who was the inventor of the bouncing bomb dropped by the RAF during the Second World War?

15 In Spain, what status do the letters SA indicate after a company name?

16 What wine comes from Worms?

17 What country is the world's no. 1 car producer?

18 The Italians call this fruit 'ananas'. What do we call it?

19 What British institution is the world's fourth-largest employer?

20 Cartoon character Captain Pugwash is named after a British naval hero. What is his first name?

21 Where can footballers' wives and girlfriends, and everyone else, drive a car with the international oval identifier 'WAG'?

22 What Shakespeare character says the immortal line, 'Friends, Romans, countrymen, lend me your ears'?

23 Where would you find a Rhodes Scholar?

24 To signal using semaphore, what do you use to communicate?

25 Which distinction does the 'London Gazette' newspaper hold?

26 What is the cathedral of the diocese of London?

27 From which London railway station do trains normally leave for Manchester?

28 The 'War Cry' is the newspaper of what religious and charitable organisation?

29 The TGV is France's record-breaking high-speed train. What do the letters TGV stand for?

30 In geometry, what name would you give a triangle in which all the angles are equal?

Quiz 14

1. What gas is needed for combustion to take place?

2. What colour of flame does calcium produce in a flame test?

3. What element is present in every organic compound?

4. Roughly what speed is terminal velocity in human beings?

5. The boiling point of water is 100 ºC. What is that in Fahrenheit?

6. All matter is made up of atoms. What is the centre of each atom called?

7. What metal is the best conductor?

8. There are three metallic liquids on the Periodic Table. Name two.

9. The subatomic particles 'quarks' took their name from a passage written by which Irish author?

10. What name would you give a scientist who studies earthquakes?

11. 'When a force acts on an object, the object exerts equal force in the opposite direction.' What scientific law is this?

12. Simple life forms began to develop on Earth how many thousand million years ago (to the nearest 500 million)?

13. It's the first element in the Periodic Table, with the atomic number 1 and the symbol H. What is it?

14. What name is given to the type of substance, such as wood, that cannot conduct electricity?

15. Radar was first put to good use in Britain during the Second World War. But what does the acronym 'Radar' stand for?

16 What name is given to the type of rock that has been molten then cools to a solid?

17 In chemistry, what are the three possible states of matter?

18 Altocumulus, stratus and cirriform are all types of what?

19 What are the shortest, highest-frequency waves on the electro-magnetic spectrum?

20 Earth's geological history is divided into time periods, such as Jurassic or Carboniferous. What is the present period called?

21 What family has won a hat-trick of Nobel prizes?

22 What gas is used to make dry ice?

23 Earthquakes happen in the southwestern US because of a fault in the Pacific and North American plates. What is the fault called?

24 'If I had only known, I would have become a watchmaker.' What was Albert Einstein talking about?

25 What American astronomer discovered that the Universe is still expanding?

26 Bauxite ore is the main source of what common metal?

27 What everyday item is sand used to make?

28 English physicist James Chadwick was awarded the Nobel Prize for his discovery of what?

29 What is sodium chloride better known as?

30 What name is given to the area on the Earth's surface directly above an earthquake?

Quiz 15

These themes were also chart hits. Name the movies they came from.

1   'Love Is All Around'

2   'Eye of the Tiger'

3   'Everything I Do (I Do It For You)'

4   'My Heart Will Go On'

5   'Beautiful Stranger'

6   'Gangsta's Paradise'

7   'Nothing's Gonna Stop Us Now'

8   'Show Me Heaven'

9   'Stayin' Alive'

10   'Stuck in the Middle with You'

11   'When the Going Gets Tough, the Tough Get Going'

12   'I Don't Want to Miss a Thing'

13   'Build Me Up Buttercup'

14   'Take My Breath Away'

15   'Fight the Power'

16 'Everybody Wants to Rule the World'

17 'I Will Always Love You'

18 'You're the One that I Want'

19 'Lady Marmalade'

20 'Can You Feel the Love Tonight'

21 'Up Where We Belong'

22 'A Whole New World'

23 'Pure Shores'

24 'You Sexy Thing'

25 'Lose Yourself'

26 'Glory of Love'

27 'Power of Love'

28 'I Like to Move It, Move It'

29 '(I've Had) The Time of my Life'

30 'It Had to Be You'

Quiz 16

1   The Western Wall, the Dome of the Rock and the Church of the Holy Sepulchre are all in which city?

2   There are two great Lamas of Tibet. One is the Dalai Lama; who is the other?

3   How is the appointment of a new pope announced?

4   Who is the only Archbishop of Canterbury to be murdered inside his cathedral?

5   This saint is the patron of animals, ecologists and Italy. Who is he?

6   What is the Society of Friends more commonly known as?

7   The Bible states that Joshua brought down the walls of Jericho, but where is modern-day Jericho?

8   King Solomon was famous for his wisdom. Who was Solomon's father?

9   'Thou shalt have no other gods before me.' Which Commandment is this?

10 What is a member of the Society of Jesus generally known as?

11 Who is credited with converting the English to Christianity in the early 7th century?

12 Who nailed his document of 95 Theses to the church door in Wittenberg in 1517, sparking the Protestant Reformation?

13 For how many days does Diwali, the Hindu festival of lights, last?

14 Who is the patron saint of tax collectors?

15 Which book of the Bible has the stories of Noah and the Ark, Abraham, and Joseph and his Many-Coloured Coat?

16 What were Trappist monks not allowed to do by daytime until the 1960s?

17 St Paul was travelling on a road when he experienced his conversion. Where was the road going?

18 According to the Bible, what was Jesus's trade?

19 Which Protestant reformer taught Predestination – that each person was predestined to eternal damnation or salvation?

20 He's the Patriarch of the West, the Primate of Italy and the Bishop of Rome. What is he better known as?

21 What is the name of the tower in a mosque from which Muslims are called to pray?

22 In which Bible book can you read about the Hebrews' escape from Egypt into the desert?

23 What is the name of the seven-branched candelabrum that is an emblem of Judaism and badge of Israel?

24 'Adeste Fideles' is the original Latin version of what famous Christmas carol?

25 Who founded the Christian Science movement?

26 The Christian festival of Easter falls around the same time as what major Jewish festival?

27 What name is given to the week immediately preceding Easter?

28 What is the official name of the Mormon church?

29 Brahma, Vishnu and Shiva are gods in which religion?

30 What Islamic festival requires believers to fast during daylight hours?

Quiz 17

1   Which car, still in production, was born out of Adolf Hitler's desire for a 'people's car' for the working man?

2   If you leave Britain with LAX on your luggage, to what airport are you headed?

3   In Italy, how would you travel on a vaporetto – through the air, on the road or on the water?

4   What is the UK's largest railway station?

5   Quantas, the Australian state airline, is reputedly the world's safest. What do the letters in Quantas stand for?

6   Airship travel ended with the explosion of the Hindenburg. In what year did it happen?

7   The famous clipper 'Cutty Sark' took its name from a reference in which famous poem?

8   Where in Britain is the National Railway Museum?

9   On a ship, what is kept in the binnacle?

10   Alex Issigonis designed which modern British icon?

11   Who made the first non-stop solo Atlantic crossing by aeroplane in 1927?

12   Four British cities have underground railways. One is London; what are the other three?

13   What nationality is El Al airline?

14   What was the nickname of the 1969 Dodge Charger driven by Bo and Luke in 'The Dukes of Hazzard'?

15   The first flights of Concorde and the Boeing 747 took place in the same year. What year was it?

16 To qualify as a veteran, a car must have been built before the end of what year?

17 What was the ship on which Francis Drake sailed around the world in 1580?

18 The 'Rainbow Warrior' was sunk by French intelligence in Auckland harbour in 1985. To which organisation did it belong?

19 In France, what kind of travel service do SNCF run – air, rail, bus or tram?

20 What first made their appearance on car windscreens in 1921?

21 Liverpool's airport was called Speke; what is it known as now?

22 Traffic wardens and parking meters both made their first appearance on British streets in this year. When was it?

23 John Denver wrote a song about the most famous ship of oceanographer Jacques Cousteau. What was it?

24 What was the world's first mass-produced car?

25 Which motorway runs between Cardiff and Swansea?

26 Francis Chichester sailed single-handed around the world in 1966-67. What was the name of his yacht?

27 What colour of light does an aeroplane or ship carry on its starboard side?

28 What was the ship that took Charles Darwin to the South American islands where he made the observations that led to his theories on evolution?

29 In what city would you find Logan Airport?

30 The 'Titanic', which sank in April 1912, was the flagship of which shipping line?

Quiz 18

1. What name is given to a picture painted directly onto a wet-plaster wall?

2. What famous German school of modern art and design was closed by the Nazis in 1933 for being unGerman?

3. 'Chiaroscuro' is a term used to describe painting such as candlelit scenes. What does the word literally mean?

4. What gallery holds Britain's primary collections of modern art?

5. Who painted the famous painting of Henry VIII as a powerful middle-aged man?

6. What two renowned painters would trade insults on the streets of 16th-century Florence?

7. What famous painting by Edvard Munch was stolen from the Munch Museum in Oslo in 2004 and recovered in 2006?

8. With what art movement is Salvador Dali most commonly associated?

9. What sculpture by Anthony Gormley stands on the site of an old mine by the A1 in Gateshead?

10. What was unusual about Van Gogh's painting 'Red Vineyard'?

11. What is the world's largest art gallery?

12. A famous American painting held in the Louvre is officially called 'Arrangement in Grey and Black No. 1'. What is it more commonly known as?

13. In which city can you see da Vinci's painting of 'The Last Supper'?

14. Who painted 'The Last Judgement' on the wall behind the altar of the Sistine Chapel in Vatican City?

15. The 1978 hit 'Matchstalk Men and Matchstalk Cats and Dogs' celebrated the life and work of which English painter?

16   Which Impressionist drew inspiration from his garden at Giverny?

17   What stealthy English street artist's work combines graffiti and stencilling with anti-establishment and satirical themes?

18   What famous Spanish artist was expelled from art school after declaring that his teachers were not good enough to examine his work?

19   A painting by Belarusian painter Marc Chagall was the inspiration for the title of what multi-award-winning musical and movie?

20   Whose finger is Adam's pointing to in the painting 'The Creation of Adam' on the Sistine Chapel ceiling?

21   What Turner Prize-nominated artist famously exhibited a work entitled 'My Bed' at the Tate Gallery?

22   What substance is used for priming a canvas, wood, or other material before it's painted?

23   What American painter's work with horizontal canvases and liquid paint earned him the nickname 'Jack the Dripper'?

24   What black-and-white painting by Picasso depicted Nazi bombing of a Basque town during the Spanish Civil War?

25   What pair, originally known as performance artists, are famous for their photo montages and won the Turner Prize in 1986?

26   What rustic-themed painting by John Constable won second place in a 2005 poll to find the Greatest Painting in Britain?

27   What gallery takes up one side of London's Trafalgar Square?

28   What diminutive Impressionist's paintings of can-can dancers came to represent late-19th-century Paris?

29   What painter depicted the burning of the Houses of Parliament in 1834?

30   What British artist's work typically includes dead animals preserved in formaldehyde?

Quiz 19

Can you name the works these first lines come from?

1   All children, except one, grow up.

2   It is a truth universally acknowledged, that a single man in possession of a good fortune, must be in want of a wife.

3   The great fish moved silently through the night water, propelled by short sweeps of its crescent tail.

4   Robert Langdon awoke slowly.

5   These two very old people are the father and mother of Mr Bucket.

6   Marley was dead, to begin with.

7   Last night I dreamed I went to Manderley again.

8   The Mole had been working very hard all the morning, spring-cleaning his little home.

9   He was an old man who had fished alone in a skiff in the Gulf Stream and he had gone 84 days now without taking a fish.

10   Mathias cut a comical figure as he hobbled his way along the cloisters, with his large sandals flip-flopping and his tail peeping from beneath the baggy folds of an oversized novice's habit.

11   Someone must have been telling lies about Joseph K, for without having done anything wrong he was arrested one fine morning.

12   Once there were four children whose names were Peter, Susan, Edmund and Lucy.

13   Call me Ishmael.

14   Mr and Mrs Dursley of number four, Privet Drive, were proud to say that they were perfectly normal, thank you very much.

15   Amerigo Bonasera sat in New York Criminal Court Number 3 and waited for justice, vengeance on the men who had so cruelly hurt his daughter.

16 In the beginning God created the heavens and the earth.

17 Mrs Rachel Lynde lived just where the Avonlea main road dipped down into a little hollow.

18 It was a bright cold day in April, and the clocks were striking thirteen.

19 Scarlett O'Hara was not beautiful, but men seldom realized it when caught by her charm as the Tarleton twins were.

20 Far out in the uncharted backwaters of the unfashionable end of the Western Spiral Arm of the Galaxy lies a small unregarded yellow sun.

21 Mr Phileas Fogg lived, in 1872, at No. 7, Savile Row, Burlington Gardens, the house in which Sheridan died in 1814.

22 When shall we three meet again, In thunder, lightning or in rain?

23 What passing bells for these who die as cattle? Only the monstrous anger of the guns.

24 It was the day my grandmother exploded.

25 'Mother, have you heard about our summer holidays yet?' said Julian at the breakfast-table. 'Can we go to Polseath as usual?

26 I hope I will be able to confide everything to you, as I have never been able to confide in anyone, and I hope you will be a great source of comfort and support.

27 Lyra and her daemon moved through the darkening Hall, taking care to keep to one side, out of sight of the kitchen.

28 When the doorbell rings at three in the morning, it's never good news. Alex Rider was woken by the first chime.

29 If you want to find Cherry Tree Lane all you have to do is ask the Policeman at the cross-roads.

30 A mouse took a stroll through the deep dark wood. A fox saw the mouse and the mouse looked good.

Quiz 20

1 A KG is a Knight of the Order of the Garter, but what is a KT?

2 'http' appears before most web addresses, but what does it mean?

3 If a child receives the MMR vaccine, what diseases are they inoculated against?

4 Cars over 3 years old in Britain have an MoT certificate. What does MoT stand for?

5 American civil rights campaigner Martin Luther King worked with the NAACP. Who were they?

6 What would you find in an ICU?

7 The FANY, an all-female unit, were founded in 1907 and served with distinction in both world wars. What do the initials stand for?

8 The word 'laser' is an acronym. What do its letters stand for?

9 It was a trendy acronym in the 80s, but what is a DINKY?

10 The letters 'INRI' were inscribed above Jesus's head on the cross. What did the letters stand for?

11 If an American is a member of MADD, to which organisation do they belong?

12 If someone is an FRCP, what would you expect their profession to be?

13 The GAA is which sporting body in Ireland?

14 A senior soldier may have a staff member called an ADC. What do the letters stand for?

15 What do the letters HB in a pencil stand for?

16 If someone has ADHD, what are they suffering from?

17 In computing terms, what does ASCII mean?

18 The BEF were sent to France to fight in 1914 on the outbreak of war. What was their full name?

19 The FTSE 100 Index tracks the country's top traded shares. But what do the letters stand for?

20 Why might you not expect a friendly outcome if a MFH met a member of the LACS?

21 Mad Cow Disease is more properly known as BSE. What do the letters stand for?

22 What is the full name of the type of cycling known as BMX?

23 MRSA virus is a challenge to many British hospitals. What do the letters stand for?

24 P&O is a famous British company. What do the P and O letters stand for?

25 In diving, what does the acronym 'scuba' mean?

26 The letters NB often indicate a point that an author wants to emphasise. What does NB represent?

27 3.26 light years is a parallax second. What is it abbreviated to?

28 What's a shorter way of describing the material Polyvinyl Chloride?

29 In the Second World War, ARP wardens patrolled streets to supervise the Blackout. What do the initials represent?

30 On the back of this book you'll find the numbers that make up its ISBN. What do the letters stand for?

Quiz 21

Identify the following movies by their taglines.

1   May the Force be with you

2   See our family. And feel better about yours.

3   We Scare Because We Care

4   They'll never get caught. They're on a mission from God.

5   Who ya gonna call?

6   Just when you thought it was safe to go back in the water...

7   'For God's Sake, Get Out!'

8   A woman's heart is a deep ocean of secrets

9   Part man. Part machine. All cop. The future of law enforcement.

10 The Devil Inside

11 The Toys Are Back!

12 He was never in time for his classes... Then one day he wasn't in his time at all.

13 Prepare for glory!

14 Fridays will never be the same again.

15 Get Carried Away.

16 He's survived the most hostile and primitive land known to man. Now all he's got to do is make it through a week in New York.

17 With great power comes great responsibility.

18 Break The Codes

19 Four men ride a wild river. A weekend turns into a nightmare.

20 In a world of 1s and 0s... are you a zero, or The One?

21 ...All it takes is a little Confidence.

22 At the End of the World, the Adventure Begins

23 Where History Comes To Life

24 Trick or treat... or die.

25 Their war. Our world.

26 40 stories of sheer adventure!

27 See the movie that's controversial, sacrilegious and blasphemous. But if that's not playing, see...

28 The last man on earth is not alone

29 One Ring To Rule Them All.

30 We've always believed we weren't alone. Pretty soon, we'll wish we were.

Quiz 22

Identify the speakers of these quotes.

1 'Life is what happens to you while you're making other plans.'

2 'Power is the ultimate aphrodisiac.'

3 '...finishing it was the most remarkable feeling I've ever had... When I finished one chapter near the end I absolutely howled.'

4 'When the President does it, it means that it is not illegal.'

5 '1992 is not a year I shall look back on with undiluted pleasure... it has turned out to be an "annus horribilis".'

6 'There is no such thing as society. There are individual men and women, and there are families.'

7 'All I need to make a comedy is a park, a policeman and a pretty girl.'

8 'The Beatles and the Rolling Stones were rulers of pop music, Carnaby Street ruled the fashion world... and me and my brother ruled London. We were f***ing untouchable.'

9 'As I look ahead I am filled with foreboding. Like the Roman, I seem to see "the River Tiber foaming with much blood".'

10 'Vive le Québec libre!'

11 'An alcoholic is someone you don't like who drinks as much as you do.'

12 'I have to inform you that no such undertaking has been received and consequently, this country is at war with Germany.'

13 'I want to be the white man's brother, not his brother-in-law.'

14 'Remember that you are an Englishman, and have consequently won first prize in the lottery of life.'

15 'The nation had the lion's heart. I had the luck to give the roar.'

16 'The worst part of being gay in the 20th century is all that damn disco music to which one has to listen.'

17 'You can get much further with a kind word and a gun than you can with a kind word alone.'

18 'I don't mind how much my ministers talk, as long as they do what I say.'

19 'Hell is other people.'

20 'This above all: to thine own self be true, And it must follow, as the night the day, Thou canst not then be false to any man.'

21 'A week is a long time in politics'

22 'I am the greatest!'

23 'Turn on, tune in, drop out'

24 '...The unacceptable face of capitalism'

25 'Most of our people have never had it so good'

26 'Science without religion is lame, religion without science is blind.'

27 'The way to capture machine guns is by grit and determination.'

28 'Modern art is a disaster area. Never in the field of human history has so much been used by so many to say so little.'

29 'Tough on crime and tough on the causes of crime.'

30 'In the future everyone will be famous for fifteen minutes.'

Quiz 23

Can you name these establishments from TV, the movies and books?

1   Rick's Café Americain

2   The Prancing Pony

3   Central Perk

4   Mos Eisley Cantina

5   The Queen Vic

6   Moe's Tavern

7   Café Nervosa

8   Madam Puddifoot's Tea Shop

9   The Bada Bing Club

10 Luigi's Wine Bar & Restaurant

11 Ten Forward

12 The Rovers Return

13 Lassiter's

14 The Bronze

15 Holt's Diner

16 The Woolpack Inn

17 Pocket and Sweet

18 Louis' Italian American Restaurant

19 Café René

20 The Railway Arms

21 Mrs Miggins' Coffee Shop

22 The Leaky Cauldron

23 The Admiral Benbow Inn

24 Dog in the Pond Pub

25 Fitzgerald's

26 The Bull

27 The Kit Kat Club

28 The Nag's Head

29 The Kebab and Calculator

30 The Gem Saloon

Quiz 24

1   What famous Mongol emperor did explorer Marco Polo meet on his travels in the late 13th century?

2   According to Coleridge's poem 'Kubla Khan', what did Kubla Khan decree in Xanadu?

3   Who was Prime Minister when London's Millennium Dome first opened?

4   Which classic children's TV programme did Tony Hart present with Pat Keysell from 1964 to 1977?

5   In 1858 Bernadette Soubirous had a vision of the Virgin Mary in which French market town?

6   Which pop icon has a daughter named Lourdes?

7   Madonna's 'Like A Prayer' video was voted Most Groundbreaking of All Time in a 2006 MTV poll. What came second?

8   'A Brief History of Time' was on the best-seller lists in Britain for several years. Who wrote it?

9   What is the smallest bird of prey used in hawking in the UK?

10   Merlin was the wizard of which British king?

11   What sacred object did Arthur and his Knights of the Round Table spend years on a quest for?

12   The author of what bestselling novel was sued for allegedly infringing the copyright of the 1980s book, 'The Holy Blood & The Holy Grail'?

13   During the Second World War, Allied codebreakers at Bletchley Park cracked which supposedly unbreakable code?

14   Which mathematician, considered to be the father of computing science, was central to breaking the Enigma Code?

15   Who portrays minor media personality Alan Partridge?

16 Steve Jobs was the founder and CEO of what blue-chip company?

17 Apple Records was the label of which 1960s pop supergroup?

18 What was the name of the first Beatles hit single in the UK?

19 Eros, the Greek God of Love, was the son of Aphrodite, the goddess of Love, and Ares, god of – what?

20 'War is peace. Freedom is slavery. Ignorance is strength.' Which book does this quote come from?

21 The people in 1984 are kept under constant surveillance by which party leader who has also given his name to a popular Channel 4 show?

22 Who first recorded the Grammy-award-winning song about a mining disaster, 'Big Bad John', in 1961?

23 Jimmy Carter was 39th president of the US, from 1977 to 1981. Who was his successor?

24 John Hinckley Jr, convicted of trying to assassinate President Reagan in 1981, claimed he did it to impress which American actress?

25 In the children's nursery rhyme, which town did Dr Foster go to in a shower of rain?

26 Which river does the town of Gloucester lie on?

27 Tolls are collected on the Severn Bridge, but one way only: are they taken crossing into England or into Wales?

28 In what year was Prince Charles invested Prince of Wales?

29 What seminal rock festival, advertised as '3 Days of Peace & Music', was held in New York state in the summer of 1969?

30 Woodstock the bird, named after the rock festival, was a character in which cartoon strip?

Quiz 25

1   What famous cricketer was the first recorded to score six 6s in one over?

2   How many innings are there in a game of baseball?

3   One team has dominated the English Premier League since its inception in 1993. Who are they?

4   There are four boxing regulatory bodies, each with their own championship. Name any two of them.

5   How many players from one team are on the field at any one time in an American football match?

6   Where were the World Fly Fishing Championships held in 2008?

7   Cricket's Twenty20 Cup replaced which trophy after a ban on tobacco advertising in Britain?

8   In racing, at what age does a filly become a mare?

9   Which 1950s British racing driver was four-times runner up but never won the Formula 1 championship?

10   The oldest and youngest winners of the British Open golf tournament were a father and son with the same name. What was it?

11   Which former Olympic swimming champion became a movie star, playing Tarzan?

12   How many players are there in a baseball team?

13   One country has dominated world archery in the 21st century. Which one is it?

14   There are five sports represented in the modern pentathlon. What are they?

15   What baseball team plays at Fenway Park and were winners of the first-ever baseball World Series in 1903?

16 Why was 1890 an important landmark in English competitive cricket?

17 If you were watching the Seasiders play football, who would you be watching?

18 How many points is a field goal worth in American Football?

19 The British Open is golf's oldest major tournament. What's the youngest?

20 Who was the first black player to win a full England football cap?

21 What racecourse is the venue for the Irish Grand National?

22 Which player makes the first move in a chess game?

23 One team dominated Rugby League's Challenge cup with eight consecutive wins from 1988 to 1995. Who were they?

24 What does the 500 signify in the Indianapolis 500 race?

25 Which male golfer has won the most major tournaments in his career up to 2008?

26 There are the four events in women's gymnastics; what are they?

27 This famous yachting competition was founded in 1851 and is held every three or four years. What is it?

28 How many players take to the field for each team in a polo game?

29 What do Imola, Estoril, Monza and Hockenheim have in common?

30 The Tour de France is one of the three major cycle tours. Name one of the other two.

Quiz 26

1   On the London Underground map, what colour is the Central Line?

2   Who defeated Ken Livingstone for the job of London mayor in 2008?

3   At which north London hill does legend say Dick Whittington turned back to the city of which he eventually became lord mayor?

4   In what century was the Tower of London first founded?

5   Monument, in the old City, is 202 feet high and was designed by Christopher Wren. What is it a monument to?

6   Which two royal sisters, both queens, are buried in Westminster Abbey?

7   Designed by architects David Marks and Julia Barfield, it stands near Westminster Bridge and was opened in 2000. What is it?

8   A salute of how many guns is fired for the opening of Parliament?

9   London's Imperial War Museum is housed in the remaining part of what infamous hospital?

10   What famous London church was destroyed in the Great Fire of 1666?

11   It was built to house the Great Exhibition of 1851, gave its name to a football team and burnt down in 1936. What is it?

12   1863 saw the world's first underground railway open in London. One terminus was Farringdon Street; what was the other?

13   Where in London did the fictional detective Sherlock Holmes live?

14   Which poet stood 'Upon Westminster Bridge' in 1802 to write in praise of London?

15   A statue depicting what quality stands outside the Old Bailey in London?

16 What is housed in St Stephen's Tower at the Palace of Westminster?

17 Its terminus until 2007 was Waterloo, but where would you go now to catch the Eurostar?

18 What is One Canada Square in London better known as?

19 True Cockneys are born within the sound of the bells of what church?

20 How many lines are there on the London Underground?

21 What London band had a no. 2 hit in 1967 with 'Waterloo Sunset'?

22 What London hospital was founded in the 12th century?

23 What American actor and director was the driving force for the reconstruction of Shakespeare's Globe Theatre?

24 How many London football teams play in the Premier League?

25 London only became the seat of English government in the 11th century. What town had been the capital until then?

26 What major gallery is located in St Martin's Place?

27 What London street became synonymous with fashion in the 1960s?

28 What famous author lived at 48 Doughty Street?

29 What London museum holds the national collections of design and the arts?

30 What is the only building to have the postcode SW1A 1AA?

Quiz 27

1 It was voted the Best Song of the 20th century, it's the most-covered song in history, the Beatles never released it as a single, and Paul McCartney dreamt it. What is it?

2 The Marmalade had a no. 1 hit in 1969 with what Beatles song?

3 Where did George Harrison meet his future wife, Pattie Boyd?

4 What Indian sitar player was a major influence on the Beatles in the late 60s?

5 Which Beatle was the last one to join the group?

6 Who did Paul McCartney say he had written the Beatles' 1968 single 'Hey Jude' for?

7 What was the Beatles' last chart hit before they split?

8 What musician bought the publishing rights to most of the Beatles' songs in 1985, outbidding Paul McCartney and Yoko Ono?

9 He produced or co-produced all the Beatles' original recordings, playing instruments on some. Who is he?

10 In what year did Paul McCartney marry Linda Eastman?

11 What Welsh singer's 1968 debut single was produced by Paul McCartney, released on the Beatles' own record label and reached no. 1 in the charts?

12 Paul McCartney wrote a song for the duo Peter and Gordon, which reached no. 1 in 1964. What was the song?

13 The Beatles had a record number of consecutive no. 1s from 1963 to 1966. How many?

14 What was the double A side that in 1967 stalled the Beatles' straight run of no. 1s?

15 What Lennon/McCartney song was an early hit for the Rolling Stones?

16 Who had a hit in 1974 with the Beatles' 1967 song 'Lucy in the Sky with Diamonds', featuring John Lennon on guitar and backing vocals?

17 In what year did Paul McCartney form Wings after the break-up of the Beatles?

18 Which Beatle's home, at 251 Menlove Avenue, is now owned by the National Trust?

19 Paul McCartney said of whom, 'If anyone was the Fifth Beatle, it was...' Who did he name?

20 George Harrison's first solo recording after the Beatles split was a worldwide no. 1. What was it?

21 How many children do the Beatles have in total?

22 The Scaffold pop, poetry and comedy trio had a brother of one of the Beatles in their line-up. What is his stage name?

23 'Judy in Disguise (with Glasses)' parodied the Beatles' 'Lucy in the Sky with Diamonds'. Who recorded it?

24 What actress and former Bond girl did Ringo Starr marry in 1981?

25 What was the record label the Beatles set up in 1968?

26 After a course with Maharishi Mahesh Yoga in Rishikesh, which Beatle was reported to have described it as being 'a bit like Butlins'?

27 Which Beatle set up a film production company to finance Monty Python's 'Life of Brian'?

28 What was Ringo Starr's first top 10 hit after the Beatles split?

29 Which blonde bombshell appears in the front row of the group on the cover of 'Sergeant Pepper's Lonely Hearts Club Band'?

30 Which Beatle is left handed?

Quiz 28

1   What is Ireland's most northerly county?

2   What city does the River Lagan flow through?

3   The Irish national anthem is 'Amhrán na bhFiann' but what is its name in English?

4   What traditional instrument is the emblem of the Irish State?

5   What is the name of the Dublin brewery where Guinness is brewed?

6   How many counties of Ulster are not included in Northern Ireland?

7   Ireland's two women presidents to date both have the same first name. What is it?

8   In what county would you find the Blarney Stone?

9   What book by Frank McCourt told of his childhood in Limerick?

10   Where in Ireland was the RMS 'Titanic' built?

11   In what county are the Mountains of Mourne?

12   The Irish pancake boxty is made from what ingredient?

13   What is the only college of Dublin University?

14   What plant is the emblem of St Patrick?

15   What Neolithic passage tomb in County Meath is built in alignment with the midwinter sunrise?

16 How many counties in Ireland are part of the UK?

17 Who was the first First Minister of Northern Ireland?

18 What canal is mentioned in Brendan Behan's song, 'The Auld Triangle'?

19 What 19th-century nationalist song was voted the World's Most Popular Song in a 2002 BBC World Service global poll?

20 What is Ireland's longest river?

21 What song is sung by the all-Ireland national rugby team in addition to the Irish national anthem?

22 From what Dublin building was the Proclamation of the Irish Republic read, marking the start of the Easter Rising of 1916?

23 What was the political party founded by Arthur Griffith in 1905?

24 What is the name of the Irish Parliament?

25 What two Irish leaders died within 10 days of each other during the Irish Civil War in 1922?

26 When did Ireland officially become a republic?

27 The first woman elected to the House of Commons was a Sinn Fein MP. Who was she?

28 What name was given to the period of conflict in Northern Ireland from 1968 to 1998?

29 What was the name of the agreement that brought peace to Northern Ireland in 1998?

30 Ireland is a producer of a high-quality fabric made from flax. What is it?

Quiz 29

1   According to an old British superstition, if you were downcast, what animal was said to be on your shoulder?

2   In Ancient Greek mythology, what type of animal was Pegasus?

3   What is the world's biggest land animal?

4   What is ophidiophobia the fear of?

5   In the 'Tintin' comics, what is the name of Tintin's dog?

6   What type of animal features in the Landseer painting, 'Monarch of the Glen'?

7   Which animal is used in heraldry to represent England?

8   Which Derby winner was allegedly kidnapped by the IRA in 1983 and was never seen again?

9   What was the name of the first dog in space?

10 What is the name of the cat belonging to Hogwarts' caretaker Argus Filch in the Harry Potter series?

11 How many million years were the dinosaurs on earth (to the nearest 10)?

12 In the Christmas story, what animals were said to be present in the stable where Jesus was born?

13 What is the state animal of California?

14 What creatures was it said that St Patrick banished from Ireland?

15 Crimson Rosella, Port Lincoln and Greater Red-Cheeked are all types of what?

16 In which story does the Cheshire Cat appear?

17 The Ancient Greeks believed a fearsome three-headed dog guarded the entrance to Hades. What was his name?

18 What creature was believed to have carried and transmitted the Plague, or Black Death in the 14th century?

19 What British journalist said, 'I don't often agree with the RSPCA as I believe it is an animal's duty to be on my plate at suppertime.'

20 In 'The Lord of the Rings', what was the name of Gandalf's horse?

21 Bengal, Burmese and Abyssinian are all types of what?

22 'The Boy Who Cried Wolf', 'The Wolf in Sheep's Clothing' and 'The Tortoise and the Hare' all come from what collection of moral tales?

23 What name is given to young fish?

24 What type of animal lives in a drey?

25 What book by George Orwell is an allegory on the dangers of Soviet Communism?

26 What animal was said to have been slain by St George, patron of England?

27 If you wore an ermine coat, you'd be wearing the fur of which animal?

28 What is the full name of the pressure group PETA?

29 Where on a horse would you find feathers?

30 Two animals appear on the United Kingdom coat of arms. What are they?

Quiz 30

1 What is the highest mountain in Europe?

2 What is the world's deadliest spider?

3 Which musical act has achieved more UK number 1s than any other?

4 Which Shakespearean character has most lines than any other (in a single play)?

5 Who was the USA's youngest president on taking office?

6 Brazil is the fastest deforesting country in the world. But which is the fastest reforesting?

7 What is the biggest-grossing film of all time?

8 Which industry spends more money advertising its products than any other?

9 What country had the world's first woman prime minister?

10 Who scored more goals throughout his career than any other professional footballer?

11 What is the world's most cultivated cereal crop?

12 At 77, he is the oldest man to have flown in space. Who is he?

13 What was the first British team to win a European footballing competition?

14 What is the world's most poisonous snake?

15 What country has the world's highest Jewish population?

16 What is the most common element in the Universe?

17 According to Interpol, which is the most stolen make of car?

18 What was the first city with a population of over a million?

19 What is Britain's oldest public-access museum?

20 Which country has more pets than any other?

21 Tesco is big in Britain but it's small fry compared to the world's biggest retailer. Who is it?

22 A painting by which artist was the first to sell at over $100 million in public auction?

23 What world boxing heavyweight champion has won most fights ever?

24 What country consumes more coffee per head of population per day than any other?

25 What country has more active volcanoes than any other in the world?

26 What is the world's number one non-food crop?

27 Which country has more native Spanish speakers than any other?

28 Who is estimated to be the world's highest earning sportsman?

29 Which country buys more video games per head of population than any other in the world?

30 Which country produces more films per year than any other?

Quiz 31

1 Rapper Calvin Broadus is better known by what stage name?

2 One of Britain's most famous novelists sometimes wrote under the name 'Boz'. Who was he?

3 Comic-book baddie Oswald Chesterfield Cobblepot is better known by his sinister alias. What is it?

4 Her assumed name was Mary Westmacott but she's far better known by her own name which appeared on dozens of her books. Who is she?

5 Singer Damian Gough performs under what name?

6 Professional wrestler James Helling is better known by his stage name. What is it?

7 Singer and DJ George O'Dowd performs under what instantly recognisable stage name?

8 Cartoon character Billy Batson is better known by what superhero name?

9 This actor's name was Peter Jeremy Huggins. But can you deduce his stage name?

10 The last unelected president of the United States was born Leslie King. By what name is he better known?

11 Sex Pistol Johnny Rotten now goes by his own name. What is it?

12 Turkish hero, patriot and moderniser Mustafa Kemal is better known under what other name?

13 The professional name of actor and martial artist Lee Yuen Kam is well known. What is it?

14 Iconic pop and rock star Alecia Moore is better known under her stage name of – what?

15 His mother knew him as Edson Arantes Do Nascimento. What does the footballing world knows him as?

16 This animated hero's real name was Paul Metcalfe. While he worked for SPECTRUM, he was better known as what?

17 Dwayne Johnson is more recognisable in his professional rose as which actor and wrestler?

18 Cecilia Kalogeropoulos is better known as which 20th-century operatic diva?

19 Rapper and actor Marshall Mathers III goes by what stage name?

20 Ethiopian Emperor Ras Tafari Makonnen is also known by his imperial title of – what?

21 The Clash's John Mellor was better known by what name?

22 Irish-American Sean O'Fearna is one of the great film directors. What name did he go by?

23 This celebrity's own name is Katie Price. What's her professional name?

24 Icelandic-born Magnus Sigursteinnson was one of Britain's best-known TV faces. By what name is he known?

25 Audrey Ruston is seen as the epitome of elegant chic. What's she better known as?

26 Seekers after enlightenment recognise the name Siddhartha Gautama. But he's better known to the world as what?

27 Singer Paul Hewson is better known by his stage name. What is it?

28 Vladimir Ilyich Ulyanov was a pivotal figure in 20th-century history. What does the world known him as?

29 Farrokh Bulsara fronted a famous British rock band of the 70s and 80s. Who was he?

30 This film star had four legs, a rust-and-white coat, communicated with humans and answered to the name 'Pal'. What was the star better known as?

Quiz 32

1   When it was established, the EU was known as the EEC. What do the letters EEC stand for?

2   What famous landmark would you find at Étoile in Paris?

3   In what country is the source of the River Rhine?

4   What is the largest European land animal?

5   What island was awarded the George Cross for bravery in 1942?

6   On what date was the Euro first introduced as currency in affected states?

7   What European country is the world's most popular destination for tourists?

8   The Prado Museum is in which European capital?

9   How many states did Yugoslavia split into between 1999 and 2006?

10 Clear Island is at the southernmost tip of what country?

11 In what year did Ireland join the EEC?

12 Nuuk is the capital of which island country?

13 Which country would you be in if you were reading 'Diario Popular' newspaper?

14 The Greeks call it Kypros and the Turks call it Kibris. What do we call it?

15 What famous European unifier was born on Corsica in 1769?

16 What feature keeps Europe warmer than other places on similar latitudes around the globe?

17 Who were the six original members of the EU's forerunner, the EEC?

18 What country is Bratislava the capital of?

19 Three countries outside Europe are members of the military alliance NATO. Who are they?

20 Which famous church in Istanbul was built as a Christian cathedral, was later a mosque and is now a museum?

21 What city was the West German and then the united German capital from 1949 to 1999?

22 What English architect designed Paris's Pompidou Centre?

23 In which two cities does the EU parliament meet?

24 What Italian island, a resort since Ancient Roman times, has given its name to a pair of cropped trousers and a classic Ford coupé?

25 What European nation has the tallest people in the world?

26 What former British cabinet minister, who resigned from office twice, is now Britain's representative in the European Commission?

27 The centre of what European capital stands on 14 islands?

28 What country was the birthplace of the Renaissance in the 14th century?

29 What country's flag features a blue Scandinavian cross outlined in white and set on a red field?

30 What major contemporary art museum opened in 1997 in Spain's Basque Country?

Quiz 33

1   Under the metric system, how many square metres are there in a hectare?

2   Under the imperial system, how many fluid ounces are there in a gill?

3   What scale is used to judge the strength of an earthquake under the ground?

4   What is the hardest mineral on the Mohs Scale?

5   In geometry, what would you call a four-sided shape where none of the sides are parallel?

6   What measurement on a circle does the calculation pi r squared give?

7   In 1752 the Julian calendar, which was increasingly inaccurate, was dropped in favour of what calendar?

8   If a ship is travelling at 20 knots, how many miles per hour is it doing?

9   What is the name of a unit used to measure energy?

10   The average speed travelled between two points is measured by the distance divided by what other measurement?

11   What is the Dewey Decimal System used to categorise?

12   What name is given to a triangle with three unequal sides?

13   What is the national speed limit on single-carriageway roads in Britain?

14   A horse's height is measured in hands. How wide is a hand?

15   Sound is measured in decibels, with the human voice at roughly 55–65 dB. What level is the pain threshold?

16 Winds of 100 km per hour (roughly 60 mph) would be measured as what on the Beaufort wind scale?

17 What celestial body did navigators traditionally use for night-time navigation?

18 What space in central London was laid out to be a hectare in size?

19 What direction lies at 90° on the compass?

20 How many degrees of longitude equal 1 hour in time?

21 What is the unit of measurement used to measure force?

22 What are the lines on a weather chart which outline areas of similar atmospheric pressure?

23 What number is the International System of Units (SI System) based on?

24 What instrument is used to measure atmospheric pressure?

25 What is the Mercalli Scale used to measure?

26 How many Carats are there in gold that is 100% pure?

27 On which day of the Roman month did kalends fall – beginning, middle or end?

28 What unit of measurement is used to measure power?

29 A barrel of oil contains how many imperial gallons?

30 How many square metres are in an are?

Quiz 34

1   Which fashion shop and label was founded by Barbara Hulanicki?

2   What is the name of the heelless slipper traditionally worn in Turkey and the Arab world?

3   What colour was the cap of liberty worn by supporters of the French Revolution?

4   Americans call them 'suspenders'. What do we call them?

5   In which decade did Levi Strauss first begin producing his denim jeans?

6   If a woman were wearing a mantilla, where would she wear it?

7   How can you tell if a piece of cloth has been cut with pinking shears?

8   Which British designer was the Queen's dressmaker for 50 years?

9   Hawaiian women wear this and so did Homer Simpson in 'The Simpsons' episode 'King-Size Homer'. What is it?

10 What was the name of the cloth bindings that First World War soldiers wound around their lower legs to keep water out of their shoes?

11 This designer's popularity grew after his designs featured in the 1974 movie 'The Great Gatsby'. Who is he?

12 In France it's a sabot; in Holland, a klomp. What do we call this footwear?

13 The skull cap worn by Jewish men is called a what?

14 This iconic French designer who died in 2008, helped popularise high fashion in the 60s with his innovative ready-to-wear clothes. Who was he?

15 Seafarers might wear this waterproof hat with a very broad rear brim. What is it called?

16 Which French designer caused a sensation with his ostentatious New Look after the austerity of the Second World War?

17 'Haute couture is finished because it's in the hands of men who don't like women.' These were the words of which French fashion designer?

18 What part of the body would you wear a wimple on?

19 This cashmere shawl, highly fashionable in the 90s, is made from the underfur of a Tibetan goat. What is it?

20 What name was given to the starched and elaborately folded pieces of fabric worn around the neck in Elizabethan times?

21 What fabric did Roman Emperor Augustus restrict by law because he thought it too effeminate?

22 'I remember every detail. The Germans wore grey. You wore blue.' What movie is this line from?

23 What red, rimless, black-tasselled hat was worn in the Near and Middle East as well as by comedian Tommy Cooper?

24 What designer invented the wrap dress?

25 Where would a warrior normally have worn a torc?

26 'It's always the badly dressed people who are the most interesting.' To what fashion designer are these words attributed?

27 Which fashion designer ran a shop called Sex at 430 King's Road, London, in the 1970s?

28 What was the first fashion house Stella McCartney joined after graduating?

29 Which fashion house produces the perfumes Paris and Rive Gauche?

30 Which British wit is said to have remarked, 'Fashion is what you adopt when you don't know who you are'?

Quiz 35

1   Which classic 80s group had a hit album called 'Lexicon of Love'?

2   She got the boy at the end of 'Gregory's Girl' and she was the lead singer of Altered Images. Who was she?

3   Mary Sandeman had a no. 1 hit in 1981 with 'Japanese Boy'. What was her stage name?

4   Mike and the Mechanics had hits throughout the decade, but which more famous band did Mike also belong to?

5   Kylie Minogue's first UK no. 1 was in the 80s, when she recorded simply as 'Kylie'. What was the song?

6   A group of primary-school children knocked the recently deceased John Lennon off the no. 1 spot in December 1980. With which song?

7   A former member of Clannad reached no. 1 in 1988 with her song, 'Orinoco Flow'. What is her name?

8   This seminal 80s band were a five-piece outfit, with three unrelated members all called Taylor. Who were they?

9   What was the last no. 1 of the 70s that held on to become the first no. 1 of the 80s?

10 Katrina and the Waves represented Britain in the 1997 Eurovision Song Contest. But what was their first 1985 hit?

11 They're twins; one of their songs is a Scotland football 'anthem'; and their first hit, in 1987, was 'Letter from America'. Who are they?

12 When The Tourists split, two members formed a duo that were a defining look and sound in the 80s. Who were they?

13 Which tousle-haired trio, later a massive success in their own right, sang backing vocals on Fun Boy Three's 'It Ain't What You Do...'?

14 Who had three consecutive no. 1s in the early 80s with 'Going Underground', 'Town Called Malice' and 'Beat Surrender'?

15 What band did Mick Jones form after being fired from The Clash?

16 The Irish traditional ballad 'She Moved Through the Fair' provided the music for what Simple Minds 1989 chart-topper?

17 Which 80s song mentions, among other places, Carlisle, Dundee, Leeds, Grasmere and Dublin?

18 Vince Clarke was once a member of this band, writing one of their early hits, 'Just Can't Get Enough'. Who are they?

19 Ultravox's 'Vienna' was famously kept at no. 2 in the charts in 1980 by what novelty no. 1?

20 His band The Teardrop Explodes had a top 10 hit with 'Reward'; he later wrote the bestselling 'The Modern Antiquarian'. Who is he?

21 Which single was trashed on air by Radio 1 DJ Mike Read, banned by the BBC and went on to spend 48 weeks on the charts in 1983–84?

22 Two songs called 'Who's That Girl' were hits in the 80s. Whose made no. 1?

23 What two artists teamed up for the 1982 no. 1, 'Ebony and Ivory'?

24 In 1986 singer Elvis Costello married which member of the Pogues?

25 What singer, herself the daughter of a folk singer, had a hit with Billy Bragg's 'A New England' in 1985?

26 Paul Hardcastle's 1985 hit 'Nineteen' was about the average age of what?

27 How many band members were in the 80s ska group Fun Boy Three?

28 Two English easy-listening artists had a top 10 hit with 'The Skye Boat Song' in 1986. Who were they?

29 She was the face of Chanel perfume Coco; her partner is Johnny Depp; and her first hit was in 1988 with 'Joe Le Taxi'. Who is she?

30 What is the connection between the Style Council and the Jam?

Quiz 36

1. What do the letters in the educational qualification PhD stand for?

2. Only two pieces can make the first move in a chess game. What are they?

3. In what American state would you find Disneyland?

4. What is the only circumstance in which healthy UK drivers are allowed to drive without a seatbelt?

5. What country lies to the east of New Zealand across the South Pacific Ocean?

6. If a pudding is served à la mode, with what accompaniment does it come?

7. What edition of which British soap has pulled in the highest viewing figures ever?

8. Where in Britain would you find the Golden Mile?

9. Where does proper port wine come from?

10. What nationality was Chaim Herzog, sixth president of the State of Israel?

11. What colour is a €20 banknote?

12. How many draughts pieces does a player begin a game with?

13. What major city was originally called New Amsterdam?

14. What famous tourist nightclub in Paris's Montmartre is associated with the dance, the Can-Can?

15. What Italian cheese from Campania is made from buffalo milk?

16 On what continent is the highest mountain outside Asia?

17 Which is the first US state, alphabetically speaking?

18 What is the largest Spanish-speaking country?

19 Is Value Added Tax a direct or an indirect tax?

20 What is the equivalent of a Lord Mayor in Scotland?

21 In which craft would you find garter rib, purled ladder and little pyramid?

22 What religious group meets in Kingdom Halls?

23 What region of France produces wines such as Graves, Sauternes and Médoc?

24 The New York state village of North Tarrytown was renamed what in 1997 in honour of a Washington Irving short story?

25 What British Army institution celebrated its centenary in 2008?

26 How many blue triangles are on the Union Flag?

27 Some systems of proportional representation use the STV system. What does STV stand for?

28 What is the lower house of the American parliament called?

29 What night-time event does a oneirologist study?

30 What North American state or province lies directly across the North Atlantic from Ireland?

Quiz 37

Fill in the missing word in the following sayings.

1 — goes in like a lion and goes out like a lamb.

2 — is the thief of time.

3 A — days' wonder

4 — will move mountains.

5 Zeal without knowledge is like fire without —

6 Revenge is —

7 Rome was not built in —

8 — is mightier than the sword.

9 A stitch in time saves —

10 The road to Hell paved with —

11 What can't be cured must be —

12 Time is a great —

13 — is the mother of invention.

14 Live and let —

15 He who pays the piper calls —

ANSWERS PAGE
301

16 There is more than one way to —

17 Nothing moves faster than —

18 As you —, so shall you reap.

19 — is thicker than water.

20 The apple doesn't fall far from —

21 — is golden.

22 All roads lead to —

23 — always desert a sinking ship.

24 — makes perfect.

25 All that glitters is not —

26 — is the spice of life.

27 You can't — everyone.

28 — is the great leveller.

29 — is the best policy.

30 — helps those who help themselves.

Quiz 38

1 The Pacific Ocean is the world's largest. Roughly what percentage of Earth's surface does it cover (to the nearest 2%)?

2 What country has the greatest area of inland water?

3 What name is given to the stranded loop of a river on a flood plain?

4 Which falls lie between Zambia and Zimbabwe?

5 What sea area lies off Cardiff, Swansea and the north Cornish coast?

6 What is the longest river in the British Isles?

7 In Watch periods at sea, what name is given to the period from 8pm till midnight?

8 The different levels of the ocean are called zones. The Sunlit Zone is top, and 200m deep. What is the next zone?

9 Which river is over 4000 miles long, flows north into the Mediterranean and has the Valley of the Kings on its west bank?

10 What strait lies between North and South Islands of New Zealand?

11 What two pressures cause tides?

12 Multicellular marine algae is better known as what?

13 What is the French name for the English Channel?

14 What two continents does the Bosporus separate?

15 What is the biggest of the five North American Great Lakes?

16 What is the only river that flows both north and south of the Equator?

17 90% of the fresh water in the world can be found where?

18 What sea area lies between Miami, Bermuda and Puerto Rico?

19 The Danish Strait separates what two island countries and former Danish possessions?

20 Roughly what percentage of the Earth's surface is water?

21 Baffin Bay lies between what two oceans?

22 Where around Australia would you find the Bass Strait?

23 Around what latitude is the sea area known as the Doldrums?

24 Daytona Beach, tourist magnet and a home of NASCAR racing, is on the shores of what body of water?

25 What name is given to a high tide when the Sun's gravity reinforces that of the Moon?

26 What David Attenborough series for the BBC explored Earth's seas and oceans and the life in them?

27 The credits to what TV show give a bird's-eye view of the Thames for part of its route?

28 The world's longest coral reef is over 1400 miles long. What is it called?

29 The world's highest free-falling waterfall is the Angel Falls, at 3212 feet. In what country is it?

30 What type of famous sailing ship was used in the New World explorations of the 16th and 17th centuries?

Quiz 39

Identify the movies these famous quotes come from.

1 'I wanted to marry her when I saw the moonlight shining on the barrel of her father's shotgun.'

2 'You're not too smart, are you? I like that in a man.'

3 'You! My room, 10.30 tonight.' (to another) 'You! 10.45. And bring a friend.'

4 'I am no man!'

5 'I'll make him an offer he can't refuse.'

6 'They may take our lives, but they'll never take our freedom!'

7 'I do wish we could chat longer but I'm having an old friend for dinner.'

8 'Look, Heather left behind one of her swatches. She'd want you to have it, Veronica. She always said you couldn't accessorise for shit.'

9 'Marriage is like the Middle East. There's no solution.'

10 'You killed my pine, you space bastard!'

11 'But being as this is a .44 Magnum, the most powerful handgun in the world, and would blow your head clean off, you've got to ask yourself one question: Do I feel lucky? Well, do ya, punk?'

12 'I'll be back.'

13 'Show me the money!'

14 'You're going to need a bigger boat.'

15 'I wish I knew how to quit you.'

16 'I see dead people.'

17 'Pay no attention to that man behind the curtain!'

18 'Leave the gun. Take the cannoli.'

19 'I don't mind if you don't like my manners. I don't like them myself. They're pretty bad. I grieve over them long winter evenings.'

20 'The judge has left town, Harvey's quit, and I'm having trouble getting deputies.'

21 'That's not a laser. It's a little lightbulb that blinks.'

22 'We are the future, Charles. They no longer matter.'

23 'The ground shakes. Drums, drums in the deep. We cannot get out. A shadow moves in the dark. We cannot get out. They are coming.'

24 Are you not entertained? Are you not entertained?! Is this not why you are here?'

25 '...apart from the sanitation, medicine, education, wine, public order, irrigation, roads, the fresh-water system and public health, what have the Romans ever done for us?'

26 'You were only supposed to blow the bloody doors off!'

27 'I hate the British! You are defeated but you have no shame. You are stubborn but you have no pride. You endure but you have no courage. I hate the British!'

28 'Welcome to Sherwood, my lady!'

29 'Why can't I worship the Lord in my own way: by praying like hell on my deathbed?'

30 'Infamy! Infamy! They've all got it in for me!'

Quiz 40

1   What was the first full-length movie made entirely on computer?

2   What satellite broadcast the first TV pictures across the Atlantic and was celebrated in a single by the Shadows in 1962?

3   The first small home computer to sell in great numbers, appeared in 1975. What was called what?

4   How many bits are in a byte?

5   A web address is called a url. What does 'url' stand for?

6   What is the aspect ratio of widescreen view on a UK TV?

7   In a digital image, what is a picture element better known as?

8   In what year was the CD launched?

9   What term, taken from Greek mythology, is used to sneak programs onto a computer by stealth and without the user's consent?

10 The character Forrest Gump from the book and movie of the same name, becomes a millionaire by accidentally buying shares in which company?

11 The World Wide Web was created in 1989 but when was it first released?

12 What name is given to the attempt to inquire sensitive personal information, such as bank account details, by digital scam?

13 In what movie does the hero find himself digitised and forced to play computer games for real by the Master Control Program?

14 What Englishman designed the iMac?

15 Some domain names have country identifiers, such as Britain's (dot) uk. What is Denmark's identifier?

16 If you type in a webpage that cannot be found, what error is returned?

17 AirPort is whose wireless technology?

18 Where in California is Silicon Valley – north or south?

19 What company invented the floppy disk?

20 What word is used in computing terms to describe hostile or malicious software?

21 Where would you be dialling in the UK if the number started with 02?

22 How many colours are used to print a normal colour document?

23 What was the name of the computer that was asked the ultimate answer to Life, the Universe, and Everything in 'The Hitch-hiker's Guide to the Galaxy'?

24 What name is given to the stage of development when software is given a limited public release for testing and refinement?

25 How is the signal carried from a TV remote to the sensor in the TV monitor?

26 What is the name given to those who buy domain names hoping to sell them on at a profit?

27 What does IMAX (of IMAX cinema) stand for?

28 Where in the US is the headquarters of Microsoft Corporation?

29 What name is given to a deliberately hidden message on a CD, DVD, video game or other media?

30 What is the common name for the modulator-demodulator that allows the transmission of information from a computer over a telephone line?

Quiz 41

1   What Italian city is home to the world's biggest opera venue?

2   What love story immortalised by Shakespeare was set in Verona?

3   Romeo is the second son of what famous celebrity couple?

4   In what year did David Beckham play his first Premier League game for Manchester United?

5   A terrorist attack in the US killed 168 people in 1995. In what city did it take place?

6   Oklahoma is one of the central states that suffers most from tornadoes. What is this tornado-prone area commonly called?

7   What classic musical tells the story of a girl blown by a tornado into a fantasy land?

8   Which companion does Dorothy meet first in Oz – the Tin Man, the Scarecrow or the Cowardly Lion?

9   In the classic ITV series about a scarecrow, 'Worzel Gummidge', the lead role was played by what actor?

10 Jon Pertwee is famous for his role as the Doctor in 'Doctor Who'. What incarnation of the Doctor did he play?

11 Released in 2000, what was Robbie Williams' third no. 1 single?

12 What DJ and TV presenter was at one time married to actress Billie Piper?

13 The 'EastEnders' character Pat Evans is played by what actress?

14 St Clement Danes is one of the City of London churches mentioned in what nursery rhyme?

15 Oranges and lemons are a rich source of what important vitamin?

16 Hepatitis C is a disease affecting what organ of the body?

17 What famous former Manchester United winger received a liver transplant in 2002?

18 An airport in what city has been named after George Best?

19 What two-time world snooker champion came from Belfast?

20 Professor Henry Higgins was the leading male character in which Lerner and Loewe musical?

21 What was the 1913 play on which 'My Fair Lady' was based?

22 What Nobel Prize-winning writer was the author of 'Pygmalion'?

23 British actor Martin Shaw is most famous for his role as Doyle in 'The Professionals'. What car is most associated with the show?

24 Capri is an island in what Italian bay?

25 The Bay of Naples was devastated by what natural disaster in AD 79?

26 What god did the Romans believe Mount Vesuvius was home to?

27 What TV show featured a character from the planet Vulcan?

28 What was the subtitle of the original 'Star Wars' movie?

29 Hope is one of the three Christian virtues. What are the other two?

30 What poet compared his love to 'a red, red rose, That's newly sprung in June'?

Quiz 42

1   In motor racing, what name is given to a sharp double bend?

2   What is a strike in baseball?

3   In shinty it's a caman; in hurling it's a hurley. What is it?

4   What is the lightest weight in professional boxing?

5   In bullfighting, it's red on one side, yellow on the other and is called a muleta. What do we know it as?

6   In what year was the London Marathon first run?

7   Who achieved the first televised maximum 147 break in the World Snooker Championship?

8   What does it signify when a skiing piste is graded green?

9   What colours do the Barbarians rugby team play in?

10   Who achieved the first perfect score in a women's gymnastic competition?

11   How many laps of the track do competitors complete in a normal speedway race?

12   When is the start of the grouse-shooting season?

13   Four balls are used in this sport, with two per team; red and yellow play blue and black. What is it?

14   If you use a foil in fencing, which part of your opponent are you allowed to hit?

15   There are two styles of wrestling; name one.

16 In which sport would you see competitors race in six colours according to a draw: red, blue, white, black, orange, and black-and-white stripes?

17 In which sport do competitors stop on the finish line?

18 The longest men's Wimbledon singles final was in 2008; who was the winner?

19 What are the two types of lift in Olympic weightlifting?

20 He was the great-uncle of jazz trumpeter Humphrey Lyttelton and was the first man to represent England at both cricket and football. Who was he?

21 Which sports does the WPBSA administer?

22 The Subalterns' Cup sees teams compete in which sport?

23 It's now been superseded, but what was the Gordon Bennett Trophy awarded for?

24 Who was the first black male singles champion at Wimbledon?

25 Which team was added in 2000 when rugby's Five Nations Championship became the Six Nations?

26 In tennis, what is the women's equivalent of the Davis Cup, with competing international teams?

27 Which gymnast became Britain's first-ever world champion, winning first place in the asymmetric or uneven bars competition in 2006?

28 What trophy do the Scottish and English rugby teams compete for in their Six Nations match?

29 How many Wimbledon singles titles did American Pete Sampras win?

30 What nationality was the first non-British male to win the Wimbledon singles championship?

Quiz 43

1   Which British actor and comic is the author of a series of books featuring young James Bond?

2   Who was the Children's Laureate from 1999 to 2001?

3   Which character lives in Toytown, has a friend called Big-Ears and drives a red and yellow car?

4   In 'The Lion, The Witch And The Wardrobe', the wardrobe is a gateway to which magical land?

5   'The Twelfth Of July', in Joan Lingard's 'Kevin and Sadie' series, is set in which city?

6   Which Mr Man wears a bandage wrapped around his head?

7   Which Canadian province was the setting for 'Anne of Green Gables'?

8   'Harry Potter and the Philosopher's Stone' was given a different title by its US publisher. What was it?

9   What classic story immortalised the ideas of one-legged pirates with parrots, hidden gold on tropical islands, maps marked with an X, and the Black Spot?

10 What preschool-age character has 'nobbly knees and turned-out toes and a poisonous wart at the end of his nose'?

11 What acclaimed children's series features the adventures of Lyra and Will in a set of parallel universes?

12 What animal character lives in the Hundred Acre Wood and is owned by Christopher Robin?

13 What do the letters BFG in the title of the Roald Dahl book stand for?

14 What rhyming story features Thing One and Thing Two, a disapproving fish and an unusual cat?

15 What modern classic novel of boys marooned on an island was itself inspired by the Victorian classic, 'The Coral Island'?

16 What Ian Whybrow character has a wicked uncle called Big Bad and a little brother called Smellybreff?

17 What pop star has written a successful series of books for girls entitled 'The English Roses'?

18 What colour is Thomas the Tank Engine?

19 What boy, created by Francesca Simon, has a tell-tale brother called Perfect Peter?

20 What Hans Christian Andersen fairy story features a penniless soldier, a witch and three magic dogs who guard secret treasure?

21 What is the name of the prep school, created by Willans and Searle, where Nigel Molesworth is a pupil?

22 What traditional story tells of two children who are abandoned by their father, lured into a gingerbread house and fattened up by a cannibalistic witch?

23 What poet and novelist became the Children's Laureate in 2007?

24 Who is the author of 'A Series of Unfortunate Events'?

25 The award-winning 'Erik The Viking' was written by which member of the Monty Python team?

26 In what location was Paddington Bear found sitting on his suitcase?

27 What is the first book in Anthony Horowitz's Alex Rider series, which became a movie in 2006?

28 What Gillian Cross character keeps his school in order with his hypnotic eyes, which he also plans to use for world domination?

29 What two residents of a small Gaulish village resist the might of the Roman Army with the help of magic potion and an endless string of puns?

30 What is the surname of the hero of Richmal Crompton's 'Just William' books?

Quiz 44

1   A beautiful actress and celebrity baker is married to a British satirical cartoonist. Name one of this couple.

2   What is singer Victoria Adams' married name?

3   Actress Lauren Bacall has been married twice: once to Humphrey Bogart, but who was her second husband?

4   Name one of the two famous partners of US actress Farrah Fawcett.

5   Sadie Frost and Jude Law were in the news after their divorce in 2003. But who was Sadie's first husband?

6   The singer Cher has been married twice – famously to her singing partner Sonny Bono, but which musician was her second husband?

7   Angelina Jolie is famous for her celebrity partnership with Brad Pitt. Name one of her other two actor husbands.

8   Who is the musician husband of supermodel Heidi Klum?

9   Actress Heather Locklear had an acrimonious break up with her rock-star husband in 2006. Who was he?

10 Which member of the Bee Gees was Lulu once married to?

11 Who was the wife of Roman general Mark Antony?

12 Which fashion designer was the first husband of 60s singing icon Sandie Shaw?

13 Tennis player Pam Shriver is married to which former James Bond actor?

14 Irish actress Frances Tomelty was the first wife of which English pop star?

15 Uma Thurman divorced her second husband Ethan Hawke in 2004. What English actor was her first husband?

16 Former Doctor Who companion Lalla Ward is married to what biologist and celebrity atheist?

17 Former 'EastEnders' star Shane Richie was previously married to which of the Nolan Sisters?

18 This Scottish Indy 500 winner is married to actress Ashley Judd. What is his name?

19 French President Nicolas Sarkozy married an Italian former model in 2008; who is she?

20 In 2007 Desperate Housewife Eva Longoria married which professional basketball player?

21 Oscar-winning actress Emma Thompson's marriage to actor Greg Wise is her second. Who was her first husband?

22 Chris Martin, lead singer of the band Coldplay, is married to the former fiancée of Brad Pitt. Who is she?

23 Actor Michael Douglas married which Welsh actress in 2000?

24 As Angie in 'EastEnders', she endured a nightmare marriage to Den Watts, but who is Anita Dobson's longer-lasting, real-life partner?

25 Actor Tom Cruise married for the third time to former 'Dawson's Creek' actress Katie Holmes. Name one of his previous wives.

26 Together for years, but they never made it to the altar. What English actress was Hugh Grant's long-time companion?

27 She was born Jacqueline Lee Bouvier and became one of the most iconic women of her generation. Name one of her two husbands.

28 Oasis lead singer Liam Gallagher married for the second time in 2008. Patsy Kensit was his first wife; who is his second?

29 Elvis's daughter Lisa Marie Presley has been married four times. Name her second or her third husband.

30 Two of the wives of Henry VIII outlived him; who were they?

Quiz 45

1   He was known as both Henry McCarthy and William H Bonney, and the nickname he was known by was based on the second of these names. What was it?

2   He was executed for murder, he donated his eyes to science, punk band the Adverts wrote a song about him and his last words were, 'Let's do it'. Who was he?

3   The infamous Alcatraz Prison, now closed, was in what US state?

4   In what year did Britain abolish the death penalty for murder?

5   When did Britain completely remove from the statute books capital punishment under any circumstances?

6   What did Francis Tumblety, George Chapman and Prince Albert Victor all have in common?

7   What iconic US singer became the first ever to perform in California's Folsom Prison?

8   When was the last public hanging in Britain (to the nearest 5 years)?

9   What Russian author wrote the novel 'Crime and Punishment'?

10 What name is given to the punishment that involved being hanged, cut down before death, disembowelled and emasculated while still alive, then cut up?

11 The body of what former British ruler was removed from its Westminster Abbey tomb and hanged, drawn and quartered in 1661?

12 What US serial killer and his gang escaped execution when their convicting state temporarily abolished the death sentence?

13 What famous highwayman was executed for horse-rustling in 1739 in York, where he had fled from London to escape justice?

14 What year did the last executions in Britain take place?

15 What mid 2000s US show revolves around an innocent man sent to death row after a political conspiracy?

16 The theft of £2.6 million from the Glasgow-London post train in 1963 became known as what?

17 With four billion novels sold, what British crime writer is second only to Shakespeare on the best-selling authors' list?

18 Who was the last woman to be hanged in Britain?

19 What British actor was convicted for lewd conduct in a public place with a prostitute called Divine Brown, in 1995?

20 What Nazi propagandist, not actually a British citizen, was hanged in Pentonville Prison for treason in 1946?

21 What king executed Welsh Prince Dafydd ap Gruffydd and Scot Sir William Wallace for treason against England?

22 His books featuring an Oxford police inspector were made into a perenially popular TV show that ran from 1987 to 2000. Who was the author?

23 From which country does Osama Bin Laden come?

24 Who was hanged in 1953 for the murder of a policeman, only to be pardoned 45 years later?

25 What Great Train Robber was a fugitive in Brazil until 2001?

26 The medieval practice of testing a person's innocence by making a person walk over red-hot ploughshares, was known as what?

27 What aristocrat disappeared after apparently murdering his children's nanny in 1974?

28 A Cromwellian law made it illegal to eat what traditional food on Christmas Day?

29 US terrorist Timothy McVeigh was executed for committing the second-worst terrorist act in US domestic history. What was it?

30 What cop works for Lothian and Borders CID, drinks in Edinburgh's Oxford Bar, supports Hibs and is played on TV by Ken Stott?

Quiz 46

1   The former British colony of India is now three separate states. What are they?

2   What Western power did the Vietnamese defeat at the Battle of Dien Bien Phu?

3   What city state lies at the southern end of the Malay Peninsula?

4   What did the country of Siam change its name to?

5   When did the modern State of Israel formally come into being?

6   By what name is the Chinese city of Beijing also known to English speakers?

7   In what country is the temple of Angkor Wat?

8   Which Jordanian rock-built city, now a World Heritage site, was ruled by the Romans then lost to Western view again until the 19th century?

9   What country is the world's biggest coal miner and producer?

10 Under which 18th-century Russian ruler did St Petersburg become the new capital of Russia?

11 Which is further west, Burma or Nepal?

12 When the USSR broke up, how many countries did it split into?

13 What is the biggest city in Asia?

14 The South Vietnamese capital Saigon was renamed after the country's fall in 1975. What is its name now?

15 What is the capital of Turkey?

16 Dubai is a part of which Middle Eastern state?

17 What bay does India's Ganges River flow into?

18 In what year did Hong Kong pass from British into Chinese hands?

19 If you were served Monsoon Malabar from India, what should you expect?

20 What territory did Indonesia occupy from 1975 to 1999, resulting in the deaths of around a tenth of the population?

21 What Indian province has given its name to a bay, a tiger and a cat?

22 The Indian city of Mumbai is better known in the West as what?

23 The Formosa Strait lies between China and what island?

24 The movie 'The Killing Fields' depicted the murderous regime of the Khmer Rouge in what country?

25 In what city is the Bollywood film industry based?

26 What pass through the Hindu Kush mountains separates Pakistan and Afghanistan?

27 What Indian political party, with Ghandi as its unofficial head, led the country to independence from Britain?

28 What country, birthplace of Gengis Khan, lies landlocked between Russia and China?

29 Which Asian nation is made up of 7107 islands?

30 The British founder of Singapore is remembered in the name of the city's most famous hotel. What is it?

Quiz 47

1   The object of this card game is to hold cards with a value as close to 9 as possible. What is it?

2   Name one of the red properties on a traditional Monopoly board.

3   How many tiles are there in a normal set of dominoes?

4   How many squares are there on a chess board?

5   Who is the victim in a game of Cluedo?

6   What number would you have with two little ducks in a bingo game?

7   What is the name of the best possible hand in poker?

8   How many counters has a player in backgammon?

9   How many divisions are there on a European roulette wheel?

10 What are the two letters that carry the highest 10-points value in Scrabble?

11 How many Major Arcana cards are in a tarot pack?

12 Which 1995 movie features a board game where the hazards players face in the game come to life?

13 Which previously popular parlour game involved snatching floating raisins from a jug of flaming brandy and extinguishing them by eating them?

14 What board game was found on board the wreck of the Tudor warship 'Mary Rose'?

15 In what Ingmar Bergman movie does the main character play chess with Death?

16 Which fictional Italian plumber is the mascot of the Japanese videogame company Nintendo?

17 How many rooks are there on a chess board?

18 Which board game is played at competitions and tournaments around the world, has inspired a song and is sold as 'the game that ties you up in knots'?

19 In Scrabble, how many points is the word 'quiz' worth using no blank tiles?

20 What Russian video game, featuring falling blocks dropping into a puzzle, is one of the most popular video games ever?

21 In the 1983 movie 'War Games', what game shows the US military computer the futility of playing the 'game' Global Thermonuclear War?

22 In what series of video games do players create virtual people who can settle in neighbourhoods with families?

23 In what game did Mario make his first appearance?

24 Excluding jokers, how many picture cards are in a normal deck?

25 What is the cheapest property on a classic Monopoly board?

26 Which fantasy role-play game, first published in 1974, set the standard for role-playing war games to the present day?

27 Sonic the Hedgehog is the mascot of what games company?

28 How many cards of the same suit are needed for a flush in poker?

29 What year did Nintendo GameCube arrive on the European market?

30 What are the colours on a Rubik's Cube?

Quiz 48

1   A ship flies the blue peter signal when it's about to do what?

2   What symbol appears in the centre of the Canadian flag?

3   What country's flag features a green cedar tree against a white background?

4   Apart from the flag of Wales, what is the only other national flag to feature a dragon?

5   What two colours feature on the Ukranian flag?

6   What colour is the cross on the flag of Greece?

7   Which is the only state in the USA that still uses the Union Flag on its state flag?

8   Which African country has the first letter of its name set in the centre of its flag?

9   How many stars are on the EU flag?

10   What nation's flag has an outline of the country itself set against a white background?

11   Two European countries have square flags. One is Vatican City; what is the other?

12   How many stars are on the flag of China?

13   What name is given to a national flag that is flown at the stern of a ship?

14   Where on a flag is the fly?

15   What name is given to a string of decorative small flags, commonly triangular in shape?

16 What US state flag features the constellation the Plough set on a blue field?

17 What nickname is given to the traditional pirates' flag of a skull with crossed bones set on a black background?

18 What national flag features the words 'Ordem e Progresso' (Order and Progress) on a central band?

19 What colour of flags are awarded to European beaches to show they have attained a set standard of cleanliness?

20 What two national flags are based on the British Blue Ensign with the Southern Cross in the fly?

21 What national flag is a plain green one?

22 What is the only national flag to feature a human body part?

23 What West African nation has a flag closely modelled on the Stars and Stripes of the USA?

24 What are the traditional pan-Slav colours, shared by many of the Eastern European national flags?

25 What country has a non-rectangular national flag, based on two separate pennants?

26 What are the papal colours, as represented on the flag of Vatican City?

27 What words are inscribed on the California state flag?

28 How many European countries have flags featuring the Nordic cross?

29 The old flag of the Communist USSR was abandoned in what year?

30 What flag is never flown at half mast in Britain?

Quiz 49

1   The Egyptians had two of the Wonders of the Ancient World. What were they?

2   Egyptian royal adviser Imhotep was worshipped as a god. In what 1999 movie was he a main character?

3   The Roman letters LXV represent which number?

4   Which two of the Greek gods were twins?

5   The first month of the year is named after which two-faced Roman god?

6   Ancient Egyptians used a particular plant to make boats, mats, mattresses and paper. What was it?

7   Alpha and beta are the first and second letters of the Greek alphabet. What is the third?

8   Which Greek general founded a new capital by the Nile Delta in the 4th century BC?

9   The Great Sphinx has the head of a human and the body of a what?

10 Who did the goddess Aphrodite promise as a bride for Paris, Prince of Troy, so sparking the Trojan War?

11 Place the empires in chronological order from oldest to youngest: Greek, Roman, Egyptian.

12 Who was the Egyptian god of magic, of the dead and of embalming?

13 What are the two epic Ancient Greek poems that relate the Trojan War and Olysseus's journey home afterwards?

14 Who were the two British men credited with finding the tomb of Pharaoh Tutankhamun?

15 What is the northernmost wall the Romans built in Britain to keep out hostile invaders?

16   Nike was the Greek goddess of what?

17   What did Ancient Egyptian embalmers put in canopic jars?

18   In Ancient mythology, what marked the boundary between the world of the living and the Underworld?

19   Who was the first Roman emperor to set foot in Britain?

20   At which sacred Ancient Greek site would you find the Parthenon, the Erechtheum and the Odeon?

21   In 'The Odyssey', what was the name of Odysseus's ship?

22   The 2007 movie '300' depicted a battle in 480 BC between the Greeks and Persians. What was it?

23   The Greeks knew this god as Eros, but what was his name to the Romans?

24   What was the name of the first ever Roman road, built in the 4th century BC?

25   Which Greek hero killed the Minotaur in the Labyrinth at Knossos on Crete?

26   Which Greek god was believed to give prophecies through his Oracle at Delphi?

27   Who was the Ancient Egyptian sun god, believed to have created himself and everything else?

28   What artefact, found during the Napoleonic War, let scholars decipher Ancient Egyptian hieroglyphs for the first time?

29   What was the Greek state renowned for its martial prowess and whose name became synonymous with harsh conditions?

30   Who was the last ruler of Egypt before it lost its independence to the Roman Empire?

Quiz 50

1   Newly qualified doctors take a pledge to maintain ethical principles. What is it called?

2   Which popular over-the-counter drug was first tested by its developer Dr Stewart Adams as a cure for his hangover?

3   The first heart transplant was performed by Christiaan Barnard in his hospital in South Africa. When was it?

4   What anti-depressant, hailed as a miracle drug, first came on the market in 1988?

5   Which British scientist pioneered antisepsis in the 1860s?

6   Name one of the three Canadian scientists who isolated the hormone insulin, paving the way for diabetes treatment?

7   Which famous British author practiced as a doctor before finding greater fame as a crime writer?

8   What name is given to doctors who specialise in diseases of the blood?

9   What pain-relieving drug was developed from the bark of the willow tree?

10   What is the disorder hypotension more commonly known as?

11   Moorfields Hospital in London is associated with disorders of what area of the body?

12   All royalties from the sale of which children's book go to Great Ormond Street Hospital?

13   In what year was the NHS founded?

14   In which European city are the remains of Sigmund Freud, the father of psychoanalysis?

15   What nursing reformer was known as 'The Lady with the Lamp'?

16 What medical charity, recipient of the Nobel Peace Prize in 1999, was founded in 1971 by a group of French doctors?

17 What is the only country in which euthanasia is legal?

18 Rubeola is better known as what once-common disease?

19 Discovered by Alexander Fleming 80 years ago, it changed the face of medicine and has saved an estimated 200 million lives. What is it?

20 What is laparoscopic surgery more commonly known as?

21 What name is given to the spinal injection intended to anaesthatise labour pains during birth?

22 What is the layperson's term for toxaemia?

23 Which of the senses does an aural disorder affect?

24 What American scientist developed the first inactive polio vaccine, never taking out a patent on his work?

25 At least 5% of the NHS budget is spent on helping patients with what disease?

26 What does the abbreviation DOA mean to a hospital worker?

27 If someone has DDS after their name, what part of your body would they look into?

28 A rhinologist specialises in diseases of which part of the body?

29 It's known as Montezuma's Revenge or Delhi Belly. What is this tourist's affliction?

30 What insect carries and transmits malaria and yellow fever?

Quiz 51

1 What was the name of Elvis Presley's original backing band?

2 What country won the very first Eurovision Song Contest in 1956?

3 This 50s teen idol was married to Debbie Reynolds and Elizabeth Taylor, and was one of the decade's most popular stars. What was his name?

4 The first British singles chart was compiled by NME (New Musical Express). In what year did it appear?

5 The Christmas no. 1 in 1950, based on a children's story, went on to be an all-time Christmas classic. What was it?

6 The 50s saw the start of the career of what is officially the world's longest-surviving unchanged vocal act. Who are this family group?

7 This evergreen star, who sang both at JFK's inaugural ball in 1961 and Glastonbury in 2007, had her first hit in 1959. Who is she?

8 Doris Day had two Oscar-winning songs in the charts in the 50s. Name one of them.

9 What influential rocker had a hit with 'Summertime Blues' in 1958?

10 Mel Blanc, the Man of a Thousand Voices, had a hit in 1951 with a song featuring two of his characters. What was it?

11 This performer, later a Radio 1 and Radio 2 DJ, had a series of top 10 hits including 'Chain Gang' and 'Unchained Melody'. Who is he?

12 Before the sales of singles were used for compiling the chart, sales of what were used to determine songs' relative popularity?

13 What 1959 Chuck Berry song did the Beatles use nine years later as a basis for their parody, 'Back in the USSR'?

14 What song, later featured on the soundtrack for 'American Graffiti', was a hit for doo-wop band The Platters in 1959?

15 Elvis Presley's first song reached no. 2 in the UK charts. What was it?

16 What Leiber and Stoller song, first performed by the Clovers in 1959, has been covered by The Searchers, Neil Diamond and the White Stripes and was even referenced in 'Shrek 2'?

17 What fraternal duo had a hit with 'All I Have to do is Dream' in 1958?

18 What classic 1958 song by Lord Rockingham's XI was later used in a classic ad for Maynard's Wine Gums?

19 Jazz singer Peggy Lee's voice was heard on what Disney animated feature from 1955?

20 This song was a no. 1 hit for Los Lobos in 1987 but was originally recorded by Ritchie Valens in 1958. What was it?

21 'Rockin' Robin' was covered by Michael Jackson to become his second solo hit in 1972. But who first recorded it in 1958?

22 'My Baby Just Cares for Me', first written for the 1928 musical 'Whoopee', later became the theme tune of what jazz singer?

23 A Chuck Berry song was the climax to the 1955 school dance in the movie 'Back to the Future'. What was it?

24 What song was a smash for Gene Vincent and His Blue Caps in 1956?

25 45 prm singles, introduced in 1949, took over from 78s as the singles format of choice in the 50s. What does rpm stand for?

26 What R&B singer nicknamed the Fat Man, released 'Ain't That a Shame' and later performed it in the film 'Shake, Rattle and Rock!'?

27 Who sang the classic rock and roll number, 'Rock Around the Clock'?

28 What Tennessee Ernie Ford song about coalmining reached no. 1 in the US charts in 1956?

29 Elvis Presley's movie career launched in 1956 with what musical western?

30 By what name is the iconic 50s star the Reverend Richard Wayne Penniman better known?

Quiz 52

1   Who was the first actress to play M?

2   How many full-length Bond novels did Ian Fleming write?

3   Who sang the theme to the 2006 Bond movie 'Casino Royale'?

4   In which movie did SPECTRE mastermind Blofeld first appear?

5   Ian Fleming's home shared its name with which one of his stories?

6   In which movie did the Moonbuggy appear?

7   Which movie features two of the actresses from 'The Avengers' TV series?

8   Baddie Jaws first appeared in which Bond movie?

9   In which city was the climax to 'Casino Royale' set?

10 Which British singer performed the 'Thunderball' theme?

11 Which character was 'The Man With The Golden Gun' in the 1974 movie?

12 How many actors have played James Bond in the official series of movies?

13 What does the name SPECTRE stand for?

14 'Austin Powers' baddie Dr Evil was a parody of which Bond villain?

15 Which Oscar-winning actor played the villain in 'A View To A Kill'?

16 What make of car did Bond drive in his 2006 outing, 'Casino Royale'?

17 Which actress who played a Bond baddie was married to composer Kurt Weill?

18 Who played 006 Alec Trevelyan, aka the villain Janus, in 'GoldenEye'?

19 What is the connection between 'Tomorrow Never Dies' and 'Desperate Housewives'?

20 How many non-British actors have played Bond?

21 George MacDonald Fraser, author of the 'Flashman' novels, wrote the screenplay for which Bond movie?

22 Who composed the original James Bond theme?

23 Which of the Bond movies was the first to have its theme performed by a band?

24 Michelle Yeoh, star of 'Crouching Tiger, Hidden Dragon', appeared in which Bond movie?

25 'Everyone has a past. Every legend has a beginning...' This was the tagline of which Bond film?

26 In which Bond spoof did David Niven play James Bond?

27 Which was the first Bond theme that didn't share its title with the movie?

28 Which British author who wrote the script for 'You Only Live Twice', went on to write 'Chitty Chitty Bang Bang'?

29 Which Bond assassin wore a steel-rimmed bowler hat?

30 Including 'Quantum of Solace', how many official Bond movies have there been?

Quiz 53

1   What movement did Wat Tyler and Jack Straw lead in 1381?

2   The son of which English king became the first Prince of Wales?

3   Who was the last King of England before the Norman Conquest?

4   The Battle of Gravelines between England and Spain in 1588 is better known by the name of the Spanish force on the day. What was it?

5   It was bought in 1626 for a sack of beads, cloth and ironware. It's now the centre of one of the world's biggest cities. What is it?

6   In the Wars of the Roses, which family house wore the red rose – York or Lancaster?

7   What movement, begun in 1096 by Pope Urban II, saw Western power expand into Asia?

8   In this year the Moors were expelled from Spain and Columbus discovered the Americas. What year was it?

9   Which famous Scots leader was named Guardian of Scotland in 1297?

10 What is the name of the pictorial record of the Norman invasion that was created several years after the invasion itself?

11 Who made himself the first secular head of the English church in 1534?

12 Who was charged with treason and executed in front of the Banqueting House in London on 30th January 1649?

13 What was the area in eastern Ireland, ruled directly by the English through the Middle Ages, known as?

14 He was a scurrilous gossip, worked at the Admiralty and wrote in his diary about the Great Fire of London. Who was he?

15 Who was the last Yorkist king of England?

16 James VII of Scotland was also James the – what – of England?

17 What did King John put his name to at Runnymede in 1215?

18 What Welsh leader led a revolt against the English in the early 15th century?

19 What royal was executed at Fotheringay Castle in February 1587?

20 King Alfred drove the Danes back out of his kingdom in the 9th century. What kingdom was it?

21 What is the name of the famous Moorish palace in Granada?

22 In which long war did Joan of Arc lead the fight against the English?

23 What 13th-century empire was the second-largest ever in the world, stretching from Korea to western Russia?

24 The first university to grant degrees was established in 1088 in what Italian city?

25 Who served in the 17th century as the first Protector of England, Scotland and Ireland in place of the king?

26 What was so unusual about the edition of 'The Canterbury Tales' printed by William Caxton in 1476?

27 What census of England did the Normans draw up in 1086 to help them tax the country more efficiently?

28 What order of fighting monks was established in the early 12th century to ensure safe passage of pilgrims travelling to Jerusalem?

29 What ruler did Charles II succeed when he came to the throne?

30 What Massachussetts town became infamous for a series of witchcraft trials in 1692 that saw more than 20 people executed?

Quiz 54

1 In which country would you be served Gado Gado as a native dish?

2 What name do the French give a toasted cheese sandwich with ham, topped with a fried egg?

3 If you ordered a plate of Fritto Misto di Mare in Italy, what would you get?

4 In an aioli, what is the oil or mayonnaise flavoured with?

5 'In victory you deserve it, in defeat you need it.' What drink was Winston Churchill talking about?

6 When an oven is set at Gas Mark 5, what is its temperature in degrees Centigrade?

7 Both are smoked herring, but what is the difference between a bloater and a kipper?

8 When during a meal would an Italian serve you antipasto?

9 Stilton cheese can only be made in three English counties. Name one of them.

10 Golden Boy, Early Girl and Big Boy are all varieties of what?

11 In what dish is raw minced beef served shaped into rissoles, often with a raw egg?

12 What Middle Eastern dish is made from ground chickpeas and sesame seeds with olive oil and garlic?

13 What cocktail do the ingredients gin and vermouth make?

14 Which hard-living poet declared, 'Let us have wine and women, mirth and laughter, Sermons and soda water the day after'?

15 On which Scottish island is Talisker single-malt whisky produced?

16 In the US this herb is known as cilantro; what do we know it as?

17 French liqueur Crème de Cassis is flavoured with what fruit?

18 Which Indian drink is made from yoghurt and served with salt or sugar?

19 What is the food tripe derived from?

20 Yarg is a Cornish variety of cheese that comes wrapped in what plant?

21 If you drank pastis in France, what flavour would you expect it to have?

22 What shape is the pasta farfalle?

23 Chicle, the latex from the sapodilla tree, was originally used to make what edible substance?

24 Which Indian variety is known as 'the Champagne of Tea'?

25 Oysters wrapped in bacon are called Angels On Horseback. What are Devils On Horseback?

26 To which fortified wine does the Portuguese city of Oporto give its name?

27 The French call them Cuisses de Grenouilles; what are they in English?

28 Which liqueur is used in cocktails for its blue colour?

29 Mead was once widely drunk in England. What is its main ingredient?

30 Flower of Kent, Pink Lady and York Imperial are all varieties of what?

Quiz 55

1   As well as Wimbledon, what are tennis's other Grand Slam tournaments?

2   Which celebrity chef used to play football for Glasgow Rangers?

3   What is the maximum number of clubs allowed in a golf bag?

4   What Northern Ireland football team plays home games at Windsor Park?

5   South Africa won the Rugby World Cup in 2008. Who had been the previous holders?

6   In which sport would you find a grinner, a palomar and a half-blood?

7   The Thomas Cup is a prize in which sport?

8   What is the basketball team from Dallas known as?

9   The first winner of BBC's Sports Personality of the Year was a British runner who later became ITN's first newscaster and a Tory politician. Who was he?

10 What's the highest number of points you can score with a single darts throw?

11 How many players are on the field in a normal hockey game?

12 What golfer, a multiple winner of majors, was struck by lightning on a golf course in 1975, suffering spinal injuries?

13 What team has made most appearances in an American Superbowl final?

14 The longest-ever boxing world championship fight under Queensberry rules lasted for how many rounds?

15 What sport do the Boston Celtics play?

16 What sport would you be watching at its world championships in the Crucible, Sheffield?

17 A US team and a non-European International team compete biennially for what professional golf trophy?

18 What batsman has scored most runs in test cricket to date?

19 What county cricket club's home is the Riverside Ground?

20 How high off the centre of the court is the top of a badminton net?

21 What team did Michael Jordan play his basketball for?

22 How many of tennis's Grand Slam tournaments are played on grass to date?

23 Who has scored most tries in a rugby World Cup?

24 What Grand Prix takes place at Imola?

25 What famous sports ground has been in three separate London locations, moving to its present one in 1814?

26 In which sport would you see a Flamingo, and Eggbeater and a Float?

27 What colour of belt denotes a beginner at the first grade in judo?

28 What tennis player has won more Grand Slam singles titles than any other to date?

29 Who was the last male tennis player to win all four Grand Slams in one year?

30 What constructor team was first to more than 200 Formula 1 Grand Prix wins?

Quiz 56

Name the animals from each of these TV shows or movies.

1   'Mr Ed'

2   'Flipper'

3   'Arachnophobia'

4   'Free Willy'

5   'Born Free'

6   'Black Beauty'

7   'Jaws'

8   'Ben'

9   'Ring of Bright Water'

10   'Skippy'

11   'Kes'

12   'Every Which Way But Loose'

13   'Stuart Little'

14   'Bringing Up Baby'

15   'Howard – A New Breed of Hero'

16 'Old Yeller'

17 'The Barefoot Executive'

18 'Seabiscuit'

19 'Cujo'

20 'Babe'

21 'Anaconda'

22 'The Rescuers'

23 'Watership Down'

24 'Jurassic Park'

25 'An American Tail'

26 'Lady and the Tramp'

27 'Pingu'

28 'Rupert'

29 'Jakers!' (main character)

30 'Flushed Away'

Quiz 57

1. What animal has the longest gestation period?

2. How many legs has the common centipede?

3. What type of creature is a flying fox?

4. It's a tuber, a member of the nightshade family and the world's largest food crop after the cereals. What is it?

5. The dodo became extinct around 1680. What island was its habitat?

6. What type of grass grows by 3–4 feet per day?

7. Does soft wood or hard wood come from tropical trees?

8. What British bird's eggs are the largest?

9. The Giant's Causeway in Ireland and Fingal's Cave on Staffa are made of what type of rock?

10. What type of livestock animal is the species Ovis Aries?

11. In which geological time period did the first mammals appear on Earth?

12. If a creature is amphibiotic, what change of habitat takes place between youth and maturity?

13. What is the largest member of the deer family in Europe?

14. What is the name of the biggest gem-quality diamond ever discovered?

15. What colour are the flowers on a gorse or broom bush?

16 Are koalas mammals or marsupials?

17 What gemstone is completely made of carbon?

18 What does a palaeontologist study?

19 What subsidiary of the Ministry of Defence is responsible for forecasting the UK's weather and climate movements?

20 What type of bird is a widgeon?

21 What creature has its ears on its legs?

22 Two halves of what organ in mammals are joined by the corpus callosum?

23 What is the hardest known substance?

24 What is the only bird that can fly backwards?

25 Alligators are native to only two countries. One is China; what is the other?

26 What percentage of a tree is made up of living cells – less than 80%, less than 50% or less than 1%?

27 What purpose do root hairs on plants serve?

28 These birds are known as bonxies for their habit of dive-bombing humans walking near their nest sites. What is their proper name?

29 How many points has a snowflake?

30 What country is home to more venomous snakes than any other in the world?

Quiz 58

1 What was banned by constitutional law in America between 1920 and 1933?

2 What 1890 battle saw the final defeat of the Native Americans by the US government?

3 What is the symbol of the American Democratic Party?

4 Why did people flock to California in 1848–49?

5 Which US state has the motto, 'Live Free Or Die'?

6 Two American states don't border any others. What are they?

7 There are eight prestigious Ivy League colleges and universities in the US. Which one is the oldest?

8 What was the first English settlement in the New World?

9 What was the first state to be admitted to the Union in 1787?

10 America's adoption of the Declaration of Independence is celebrated on what day?

11 Which group was given the right to vote in America in 1924?

12 What is Old Glory a nickname for?

13 At -86m, it's the lowest point in North America as well as the hottest and driest. Where is it?

14 What was the most famous dance to come out of the Jazz Age in 1920s America?

15 Who was shot in the back during a saloon poker game in Deadwood in 1876?

16 What city is the capital of New York state?

17 What was the name of the ship on which English religious non-conformists sailed from Southampton to the New World in 1620?

18 If a US address has the zip code initials MT, which state is it in?

19 What was the name of the network by which American slaves escaped from the South to the North?

20 What is the most populous state in the Union?

21 According to the old patriotic song, who stuck a feather in his hat and called it macaroni?

22 There are five boroughs in New York. One is Manhattan; name two of the others.

23 How many states were in the Confederacy that split from the Union in 1861?

24 In what state is the Pearl Harbor naval base which was bombed by the Japanese in 1941?

25 He's tall, with white hair, a goatee and a white top hat with stars on its band. He's also considered the personnification of the United States. Who is he?

26 Who is the Commander-in-Chief of the US armed forces?

27 How many stars are on the American flag?

28 What is the national bird of the United States?

29 Which Washington monument commemorates the dead and missing of the Vietnam war?

30 What is the smallest state in the Union?

Quiz 59

1   Sirius is the brightest star in the sky. What is the next brightest?

2   A cheetah is the world's fastest mammal. Which is second?

3   The largest human organ is the skin. What's second?

4   Britain was the first country to have TV with regular public broadcasting. Who was second?

5   The Open University has more students than any other UK university. Which is second?

6   North Yorkshire is England's biggest county. What's second-biggest?

7   Americans own more cars than any other country. Who is second?

8   Ben Nevis is Britain's highest mountain. What's the second-highest?

9   What world 'second' does former Indian PM Indira Gandhi hold?

10 The USA has more dentists per head of population than any other country. What Middle Eastern country is second?

11 The Bible is the best-selling book ever. What's second?

12 The world's smallest country is Vatican City. Which country is second-smallest?

13 Roger Bannister ran the first recorded four-minute mile. Who ran the second?

14 In 1903 Marie Curie became the first woman to win a Nobel Prize. Who was the second?

15 France consumes more champagne than any other nation. Who's second?

16 The Moon was the first body in our solar system to be visited by spacecraft. What was the second?

17 China's Red Army is the world's biggest. Which country's army is second biggest?

18 Christianity is the world's biggest religion. Which is second?

19 Elton John's 'Candle in the Wind 97' is the best-selling UK single ever. What's second?

20 The femur is the longest human bone. What's second?

21 The first book of the Bible is Genesis. What is the second?

22 Greenland is the world's biggest island. What's the second biggest?

23 Ronald Reagan was 77 when he left office, making him the USA's oldest president. Which 20th-century president was second oldest?

24 Michael Schumacher has more Formula 1 wins than any other driver. Who's second?

25 William Hartnell was the first Doctor in 'Doctor Who'. Who was second?

26 Hindi is India's most spoken language. What is second?

27 The USA is the world's biggest trader of goods and services. What country is second?

28 Celtic were the first side from northern Europe to win football's European Cup. Who were the second?

29 'It's All Over Now' was the Rolling Stones' first no. 1 in the UK. What was second?

30 Gordon Richards won more UK flat races than any other jockey. Who's second in the rankings?

Quiz 60

1   What does a pedologist study?

2   If someone is described as being ovine, what creature are they like?

3   What is the term for someone whose hobby is cave exploration?

4   What type of work would you expect a prestidigitator to do?

5   A navvy is a building labourer, but what does the name derive from?

6   What does a colporteur sell?

7   There are 26 letters in the English language. How many are there in the Welsh?

8   What does a funambulist walk on?

9   What does a Japanese ikebanist arrange?

10 What type of work does a pedagogue do?

11 If you were an oenologist, what would your area of study be?

12 What Italian Renaissance thinker wrote advice on governing for the Medici rulers of Florence and has given his name to a word meaning 'manipulative'?

13 In Cockney rhyming slang, if your carving knife was sitting at the Cain and Abel, who would be where?

14 What does the word 'pope' mean?

15 What does a fletcher make?

16   What does a vexillologist study?

17   What do phrenologists study?

18   If you type ROFL in an email, what would you be doing?

19   What is the most commonly used letter in the English language?

20   Homonymns sound the same, but what is different about them?

21   What is the heraldic colour 'sable' better known as?

22   'Piscine' relates to what type of creature?

23   What two Greek letters combine to make up the word 'alphabet'?

24   In Europe it's known as an elk. What is it called in America?

25   What animal would frighten an ailurophobic person?

26   What is the NATO Phonic code word for the letter 'P'?

27   Located on your face, your nares is another name for what?

28   In Morse code, what vowel is represented by a dot?

29   What is etymology the study of?

30   What is the last letter of the Greek alphabet?

Quiz 61

Give the show each of these lines comes from.

1 'I don't believe it!'

2 'Is that your final answer?'

3 'I want that one.'

4 'That's hot.'

5 'Let's be careful out there.'

6 'Ha! Ha! Ha! Boom, boom!'

7 'That boy ain't right.'

8 'Bada Bing!'

9 'Oh my God! They killed Kenny!'

10 'Isn't that a pip?'

11 'And that's magic!'

12 'Make it so.'

13 'Eat my shorts.'

14 'To me, to you.'

15 'Ta-ra, chuck.'

16   'You're fired!'

17   'Are you pondering what I'm pondering?'

18   'They don't like it up 'em!'

19   'Yabba Dabba Do!'

20   'What does this button do?'

21   'This is a local shop for local people.'

22   'Is it cos I is black?'

23   'I have a cunning plan.'

24   'Drink! Feck! Arse! Girls!'

25   'Lovely jubbly.'

26   'Suit you, sir – oooh!'

27   'What's up, Doc?'

28   'I'm free!'

29   'I've started, so I'll finish.'

30   'Which is better? There's only one way to find out – FIIIIGHT!'

Quiz 62

1   How many numbers are used in binary coding?

2   What do you call a number that divides exactly into another number?

3   The numbers on the opposite face of a dice always add up to the same total. What is it?

4   The Romans wrote this number as XL. What would it be to us?

5   If A = 1 and Z = 26, what number is Q?

6   What do you get if you multiply the number of sides in a pentagon with the number of sides in a trapezium?

7   What numbers would you key on your phone if you wanted to text 'hi'?

8   How much is the binary number 11 when expressed as a decimal number?

9   What name is given to an angle that is less than 90º?

10   How many sealed boxes are used in the Channel 4 programme, 'Deal or no Deal'?

11   In the nursery rhyme 'Sing a Song of Sixpence', how many blackbirds were baked in the pie?

12   In Douglas Adams's 'The Hitch-hiker's Guide to the Galaxy' books, what number was revealed to be the Ultimate Secret to Life, the Universe and Everything?

13   In ancient mythology, how many labours did Hercules or Heracles perform?

14   Given that a thousand is 1 followed by three noughts, what name is given to a number that is 1 followed by a hundred noughts?

15   What late-2000s US TV show features a mathematician who uses his calculations to help the FBI solve crimes?

16 The portion of a circle between the centre and two points on the perimeter is called what?

17 How many holes would a golfer play to win the British Open?

18 At what age do you become a nonagenarian?

19 How many hills was the ancient city of Rome built on?

20 'In a right-angled triangle, the square of the hypotenuse is equal to the sum of the squares of the other two sides.' What mathematical rule is this?

21 In the Roald Dahl book 'Charlie and the Chocolate Factory', how many golden tickets were enclosed with the sweet bars?

22 If the perimeter of a square is 56 cm, how long is any one side?

23 What name is given to a number that cannot be divided by any natural number other than itself and 1?

24 How many muses did the Ancient Greeks believe there were?

25 How many spots are there on a normal dice?

26 If it rains on St Swithin's Day, the 15th of July, how many days' rain does the old rhyme say must follow?

27 How many years would you have been married if you had an emerald wedding anniversary?

28 How many pairs of chromosomes are there in every human cell?

29 What is the next number in this sequence: 2, 3, 5, 7, 11, 13, 17... ?

30 How many basic letters did the Romans use in combination in their numbering system?

Quiz 63

1   What renowned American folk artist wrote 'Where Have All the Flowers Gone', 'If I Had a Hammer' and 'Turn! Turn! Turn!'?

2   What English folk-revival band had a top 5 hit in 1975 with 'All Around My Hat'?

3   From what border area of India and Pakistan does bhangra music and dance come?

4   Who is the composer of the all-Ireland anthem, 'Ireland's Call'?

5   Fado is a type of folk music associated with what country?

6   Who founded The Dubliners?

7   The traditional English song 'The Carol of the Twelve Numbers' is better known by what title?

8   Peadar Kearney, co-author of the Irish national anthem 'The Soldier's Song', was also the uncle of which Irish writers?

9   The African anthem 'Nkosi Sikelel' iAfrika' translates into English as what?

10 Who wrote and performed the classic 60s protest song, 'The Times They Are a-Changin'?

11 What Irish group was instrumental in the revival of interest in traditional music in the US in the 1960s?

12 What 1929 song that became a campaign anthem of Franklin D Roosevelt, is also the unofficial anthem of the Democratic Party?

13 The Pogues and The Dubliners had a UK top 10 hit in 1987 with what traditional Irish song?

14 What South Boston band entered the US top 20 album charts for the first time in 2007 with 'The Meanest of Times'?

15 'John Brown's Body' was a marching song for American soldiers in what conflict?

16   What British folk singer wrote both 'The First Time Ever I Saw Your Face', and 'Dirty Old Town'?

17   'Flower of Scotland' is the anthem of the Scotland rugby team, but what duo made it famous?

18   What Oklahoma musician was the author of the American folk anthem, 'This Land is Your Land'?

19   What English king was long thought to be the composer of the tune 'Greensleeves'?

20   What Chilean songwriter was one of those tortured and executed by General Pinochet's forces after their coup d'état in 1973?

21   What 13th century English song celebrates the arrival of summer?

22   Canadian folk duo Kate and Anna McGarrigle are the mother and aunt respectively of what two singer-songwriters?

23   What poet wrote the traditional carol, 'In the Bleak Midwinter'?

24   What Armagh-born musician was the Clancy Brothers' most frequent collaborator?

25   What Dublin-born writer was the composer of 'Liverpool Lou', 'The Patriot Game', 'The Merry Ploughboy' and 'McAlpine's Fusiliers'?

26   What song of the Highland Clearances, written and performed by the Proclaimers, reached no. 3 in the UK chart in 1987?

27   What Irish town is mentioned in the traditional anti-war song, 'Johnny I Hardly Knew Ye'?

28   The Welsh folksong 'Ar Hyd y Nos' represents Wales at the Last Night of the Proms, and it translates into English as what?

29   'From the mountains, to the prairies, To the oceans white with foam...' Name this Irving Berlin-penned American anthem.

30   What Breton musician, who popularised the Celtic harp, was foremost in developing Breton music in fusion with other genres?

Quiz 64

1   Who is the famous architect responsible for, among other things, the terminal at Stansted Airport and the Gherkin in London?

2   What famous construction of Barcelona architect Antoni Gaudí was begun in 1882 and is still unfinished?

3   This 18th-century architect designed the gardens at Blenheim and Kew. His first name was Lancelot but what was he better known as?

4   What London church architect, an assistant to Christopher Wren, was the subject of a novel by Peter Ackroyd?

5   The Pharos of Alexandria was a 3rd century BC Wonder of the Ancient World. What type of building was it?

6   'A house is a machine for living in.' What modern architect said this?

7   Which Scottish architect and designer redefined Art Nouveau in Britain and designed the world-famous Glasgow Art School?

8   What noted architect is married to one of the founders of London's River Café?

9   The designer of New York's Guggenheim Museum was also immortalised in a song by Simon and Garfunkel. Who was he?

10 Which annually awarded prize is often referred to as 'the Nobel Prize of architecture'?

11 This 1973 building was initially controversial but, with its sail-like roofs in a harbourside setting, is now an iconic landmark. What is it?

12 Coventry's medieval cathedral was flattened in Second World War bombing. Who designed the replacement?

13 What metal structure, built for an exhibition and meant to stand for 20 years, is now one of the most famous sights in the world?

14 Churches were traditionally built so that the priest and people would face in which direction?

15 As of 2008, what is the world's tallest building?

16 What Parisian landmark sits on top of Montmartre hill on the highest point in the city?

17 What iconic building of Imperial Rome, built by the Emperor Vespasian between 70 and 80 AD, is depicted on a 5-cent Euro coin?

18 In a traditional medieval-styled church, who would you expect to find standing or sitting in the nave?

19 What name is given to the Norman style of castle with a fortified mound and tower surrounded by a ditch?

20 In 1984, who famously described a proposed extension to the National Gallery as 'a monstrous carbuncle'?

21 What Italian city, with a basilica that is a World Heritage Site, was seriously damaged in an earthquake in 1997?

22 What is the proper name of the famous London landmark known as the Gherkin?

23 The Great Pyramid at Giza was thought to be built for what pharaoh?

24 He founded Classical English architecture, planned Covent Garden and introduced moveable scenery to the English stage. Who was he?

25 The original Crystal Palace was built in Hyde Park in 1851. What was its purpose?

26 What would you find in a castle's garderobe?

27 What French royal château, which features a room called the Hall of Mirrors, was stormed by the Paris mob in 1789?

28 What London building was originally built in 1703 as a town house for the Duke of Buckingham?

29 What London construction was destroyed by Queen Boudicca, burnt in 1163, rebuilt then replaced in 1831 and replaced again in 1973?

30 What iconic London building by Barry and Pugin was built after its predecessor burnt down, and took 30 years to complete?

Quiz 65

1   What sportsman was known as The Louisville Lip?

2   This iconic American singer was called The Man In Black. Who was he?

3   Pioneer and frontierswoman Martha Jane Canary Burke was better known as...?

4   What musician was known as Satchmo (short for Satchelmouth)?

5   This English king had two nicknames, one of which was Longshanks. Who was he?

6   Called The Father of Medicine, he was an Ancient Greek physician who lived around 400 BC. What was his name?

7   The ageless supermodel Lesley Hornby is better known by what nickname?

8   This famous 1920s athlete was known as The Flying Scotsman. Who was he?

9   First World War flying ace Manfred von Richthofen was better known by his nickname. What was it?

10   A British king notorious for his roving eye was nicknamed Old Rowley after his stallion. Who was he?

11   What is the nickname of the championship-winning Australian golfer Greg Norman?

12   This American politician was known as Tricky Dicky. What was his real name?

13   Nazi propagandist and broadcaster William Joyce was better known as what?

14   What was the nickname of the notorious suspected murderer Lord Lucan?

15   Whose nicknames include The Milk Snatcher and Atilla the Hen?

16   Who was known as The Bard of Avon?

17   This diminutive French singer was known as The Little Sparrow. Who was she?

18   Which US leader was known as The Teflon President?

19   The Maid of Orleans is better known as what?

20   This leader was known as Mahatma, or 'Great Soul'. What was his own surname?

21   Which French revolutionary was called The Sea-Green Incorruptible?

22   What batsman is known simply as The Prince?

23   Who is known in the US as The Father of His Country?

24   This Canadian former world snooker champion was known as The Grinder. Who is he?

25   This ruler was known to his contemporaries as 'The Bastard'. What was he better known as?

26   Wealthy British philanthropist William Wilberforce acquired the nickname, The Liberator. Why?

27   He was called The Wizard of Dribble and The First Gentleman of Soccer. Who was he?

28   This English soldier and leader was known as Old Ironsides. Who was he?

29   What was the nickname of England's Crusader king Richard II?

30   What was the real name of the legendary entertainer known as Ol' Blue Eyes?

Quiz 66

1   'Smallville' charts the teenage life of which American icon?

2   What is the first name of 'Dad's Army' platoon leader Captain Mainwaring?

3   What fighting group did Destiny, Harmony, Melody, Rhapsody and Symphony make up?

4   What group of superheroes work for UN law-enforcement agency Nemesis?

5   What is the surname of Buffy the Vampire Slayer?

6   How did Den Watts meet his end second time around in 'EastEnders'?

7   What is the name of the dog in 'The Magic Roundabout'?

8   The Disney TV version of what character dumped his old friend Christopher Robin for a girl called Darby in 2007?

9   From which sitcom character's apartment window can you see the Space Needle?

10   'Holby City' was a spin-off from what other show?

11   What show features customer-hating shop owner Bernard Black and his hapless assistant, Manny?

12   In what show was the chain-smoking figure known as Cancer Man a recurring character?

13   What was the name of Frankie Howerd's character in 'Up Pompeii'?

14   What is the longest-running sci-fi series ever made for TV?

15   Who was Father Ted Crilly's bishop boss in the sitcom, 'Father Ted'?

16 The Gallagher family live on the Chatsworth Estate in Manchester. In what TV show do they appear?

17 What character killed herself in the pilot episode of 'Desperate Housewives', narrating the backstory thereafter?

18 Two American sitcom characters with the surnames Truman and Adler are better known by their first names. Who are they?

19 What cartoon family live in Orbit City?

20 How many series did The Sopranos run for?

21 In the late-70s TV series, what was the Incredible Hulk's name in his everyday life?

22 What long-running series is set in County General Hospital, Cook County, Chicago?

23 Frank Pembleton is a main character what award-winning 90s homicide detective show set in Baltimore, Maryland?

24 Three separate CSI shows have been made. But what does CSI stand for?

25 What Phil Redmond-penned soap ran for 21 years on Channel 4?

26 In what two separate TV series do Chris Skelton and Ray Carling appear?

27 Ramsay Street, home to the 'Neighbours' characters, is set in what fictional suburb?

28 In what US state is the series 'South Park' set?

29 In what series is Jack Bauer a lead character?

30 How many canonical 'Star Trek' TV series were there after the original?

Quiz 67

1 The giant dinosaur Diplodocus, with elongated neck and even longer whip-like tail, was a carnivore. True or false?

2 The British farce 'Carry On Cleo' was shot on the same movie sets as the expensive Oscar-winner 'Cleopatra', with Elizabeth Taylor. True or false?

3 The driest place on Earth is in California. True or false?

4 Whisky is James Bond's favourite drink. True or false?

5 Columbus first came ashore on the American mainland at what is now Columbia. True or false?

6 It's possible to score no points with a tile in Scrabble. True or false?

7 The composer Mendelssohn lost the score for one of his overtures when he left it behind in a cab. True or false?

8 Northern Ireland's police changed their name from the RUC (Royal Ulster Constabulary) to the NIPS (Northern Ireland Police Service). True or false?

9 William Paterson, founder of the Bank of England, was actually a Scotsman. True or false?

10 The Plymouth Brethren were founded in Plymouth. True or false?

11 A 17th-century edition of the Bible misprinted one commandment as 'Thou shalt commit adultery'. True or false?

12 Albert Einstein never won the Nobel Prize for Physics. True or false?

13 Female ducks are the only ones that quack. True or false?

14 David Beckham never won the PFA Player of the Year award. True or false?

15 The Spanish city of Seville is on the Costa del Sol. True or false?

16 Water-dwelling mammals do not sleep. True or false?

17 The Arctic Tern migrates to Antarctica. True or false?

18 Lord's cricket ground is home to London County Cricket Club. True or false?

19 The biggest empire in world history has been the British Empire. True or false?

20 The organisation Amnesty International once won the Nobel Peace Prize. True or false?

21 Peacocks do not lay eggs. True or false?

22 The Portuguese national anthem has no lyrics. True or false?

23 Four European countries drive on the left. True or false?

24 Elephants are afraid of mice. True or false?

25 The planet Saturn is so light it could float in water. True or false?

26 The city of Rawalpindi is in India. True or false?

27 Jet lag is worse for a traveller flying from east to west than vice versa. True or false?

28 Astronaut Buzz Aldrin's mother's maiden name was 'Moon'. True or false?

29 A Hamas TV show featured a Mickey Mouse lookalike teaching violent extremism to Palestinian children. True or false?

30 The 100 highest mountains in the world are all located in either Asia or South America. True or false?

Quiz 68

1   What is the collective term for a group of crows?

2   What is the name of the Israeli parliament?

3   Glaciers carved out these long, narrow coastal inlets found along the coasts of Norway and New Zealand. What are they called?

4   What legendary gunfight took place in Tombstone, Arizona?

5   What date in December is the feast of St Nicholas?

6   The 1974 world heavyweight championship boxing contest became known as The Rumble in the Jungle. Where did it take place?

7   According to the Biblical proverb, 'A mild answer calms wrath, but a harsh word stirs up –' what?

8   Whose Mark 2 Jaguar, registration number 248 RPA, sold for over £100,000 at auction in 2005?

9   What name is shared by a card game and a temporary, floating bridge?

10   What European city does the River Tagus flow through?

11   In what building does the Northern Irish assembly sit?

12   How are battlesites represented on Ordnance Survey maps?

13   What name is given to the notion that any one person on Earth is an average of six steps or connections away from any other person?

14   What name is given to the study of ancient peoples' observation of the stars and the impact on their cultures?

15   What inspirational mountaineer declared, 'It is not the mountain we conquer, but ourselves'?

16 Who was the first British Prime Minister to appear on live TV?

17 And who was the first US president to appear on TV?

18 What is the densest major body in the solar system?

19 Mr Plod the policeman features in what series of children's books?

20 How often does the Queen perform the State Opening of Parliament – once a year, every two years or once in every Parliament?

21 Who is the hero of Philip Ardagh's novels set in Victorian London and described as 'a cross between Dickens and Monty Python'?

22 What mast on a three-masted ship is the mizzen mast – front, middle or rear?

23 What name describes the coat of a horse which is reddish brown with a black mane and tail?

24 The Gulf of Venice is the northernmost point of what sea?

25 What colour is the number 1 on a European Roulette wheel?

26 Transylvania, the home of Count Dracula, is in which modern-day country?

27 What notoriously wild town on America's Santa Fe Trail was home for a time to legendary frontier lawman Wyatt Earp?

28 What bodily organ can a giraffe put into its ears?

29 What psychiatric disorder's name comes from a Greek term meaning 'without appetite'?

30 What children's character's favourite food is marmalade sandwiches and cocoa?

Quiz 69

1   What David Bowie song did Lulu take to no. 3 in the UK charts in 1974, with Bowie producing and playing sax?

2   What comedy act had top 10 hits with 'The Funky Gibbon' and 'Black Pudding Bertha'?

3   Greg Lake's Christmas classic, 'I Believe in Father Christmas', is adapted from a piece of music by which classical composer?

4   What singer-songwriter was 'Glad to be Gay' in 1976?

5   What late comedian and 'EastEnders' star had a 1975 hit with 'The Ugly Duckling'?

6   Who had a hit in 1976 with 'I'm Mandy Fly Me'?

7   What was T Rex's first no. 1 hit in the UK?

8   Whose best-selling version of 'God Save the Queen' was kept off the no. 1 spot in the week of the Queen's Silver Jubilee?

9   Which well known punk band included members Johnny Fingers and Pete Briquette?

10 What American New Wave band, fronted by a former 'Playboy' Bunny, broke into the UK album chart with their second album, 'Plastic Letters'?

11 'Sex and Drugs and Rock and Roll' was first released in 1977 and banned by the BBC. Who performed it?

12 What was Slade's first no. 1 hit in the UK?

13 Which song did Don McLean write and perform as a tribute to dead rock and roller Buddy Holly?

14 Who had a no. 1 hit in the summer of 1974 with the novelty song, 'The Streak'?

15 'Waterloo' was Abba's first big hit in Britain in 1974, but what song had they had in the lower reaches of the charts the previous year?

16 Whose alter egos have been Ziggy Stardust and The Thin White Duke?

17 What novelty song by comedian Benny Hill was no. 1 at Christmas 1971 and was chosen by David Cameron as a favourite on Desert Island Discs in 2006?

18 Chelsea FC squad recorded 'Blue is the Colour' in 1972 for what event?

19 'Love Me for a Reason' was Boyzone's first hit single in 1994. But which group had already taken it to no. 1 in 1974?

20 Their albums included 'Setting Sons', 'All Mod Cons' and 'In The City'. Who were they?

21 Village People had several hits through the 70s and 80s. What were the six characters in the band?

22 A song about an encounter with a transvestite went to no. 2 in the charts for the Kinks in 1970. What was the song called?

23 Andy Gibb, younger brother of the Bee Gees, had a major hit in 1977 with a song written by his brother Barry. What was it?

24 Who replaced Glenn Matlock on bass guitar for the Sex Pistols in 1977?

25 In the Charlie Daniels song 'The Devil Went Down to Georgia', what prize is Johnny, the boy in the song, playing for?

26 The Simon Park orchestra had a hit in 1973 with 'Eye Level', the first TV theme to reach no. 1; but what show was it the theme to?

27 What song became the first ever to be played on MTV in 1979?

28 Which band wanted an 'Alternative Ulster' in 1978?

29 What was Wings' only no. 1 single in Britain?

30 What Manchester punk band, formed in the 70s by Pete Shelley and Howard Devoto, had a BBC TV show named after them in the 90s?

Quiz 70

Identify the movies from their taglines.

1   They came. They thawed. They conquered.

2   Protecting the earth from the scum of the universe.

3   Expect the impossible.

4   You don't assign him to murder cases, you just turn him loose.

5   The story of a man who was too proud to run.

6   Be afraid. Be very afraid.

7   You won't know the facts until you've seen the fiction.

8   Get ready for the rush hour.

9   You'll laugh. You'll cry. You'll hurl.

10   Drink from me and live forever.

11   How do I loathe thee? Let me count the ways.

12   Five criminals. One line-up. No coincidence.

13   They lost half a million at cards but they've still got a few tricks up their sleeve.

14   In space no one can hear you scream.

15   They're not just getting rich... They're getting even.

16 Life's greatest adventure is finding your place in the Circle of Life.

17 How'd you like to tussle with Russell?

18 What kind of man would defy a king?

19 You'll like him when he's angry.

20 Eight friends. One extraordinary year.

21 If he were any cooler, he'd still be frozen, baby!

22 Heads will roll.

23 Welcome to Girl World.

24 Make your last breath count.

25 You Can't Stop The Beat.

26 First dance. First love. The time of your life.

27 His whole life was a million-to-one shot.

28 The German Democratic Republic lives on – in 79 square metres!

29 A Singing Plant. A Daring Hero. A Sweet Girl. A Demented Dentist.

30 This school rocks like no other!

Quiz 71

1   What is the most abundant element in the universe?

2   How long does it take for the Moon to orbit the Earth?

3   The pattern of stars known as The Plough is part of a bigger constellation. What is it?

4   What is the name of the NASA probe that landed successfully on Mars in 2008?

5   After recent classification changes, what is the outermost planet in our Solar System?

6   What was the name of the space probe sent to study Jupiter in 1989?

7   The first manned space flight was by Yuri Gagarin in 1961. What was the name of his craft?

8   Which space shuttle exploded after launch in 1986, killing all its crew members?

9   The most abundant gas in Earth's atmosphere is what?

10 Name one of the three Apollo 13 crew who successfully returned to Earth after aborting their mission in 1970.

11 In what decade was the first Space Shuttle flight?

12 How many Moon landings took place under America's Apollo space program?

13 On which planet can you find the Great Red Spot?

14 What is the English name of the constellation called in Latin Piscis Austrinus?

15 What former planet in our Solar System was declassified as a planet in 2006?

16 What space mission produced the first-ever photo of the Earth from space in 1968?

17 How many billion years ago did the Universe erupt into being, according to the Big Bang theory of Creation?

18 What planet in our Solar System spins on its side?

19 What name is given to the explosion of a star?

20 What twin stars are in the constellation of Gemini?

21 NASA launched the Hubble Space Telescope in what year?

22 There are five layers that make up Earth's atmosphere. Which one contains the ozone layer?

23 Which planet in our Solar System is closest to the Earth?

24 The first Briton went into space in 1991. What was her name?

25 In what year did the Apollo Moon-landing missions come to an end?

26 What name is given to the theoretical short-cuts in the fabric of space and time?

27 What space first was achieved by Californian billionaire Dennis Tito in 2001?

28 What name is given to the invisible regions of space where gravity is so strong that not even light can escape?

29 Which was the first planet in our Solar System to be discovered with a telescope?

30 What distinction does American Edward White hold?

Quiz 72

1 Which play is considered bad luck to name and is often referred to as 'the Scottish Play'?

2 'Now is the winter of our discontent...' Which play does this quote come from?

3 What was the name of Shakespeare's wife?

4 Which Shakespearean play features rape, mutilation, cannibalism and the bloody murder of almost every major character?

5 How many sonnets did Shakespeare write?

6 In what town was Shakespeare born?

7 Whose final words were, 'Et tu, Brute!'

8 On what Mediterranean holiday island does Othello die?

9 How many children did Shakespeare have?

10 What was Shakespeare's tenth play?

11 Which of Shakespeare's plays begins with the line, 'Who's there?'?

12 What was the name of Shakespeare's theatre or playing company?

13 What theatre did Shakespeare's playing company build at Southwark?

14 What university did Shakespeare attend?

15 In 'Romeo and Juliet', what age is Juliet at her death?

16 Which of Shakespeare's characters 'had most need of blessing, and Amen stuck in my throat'?

17 What type of play did Shakespeare write more of – comedy, tragedy or historical?

18 Where was Prospero's ship sailing when it was wrecked in 'The Tempest'?

19 Who played the young Shakespeare in the 1998 movie, 'Shakespeare in Love'?

20 In what play do the 'weird sisters' appear?

21 Shakespeare's birthday is celebrated on what notable English day?

22 Shakespeare was believed to have written 'Macbeth' around 1606 for what Scottish king?

23 Shakespeare's sonnets are written in what rhyme scheme or meter?

24 Who wrote the play 'Rosencrantz and Guildenstern are Dead', based on the two characters from 'Hamlet'?

25 What, according to Prospero, is 'such stuff as dreams are made on'?

26 The Royal Shakespeare Theatre stands on the banks of what river?

27 What then-married couple played the lovers Benedick and Beatrice in the 1993 film version of 'Much Ado About Nothing'?

28 What ceremony does the 'bell, book and candle' mentioned in 'King John' refer to?

29 Which of Shakespeare's plays features within it a play called 'The Murder of Gonzago'?

30 What character in 'Julius Caesar' declares, 'There is a tide in the affairs of men Which, taken at the flood, leads on to fortune'?

Quiz 73

1   What actor's autobiography is titled, 'What's It All About'?

2   Where was actress Nicole Kidman born?

3   What is the real first name of actor Brad Pitt?

4   Who was actor Tom Cruise's first wife?

5   What British musician is American actress Gwyneth Paltrow married to?

6   What celebrity, then his fiancée, was Paul McCartney's inspiration for 'And I Love Her'?

7   Celebrity Myleene Klass was originally a member of what TV band?

8   Which of the Three Tenors died in 2007?

9   What was the given name of Buzz Aldrin, second man to walk on the Moon?

10 What actress is married to English director Sam Mendes?

11 Who is Charlotte Church's rugby-playing partner?

12 She starred in the 80s comedy sketch show 'Three of a Kind'; she had a handful of UK chart hits; and her US TV show gave 'The Simpsons' their break. Who is she?

13 What cricketer-turned-politician did Jemima Goldsmith marry in 1995?

14 What nationality is former 007 Pierce Brosnan?

15 In which country was actress Audrey Hepburn born?

16 Who is the only non-English member of Girls Aloud?

17 Which footballer married his childhood sweetheart at a ceremony on the Italian Riviera in 2008?

18 What celebrity couple named their first-born biological child Shiloh?

19 An exhibition of this singer's costumes, spanning 20 years, has drawn an estimated half-million viewers since 2005 in Australia and Britain. Who is she?

20 What world-famous supermodel has a police record after violent behaviour stretching back to 1998?

21 What famous family moved from Madrid to Los Angeles in the summer of 2007?

22 Which celebrity is regarded as the most powerful woman in America?

23 What Scottish-born TV presenter is the daughter of Ryder Cup golfer Bernard Gallacher?

24 What world statesman celebrated his 90th birthday in 2008?

25 What multiple-majors-winning golfer and Grand-Slam-winning tennis player tied the knot together in summer 2008?

26 Actress Heather Locklear was married to what two rock musicians?

27 What BAFTA-winning presenter found fame with Ant & Dec, co-presented American Idol in the US then returned home to host 'So You Think You Can Dance'?

28 What celebrity couple first met in 2004 on the set of 'I'm a Celebrity... Get Me Out of Here!'

29 Which long-legged dancing star of 'Singin' in the Rain' died in 2008 aged 86?

30 What actress was Tom Cruise's girlfriend between his marriages to Nicole Kidman and Katie Holmes?

Quiz 74

1   It's now a part of Sydney but was once a feared destination for transported British convicts. Where is it?

2   'The only invention to have come out of Australia, ever, is the rotary washing line.' Which British writer and journalist said this?

3   Perth is the capital of which Australian territory?

4   What large Australian city lies closest to Tasmania?

5   What Pacific Ocean country gained its independence from Australia in 1975?

6   What is the coastline south of Brisbane known as?

7   Australian band Men at Work had simultaneous no. 1 hits in the UK and US singles charts in 1983 with what song?

8   The world's largest monolith is in Australia. What is it?

9   What renowned New Zealand film director owns Weta Digital visual effects company?

10 What is the capital of New Zealand?

11 What constellation appears on the flags of both Australia and New Zealand?

12 What bloody First World War battle was the first major engagement for the combined ANZAC force?

13 Van Diemen's Land was once a colonial outpost for convicted felons. What is it known as today?

14 A series of comedy blockbusters between 1986 and 2001 featured the exploits of what Australian bushwhacker in the Outback and the big city?

15 What is the New Zealand national bird and the nickname for a New Zealander?

16 What shape is the field in Australian rules football?

17 Canberra is the capital of Australia; but what territory is it in?

18 What famous New Zealand operatic soprano, now a dame, sang at the wedding of Prince Charles and Diana Spencer in 1981?

19 Is New Zealand's largest city, Auckland, on North Island or South Island?

20 What is the most northerly city in Australia's Northern Territory?

21 Which New Zealand city, traditionally a final port of call for Antarctic explorers, is known as the Gateway to the Antarctic?

22 What is the name of New Zealand's famous rugby team?

23 What New Zealand-born actor won the Best Actor Oscar in 2001 for his role in 'Gladiator'?

24 What town is closest to the geographic centre of Australia?

25 Marsupials are the dominant Australian mammal type. What is a baby marsupial called?

26 What Australian state is nicknamed 'The Sunshine State'?

27 Hobart is the largest city in which Australian province?

28 What series of record-breaking movies were made in New Zealand in 2000 for release in each of the following three years?

29 What Oscar-winning Australian actress is an artistic director of the Sydney Theatre Company?

30 What sea lies between Australia and New Zealand?

Quiz 75

1   Napoleon was finally defeated at Waterloo; but what country is Waterloo in?

2   There were two major 18th-century Jacobite risings in Scotland in support of the deposed Stuart kings. Give the date of one.

3   The Women's Institute was founded in 1897. In what country?

4   What nation gifted the Statue of Liberty to America in 1886?

5   In 1753, the Treaty of Paris saw French North American territory pass to Britain. Which territory was it?

6   Which country sought to push imports of the restricted drug opium into China, resulting in the Opium Wars?

7   What day, the anniversary of a famous battle, falls on 21st October?

8   What did engineer Joseph Bazalgette design that eliminated both London's infamous 'Great Stink' and its recurrent cholera epidemics?

9   What territory broke away from Mexico in 1846 to join the United States in 1850?

10 James Watt's improvements to what engine supplied the power that drove Britain's Industrial Revolution?

11 What self-taught civil engineer, builder of the Menai Suspension Bridge, was known as the 'Colossus of Roads'?

12 The ideas of this German philosopher, which included nihilism and a declaration that 'God is dead', were later used by the Nazis. Who was he?

13 Who commissioned the building of the Arc de Triomphe?

14 This group outlined in The People's Charter of 1838 their aims of universal male suffrage, secret ballots, and annual parliaments to hold MPs accountable. Who were they?

15 What nationwide 1926 strike was sparked by concerns over enforced pay cuts and dangerous conditions in Britain's mining industry?

16　What country was once known as 'The Workshop of the World'?

17　Who unified the separate states of Italy in 1861 and also gave his name to a currant-and-shortcake biscuit?

18　What poet wrote about the 'dark Satanic Mills' of England's cities?

19　What self-educated British engineer built the world's first public railway line and devised the standard gauge for railway lines that is still used today?

20　What British city was known as 'Cottonopolis'?

21　What Scots-American steel magnate and philanthropist has been estimated to be the second-richest man in history?

22　What humanitarian Quaker grocer founded a Birmingham company that became one of the world's biggest chocolate makers?

23　What country became the first to stop its slave trade, in 1792?

24　What constitutional change took place in France on 22nd September 1792?

25　What still-popular art movement began in Paris in the 1860s with painters including Monet and Renoir?

26　The German states were unified in 1871 by what Prussian leader?

27　What Austrian Jewish physician, called the 'Father of Psychoanalysis', fled his homeland in 1938 to settle in London?

28　What Irish leader, called the 'Uncrowned King of Ireland', took his country to the brink of Home Rule until he was brought down by a divorce scandal?

29　Who did John Wilkes Booth assassinate in 1865?

30　This cigar-smoking Victorian engineer's numerous notable designs ranged from railway lines and iron-hulled ships to hospitals for the Crimean War. Who was he?

Quiz 76

1   What disease used to be known as the White Death?

2   What is the light-sensitive part of the eye called?

3   What is hippophobia a fear of?

4   What is another name for vitamin B9 which is recommended to pregnant women?

5   What is the more common name for the hallux?

6   The disease varicella is more commonly known as what?

7   What is the largest gland in the human body?

8   How many seconds on average does it take blood to circulate around the body – 23, 60 or 82?

9   What is the type of acid found in the human stomach?

10   How many bones are there in the human ear?

11   What measurement is expressed in terms of systolic over diastolic?

12   Teenagers suffer more than most from comedoes. In layman's terms, what are they?

13   What function does your epiglottis perform?

14   How many teeth should a healthy preschool child have?

15   What cells carry oxygen around your body?

16 Where in your body would you find your lingua?

17 The organs of an unborn child are fully formed after how many weeks of foetal development?

18 What name is given to the nerve cells in the human body?

19 What is the purpose of human eyebrows?

20 Roughly how many times a day does your heart beat (to the nearest 10,000)?

21 What is the normal temperature of a live human body?

22 What is deoxyribonucleic acid better known as?

23 Your tibia is another name for your what?

24 How many vertebrae are there in the adult human back?

25 Diabetes involves a malfunction of which organ of the body?

26 In which part of your body would you find your phalanx bones?

27 If you have cholecystectomy, what part of your body is removed?

28 How many days is the average human gestation period?

29 What is the largest human organ?

30 What gender of child results from an XX-chromosome pairing?

Quiz 77

Can you identify what is being spoken about from each quote?

1   'Houston, we have a problem.'

2   'This is a very bad day for South Africa. Where can white people go? There is only the sea.'

3   'It was the wrong sort of snow.'

4   'There were three of us in the marriage, so it got a bit crowded.'

5   'There can be no whitewash at the Whitehouse.'

6   'A great party is not to be brought down because of a scandal by a woman of easy virtue and a proven liar.'

7   'We have discovered the secret of life!'

8   'I have to inform you that the State of Israel has taken into custody one of the greatest of the Nazi war criminals.'

9   'It does mean... the end of Britain as an independent European state... It means the end of a thousand years of history.'

10 'The men are in splendid spirits... The wire has never been so well cut, nor the military preparations so thorough.'

11 The band was still playing. I guess all of them went down.'

12 'It's over over here.'

13 'As you watch the fire burn these unGerman books, let it also burn into your hearts love of the Fatherland.'

14 'Houston – Tranquillity Base – the Eagle has landed.'

15 They think it's all over... It is now!'

16 'Just rejoice at that news and congratulate our forces and the marines.'

17 'A billion-dollar tragedy with a fifty-cent cause.'

18 Public opinion will be led to adopt, without knowing it, the proposals that we dare not present to them directly...'

19 'We sure liberated the hell out of this place.'

20 'The Earth is blue. How wonderful. It is amazing.'

21 '...is it a book that you would wish your wives or even your servants to read?'

22 'We did it by playing football. Pure, beautiful, inventive football. There was not a negative thought in our heads.'

23 'The executioner is, I believe, very expert, and my neck is very slender.'

24 'I am just going outside. I may be some time.'

25 'This nest of vipers who have tried to sabotage the grandeur of my Germany will be exterminated once and for all.'

26 'This atrocious death will be a terrible lesson for those whose principal occupation consists in spying on and tormenting the film stars.'

27 'To our immense satisfaction we realised we had reached the top of the world.'

28 'I die a queen but I would rather die the wife of (Thomas) Culpepper.'

29 '...I was struck dumb with amazement, and when Lord Carnarvon enquired anxiously if I could see anything, it was all I could do to utter the words, "Yes, wonderful things".'

30 'You ask what is our aim? I can answer in one word: Victory. Victory at all costs... For without victory there is no survival.'

Quiz 78

1   What do the deaths of Elvis Presley and Jim Morrison have in common?

2   The gravestone of what well-known British personality bears the inscription, 'Teenage dreams, so hard to beat'?

3   According to WHO statistics, what is the most common cause of death in the world?

4   What 1994 film had to be finished by computer after its star Brandon Lee was shot during an accident in filming?

5   What comic actor's gravestone is inscribed with the Irish words that translate as, 'I told you I was ill'?

6   What 1918 event killed twice as many people as had died in the First World War?

7   What spy-novel-style death met Bulgarian dissident Georgi Markov in London in 1978?

8   What Motown star was shot dead by his own father in 1984?

9   What satirical claymation show, broadcast on MTV for four years, featured celebrities wrestling each other to the death?

10   Qin Shi Huang was the first emperor of China in the 3rd century BC. What unique funeral goods were found buried with him?

11   What iconic Briton was buried in her wedding veil and with a plaster cast of her dead husband's hand?

12   What two Roman towns were engulfed by pyroclastic surges that killed all their inhabitants in AD 79?

13   The wife of this tough-guy actor who died in 1957, placed a silver whistle inscribed with one of his lines, in the container of his ashes. Who was he?

14   What British playwright was murdered by his lover with a hammer?

15   Whose last words were, 'I'll finally get to see Marilyn'?

16 He was buried with precious furniture, decorative objects, jewellery, chariots, weapons and a large garden's worth of seeds. Who was he?

17 What Russian royal advisor and subject of a Boney M song survived stabbing, poisoning and shooting before being beaten and drowned?

18 What species of insect kills more people than any other?

19 What noted wit stated of the room where he died, 'My wallpaper and I are fighting a duel to the death. One or the other of us has to go.'

20 What pioneering 1920s dancer was strangled when her trailing scarf caught in the wheel-spokes of her open-topped car?

21 How many people are thought to have died in the Great Fire of London – under 10, under 100 or under 1000?

22 Who took over as US president when Abraham Lincoln was assassinated?

23 What noted American playwright choked to death on the cap of a medicine bottle in 1983?

24 Who died in 1955 in a Porsche 550 Spyder that he had nicknamed 'Little Bastard'?

25 According to US government statistics, how many people die in the world each day (to the nearest 10,000)?

26 What Oscar-winning English actor and star of 'The Jungle Book', killed himself out of boredom?

27 What famous 60s singer died when he skied into a tree in 1998?

28 What's the average overall life expectancy for someone born in the UK in 2007?

29 Who was the Greek god of Death and the Underworld?

30 'Ah well, I suppose it has come to this... Such is life.' The last words of what philosophical Australian bushranger?

Quiz 79

1   Roy Plomley was the first host of 'Desert Island Discs'. Who was the second?

2   They were once known as Home, Third and Light. How do we know them?

3   'Barwick Green' is the theme tune for what long-running radio show?

4   Which broadcaster's 'Letter from America' ran for over 50 years?

5   What year did Radio 1 begin broadcasting?

6   The UK has three independent commercial radio stations with a nationwide reach. What are they?

7   It ran for 50 years on Radio 4, was chaired by Humphrey Lyttelton and called itself 'the antidote to panel games'. What was it?

8   What DJ, who broadcast from 1967 for the next 37 years, was the longest-serving of the original Radio 1 DJs?

9   Mozart's 'Eine Kleine Nachtmusik' has been the theme to which long-running Radio 4 quiz show?

10 What's the name of the Archers' family farm?

11 In what country did the first radio broadcast take place in 1906?

12 What 1939 production by Orson Wells on America's CBS radio created mass panic when listeners thought Earth was being invaded?

13 What listed building in London's Portland Place is the registered HQ of the BBC and home to several BBC radio stations?

14 What DJ was the first to be heard on Radio 1?

15 When did Classic FM first begin broadcasting?

16 What famous Texas Ranger made his first-ever appearance on American radio in 1933?

17 In what year did commercial radio first arrive in Britain?

18 What name was first given in the US to radio presenters who set out deliberately to offend?

19 Who was the Canadian inventor of the walkie-talkie, CB radio, the telephone pager and the cordless telephone?

20 Which has the higher frequency, longwave or FM radio broadcasts?

21 What ground-breaking 50s American drama set in Dodge City, portrayed the brutality of the West in its realism and explicit content?

22 When did the BBC Home Service begin broadcasting?

23 What was the name of Manchester's first commercial radio station?

24 What American DJ was credited with popularising rock 'n' roll music, and appeared in music films like 'Rock Around the Clock'?

25 What comedy show, first broadcast on Radio 4, won the Douglas Adams Award for Innovative Comedy Writing in 2001?

26 What German physicist was first to show the existence of electro-magnetic waves, and gave his name to their measurement?

27 In what panel game with Nicholas Parsons do contestants talk on a subject for a period of time without repetition, hesitation or deviation?

28 What famous BBC commentator began his career on TV before moving to 'Test Match Special' where he stayed until his death in 1994?

29 What celebrated BBC news reporter helped pioneer outside broadcasts and sent back reports from Bergen-Belsen on its liberation in 1945?

30 What innovative 50s comedy show by Ray Galton and Alan Simpson introduced the new genre of situation comedy?

Quiz 80

1   What is the Olympic motto?

2   Which country always leads the Olympics' opening parade?

3   The 2012 Olympic Games will be held in London. When were the Games last held there?

4   The Games first began in 776 BC and were held in honour of which Greek god?

5   Where in Greece did the original Games take place?

6   Before the Beijing Olympics, what was the last city to host the Games in Asia?

7   What colour are the rings on the Olympic flag?

8   At which Olympic Games did Palestinian terrorists kidnap and kill 11 athletes and coaches and a local police officer?

9   When did Synchronised Swimming make its first appearance at the Olympic Games?

10   What team has won more medals than any other in the modern Olympiad?

11   Which of the five continents is the only one never to have staged the Games?

12   The Modern Pentathlon has been called 'The True Olympic Sport'. Over what period of time must its five disciplines be completed?

13   What country became the first one to host both the summer and winter Olympics in the same year?

14   Up to the 2010 Winter Olympics, Russia/USSR had the biggest winter medals tally. What country was second?

15   In what year did the first Games of the modern era take place?

16   Which swimmer famously won all seven swimming golds at the 1972 Munich Games?

17   Harold Abrahams won the UK's first sprint gold in 1924. Who won the second?

18   What British athlete won the 800m and 1500m middle-distance double gold at the 2004 Athens Olympics?

19   What two women's field events were included for the first time in the games at Sydney in 2000?

20   What part did Pierre de Coubertin play in the modern Olympic movement?

21   Protests over what accompanied the Olympic flame's progress around the world in 2008?

22   What country has won most medals in the Paralympics?

23   In what competition did Northern Ireland's Mary Peters win a gold medal in 1972?

24   After the Games in 2012, how many times will London have hosted the Olympics?

25   What figure appears on the front of an Olympic gold medal?

26   In what country were the first Winter Olympics held, in 1920?

27   What national organisation coordinates Britain's preparations and administration for the games?

28   Only five countries have competed at every summer Olympics of the modern era. Name three of them.

29   What Briton won a gold medal at each of the five Olympic Games from 1984 to 2000, and in what sport?

30   The first modern Olympiad was in Athens in 1896. What number of Olympiad will it be when London hosts the 2012 Games?

Quiz 81

1   What was the name of the Simpsons' pet dog that Homer brought home from the dog track on Christmas Eve?

2   On what TV show does 'The Itchy and Scratchy Show' appear?

3   Who is Bart's class teacher?

4   The Simpsons' neighbour, Ned Flanders has two sons. What are their names?

5   What is the shop owned by Apu in Springfield?

6   A sign outside one Springfield residence reads, 'Thank you for not discussing the outside world'. What is the building?

7   What is the first name of Bart and Lisa's grandfather, Grampa Simpson?

8   What business in Springfield does Montgomery Burns own?

9   What pioneer was the founder of Springfield?

10 How many spikes does Bart have in his hair?

11 Springfield's donut store has a statue of a giant boy on top holding a donut. What is the store's name?

12 Jeff Albertson is one of the Springfield store owners. What is his better-known nickname?

13 What nearby city is Springfield's great rival?

14 'The Simpsons Movie' had its world premiere in Springfield in which American state?

15 Who is Springfield's Bostonian-accented mayor?

16 Who is the Scottish character on 'The Simpsons'?

17 What are the names of Marge Simpson's older twin sisters?

18 What TV personality has tried to kill Bart several times?

19 What year did the Simpsons first get their own series?

20 What is the name of Homer's alcoholic best friend?

21 What brand of beer is Homer Simpson's favourite?

22 What instrument does Lisa play in the school band?

23 What character from the show features on Waylon Smithers's screen saver?

24 What is the name of Police Chief Wiggum's son?

25 Which TV-personality character was retired after the actor who voiced him died in real life?

26 Who voices Lisa's character?

27 What is the name of the church that the Simpson family attend?

28 The Treehouse of Horror episodes are shown every year in the US at what time of year?

29 What is Seymour Skinner's job?

30 What is the Simpsons' address?

Quiz 82

1 What recent TV show teamed up Sam Tyler with DCI Gene Hunt?

2 In David Bowie's song 'Life on Mars', who were 'fighting on the dance floor'?

3 What message did Lord Admiral Nelson send to his sailors at the Battle of Trafalgar?

4 Who did England beat at Wembley in 1966 to win the World Cup?

5 In what year were West Germany and East Germany reunited?

6 Graham Fagg and Philippe Cozette shook hands to seal historic new ties between Britain and France in 1990. Where did the handshake take place?

7 British comic and actor David Walliams swam the English Channel for Sport Relief in 2006. What stretch of water did he swim for charity in 2008?

8 What two bodies of water does the Strait of Gibraltar connect?

9 How many countries officially border the Mediterranean Sea?

10 Vigt-et-un is French for 21. It's also the name of a card game. Give another name by which this game is known.

11 Blackjack is one of the most popular casino games. Who famously made his big-screen comeback in 'Casino Royale' in 2006?

12 The first James Bond film was 'Dr No'. What was the second?

13 What three colours make up the Russian flag?

14 There are three colours that cannot be made by mixing other colours together. Blue and red are two of these; what is the third?

15 In multi-stage cycle races, the overall race leader wears the yellow jersey. But what rider wears the rainbow jersey?

16 America's only world chess champion died in 2008. Who was he?

17 The 2006 movie 'Bobby' depicted fictional events surrounding Senator Robert Kennedy's assassination in 1968. In what city did the events happen?

18 Los Angeles lies at coordinates 34° North and 118° West. What first-world city lies at 34° South and 151° East?

19 Australia's Pacific Highway links Sydney with what city over 600 miles away?

20 What famous band, originally from Manchester and the Isle of Man, began their music careers in Brisbane?

21 The Bee Gees wrote a movie soundtrack that remains the second-best-selling ever. What film was it for?

22 The Peggy Lee song 'Fever' mentions what famous Italian star-crossed lovers?

23 William Shakespeare wrote 'Romeo and Juliet'. Who was on the English throne when he wrote it?

24 Elizabeth I ruled England for 44 years. What year was it when Elizabeth II had ruled for 44 years?

25 What acclaimed BBC TV series, broadcast in 1996, brought together a future Doctor Who and a future James Bond?

26 For how many seasons did New York-based sitcom 'Friends' run?

27 A number system with base 10 is known as what kind of system?

28 Before decimal currency was introduced into Britain, how many pennies were in a shilling?

29 The 1957 movie '12 Angry Men' was co-produced by one of its stars. Who was he?

30 Henry Fonda's daughter Jane was previously married to what American media mogul?

Quiz 83

Name the sport associated with each of these movies.

1 'Field of Dreams'

2 'Escape to Victory'

3 'When We Were Kings'

4 'National Velvet'

5 'The Flying Scot'

6 'The Color of Money'

7 'K2'

8 'Cool Runnings'

9 'Million Dollar Baby'

10 'Slapshot'

11 'Mean Machine'

12 'Enter the Dragon'

13 'Players'

14 'Chariots of Fire'

15 'Days of Thunder'

16 'Gregory's Girl'

17 'Point Break'

18 'Varsity Blues'

19 'Aspen Extreme'

20 'The Longest Yard'

21 'Hoosiers'

22 'Fever Pitch'

23 'Raging Bull'

24 'The Cannonball Run'

25 'A League of Their Own'

26 'Stick It'

27 'Seabiscuit'

28 'The Hustler'

29 'Breaking Away'

30 'Caddyshack'

Quiz 84

1 What 20th-century British opera charts the decline in the relationship of Elizabeth I and the Earl of Essex?

2 What classical composer was a successful gambler, with his own casino, and lent money to hard-up musicians?

3 Which Rossini opera tells the story of Count Almaviva's attemps to marry his beloved Rosina?

4 What were the names of the Three Tenors?

5 How does the lead character die in Bizet's opera, 'Carmen'?

6 What is the name given to the text of an opera?

7 What music was composed by Handel in 1717 for George I and played for the king from a barge on the Thames?

8 In Wagner's 'Ring Cycle', what all-female group did Flosshilde, Wellgunde and Woglinde make up?

9 Which noted American conductor wrote the music for 'West Side Story' and 'On The Waterfront'?

10 How would you play a Portuguese machete – blow it, pluck it or play it with a bow?

11 What do the beguine, cotillon and krakowiak have in common?

12 What famous national anthem, written as the 'War Song for the Rhine Army' in 1792, is heard in Tchaikovsky's 1812 Overture?

13 This Russian composer, author of 'Peter and the Wolf', died on the same day as Stalin. Who was he?

14 The Thomas Arne opera 'The Masque of Alfred', contains which patriotic British song?

15 What American composer, a frequent collaborator with his lyricist brother Ira, wrote the opera 'Porgy and Bess'?

16 What 1981 French movie centred around a bootleg tape of a performance of the opera, 'La Wally'?

17 FE Weatherly's lyrics to the Irish folk tune 'The (London)Derry Air' are the most famous written for this music. What is the song called?

18 'The Ballad of Mack the Knife' comes originally from which work by Kurt Weill and Bertolt Brecht?

19 The characters in Bellini's Opera 'I Capuleti e i Montecchi' also appear in which Shakespeare play?

20 What do hummel, sackbut and vox humana all have in common?

21 What famous clown is mentioned in Queen's 'Bohemian Rhapsody' and is also the subject of a 1922 ballet by Sibelius?

22 What Puccini opera features the characters Lieutenant Pinkerton, Cio-Cio-San and their child, Trouble?

23 What prolific British composer lives in Orkney and became the first new Master of the Queen's Music in the 21st century?

24 What famous composer only ever wrote one opera, 'Fidelio'?

25 What classical Italian composer was a noted gourmand and had a rich dish named after him?

26 If a piece of music is to be played pianissimo, how should it be played?

27 What German composer wrote 'Hebrides Overture' after a visit to the Western Isles in 1829?

28 What Englishman is the chief conductor with the Berlin Philharmonic Orchestra?

29 What German composer who died in 2007, wrote famously experimental work such as 'String Quartet For Players In Helicopters'?

30 What name is given to the series of classical concerts that takes place mostly in the Royal Albert Hall each summer?

Quiz 85

1   What two British fliers made the first non-stop flight across the Atlantic in 1919?

2   What was the name of Portugal's famous 15th-century explorer prince?

3   What brothers took to the skies for the first time at Kitty Hawk, North Carolina?

4   What was the name of Columbus's ship in which he sailed across the Atlantic to the New World?

5   What missionary explorer was found in 1871 on the shores of Lake Tanganyika by Henry Morton Stanley?

6   Who discovered the Hawaiian islands in 1778, named them the Sandwich Islands and was killed by local natives in 1779?

7   This larger-than-life character was expelled from Oxford, travelled in disguise to Mecca, translated the 'Arabian Nights' and searched for the source of the Nile. Who was he?

8   The first expedition to cross the Antarctic continent via the South Pole was finally successful in what year?

9   What Viking is thought to have reached North America in around 1000 AD?

10 Who was the first person to reach the South Pole?

11 Which Portuguese explorer's ship, 'Vittoria', was first to circumnavigate the globe?

12 What Spanish Conquistador began the conquest of the Aztecs?

13 What English hero-explorer began his round-the-world trip in 1577?

14 What monk came from Ireland and settled on the island of Iona to teach Christianity to the Scots?

15 What famous New Zealander remarked, after reaching the top of the world, 'Well, we knocked the bastard off!'?

16 What English adventurer became the first man ever to cross Antarctica completely on foot?

17 What Scottish missionary helped promote the rights of women in Nigeria, where she was given a state funeral on her death in 1915?

18 16th-century French explorer Jacques Cartier discovered and claimed what country for France?

19 What Arctic island was colonised by Norse settlers from the 10th century until the 15th?

20 What year did Captain Scott's ill-fated Antarctic voyage end?

21 What Englishwoman held the record for the fastest solo circumnavigation of the globe until 2008?

22 Who was the first Roman leader to try to invade Britain?

23 What 6th-century Irish monk made a seven-year journey to the Isle of the Blessed, thought by some to be America?

24 What country was the first to begin exploring across the world in the Age of Discovery in the 15th century?

25 What island was first discovered in 1642 by Dutchman Abel Tasman?

26 What famous Norwegian explorer was first to navigate the Northwest Passage between the Atlantic and Pacific Oceans in 1906?

27 What Englishman sailed single-handed around the world with only one stop in 1967?

28 New Zealand was first seen and claimed by what European nation?

29 Who was the first woman to fly solo across the Atlantic?

30 The first person to discover that America was not a part of Asia, but a continent in its own right, gave his name to the place. Who was he?

Quiz 86

1   If you were served a Baked Alaska, what would you expect to find inside it?

2   What flower is the spice saffron taken from?

3   What is eaten to celebrate the rolling away of the stone from Jesus's tomb on Easter Sunday?

4   Which overweight star was said to have eaten mashed potato every night for the last year of his life?

5   According to Cervantes's character Don Quixote, what is the best sauce in the world?

6   What is the main ingredient in guacamole?

7   What type of fungus is used in the manufacture of bread and beer?

8   What drink is made from blue agave, a desert succulent?

9   What type of cake is traditionally baked for Easter Sunday?

10   The famine in Ireland in the mid 19th century was as a result of the failure of what crop?

11   Who said, 'Football and cookery are the most important subjects in the country?'

12   What method of food preservation requires that food be heated to 63 °C?

13   Which green-coloured spirit, made with wormwood, is so strong that its sale has been restricted for many years?

14   What is the ingredient that gives Worcester Sauce its flavour?

15   What type of buns are traditionally baked for Good Friday?

16 Christine, Alice and Florence are all varieties of which fruit?

17 Slivovitz is an Eastern European brandy, made from what ingredient?

18 During wartime rationing in Britain, how many fresh eggs a week were allowed per person?

19 What country does Budweiser Budvar lager come from?

20 A magnum of champagne is the size of two bottles. How many bottles' worth does a Methuselah hold?

21 What kind of dish would you expect to be eating if you were served Mulligatawny?

22 'Get yer haggis right here! Chopped heart and lungs, boiled in a wee sheep's stomach! Tastes as good as it sounds!' Which TV character said this?

23 What would you normally add to whisky to make a Whisky Sour cocktail?

24 Which country does Bull's Blood wine come from?

25 What type of pastry is used to make chocolate éclairs?

26 In 'Sing a Song of Sixpence', what was the queen doing?

27 From what American state do Cajun and Creole cuisine come?

28 What type of food is ricotta?

29 What flavour is Triple sec liqueur?

30 What do Duke of York, Ulster Chieftain and King Edward have in common?

Quiz 87

1   Created a National Park in 1951, it was the first in Britain. Which one was it?

2   Which castle was called 'the Key of England'?

3   Dunvegan Castle on Skye is home to the head of which famous Scottish clan?

4   Who was voted the Greatest Briton of All Time in a 2002 BBC poll?

5   Who came second in the same poll?

6   What colour are the seats in the House of Lords?

7   Built in 1882 and described by William Morris as 'the supremest specimen of all ugliness', it is one of the engineering wonders of the world. What is it?

8   Only one of the home countries has a patron saint's day that doesn't fall in spring. Which one is it?

9   Which is the largest castle in Wales?

10   Where in the British Isles would you find the Tynwald?

11   Who was the last British monarch to die in battle?

12   On which iconic British building will you see the words, 'In These Stones Horizons Sing'?

13   What is Britain's tallest building?

14   Where would you have to go to celebrate Maggie Thatcher Day on 10th January?

15   Which British city lies at 57° North?

16 The largest inhabited castle in the world is in Britain. What is it?

17 In what decade did Greenwich time finally replace local times in Britain?

18 What is Britain's largest area of fresh water?

19 What is the UK's highest civilian merit award?

20 The Union Flag combines the flags of which three saints?

21 What is the largest UK bird?

22 What river does Britain's longest suspension bridge span?

23 What country is the UK's favourite holiday destination?

24 What is the difference between Great Britain and the United Kingdom?

25 What emblem is under the crown on the back of a 5p piece?

26 Who is the parliamentary officer who raps on the door to summon the House of Commons to the state opening of Parliament for the monarch's speech?

27 What British political office was Robert Walpole the first person to assume?

28 Where in Britain would you find the Mathematical Bridge?

29 What major British road was officially opened by PM Margaret Thatcher in 1986?

30 What plant is associated with St David's Day?

Quiz 88

1   What British magazine that satirises Establishment incompetence and corruption, has been a magnet for libel lawsuits since its first appearance?

2   What fictional traveller visited the lands of Brobdingnag and Lilliput?

3   At which London club did Phileas Fogg end his journey and win his bet in 'Around the World in 80 Days'?

4   What well-known comic features the characters Biffa Bacon and Raffles, Gentleman Thug?

5   Who wrote the novel '2001: A Space Odyssey'?

6   What American writer was knocked down and almost killed in a traffic accident near his Maine home in 1999?

7   Thomas More's 16th-century book about a perfect society gave the English language a new word in its title. What is it?

8   What fictional character fell asleep for 20 years in the Catskill Mountains of New York state?

9   What is the motto of Alexandre Dumas's 'Three Musketeers'?

10 From 'The Lord of the Rings', name the sons of Denethor, Steward of Gondor.

11 Which one of Chaucer's pilgrims tells the first of the Canterbury Tales?

12 'The Colour of Magic' is the first book in which series by writer Terry Pratchett?

13 What fictional sleuth first made his appearance in the 'Strand' magazine in 1890?

14 In 'The Hitch-hiker's Guide to the Galaxy', what does a babel fish allow Arthur Dent to do?

15 What British newspaper was the first to publish a colour supplement?

16 She was the poet Shelley's wife, but Mary Shelley was also famous for writing what classic Gothic horror novel?

17 'The Husband', 'Velocity' and 'Life Expectancy' are all novels by what bestselling American writer?

18 What 20th-century French philosopher was a leading light of the theory of Existentialism and turned down the 1964 Nobel Prize for Literature?

19 What two famous characters first met in the labs at Barts Hospital?

20 From which novel of government surveillance and propaganda, comes the name and concept of Room 101, which contains the worst thing in the world?

21 In 1989 some Muslims called a fatwa for the death of what writer?

22 What US science-fiction writer founded the Church of Scientology?

23 What novel by American Helene Hanff tells the story of her correspondence with staff at a London bookshop in the 1950s and 60s?

24 German brothers Jacob and Wilhelm wrote children's stories including 'Cinderella' and 'Rumpelstiltskin'. What was their surname?

25 How many Sherlock Holmes novels did Doyle write?

26 What book was consistently voted Book of the Century in several end-of-century polls?

27 What county was Emily Brontë's 'Wuthering Heights' set in?

28 What rusty-voiced character from Stevenson's 'Treasure Island' dreamed of 'cheese – toasted, mostly'?

29 All the events in what modern classic novel take place on 16th June 1904?

30 Captain Hastings is the sidekick of which fictional sleuth?

Quiz 89

Can you name the advert behind each slogan?

1   If you see Sid, tell him

2   The sweet you can eat between meals without spoiling your appetite

3   It's the real thing

4   The cross-your-heart bra

5   Happiness is a cigar called...

6   The mint with the hole

7   Refreshes the parts other beers cannot reach

8   Too good to hurry mints

9   It just goes on and on and on

10 A hazelnut in every bite

11 Keeps your cat a kitten cat

12 It's not for girls

13 Tense nervous headache? Nothing acts faster than...

14 We go further so you don't have to

15 The smoker's match

16 Made to make your mouth water, Fresh with the tang of citrus, Four refreshing fruit flavours – Orange, Lemon, Strawberry, Lime!

17 Just do it

18 Put a tiger in your tank!

19 Tap it and unwrap it

20 Because you're worth it

21 Let your fingers do the walking

22 I liked it so much I bought the company

23 The soluble aspirin, the type doctors prefer

24 Nothing over sixpence

25 Wotalotlgot!

26 Bite it! Crunch it! Chew it!

27 It needn't be hell with...

28 The future's bright. The future's...

29 Prolongs active life

30 The world's favourite airline

Quiz 90

1 Who had a top 10 hit in 2000 with the 'Big Brother' theme?

2 Which previously married duo had a major hit with 'Seven Nation Army' in 2003?

3 'Shot You Down' was a hit for Nancy Sinatra in the 60s and in 2005 when she featured on a new version. Whose was it?

4 The band McFly were named after a character in what classic 80s movie?

5 Who sang about 'Stupid Girls' in 2006?

6 What group of puppets from a BBC show had a no. 6 hit with 'Number 1' in 2000?

7 'Sound of the Underground' was the Christmas no. 1 of 2002 and the first hit for what pop phenomenon?

8 What popular band, originally a boy band, reformed successfully in 2005 after almost a decade apart?

9 Liam Lynch had a top 10 hit in 2002 with what song?

10 Tony Christie teamed up with Peter Kay on the 2005 reissue of 'Amarillo' to benefit what charity?

11 Their albums include 'The Holy Bible', 'Everything Must Go' and, in 2007, 'Send Away the Tigers'. Who are they?

12 This Detroit band, fronted by Dick Valentine, have had hits that include 'Danger! High Voltage' and 'Gay Bar'. Who are they?

13 Which former Clash member produced the Libertines' albums 'Up the Bracket' and 'The Libertines'?

14 What solo singer released the album '25' in 2006 to celebrate a quarter century of his music career?

15 What new chart started in 2004?

16 Two acts have made the UK singles chart in every decade from the 1950s to the 2000s. Who are they?

17 What single was a no. 1 for Eminem from the soundtrack of his '8 Mile' movie?

18 David Gray's first top 10 hit came in 2000. What was it?

19 What movie star makes up one half of the self-styled 'greatest band on earth', Tenacious D?

20 What American glam-disco outfit has Ana Matronic, Babydaddy and Jake Shears among its members?

21 A double-A side by Westlife, featuring two covers of 70s hits, was no. 1 at the start of the millennium. What were the songs?

22 Madison Avenue became the first Australian band in 17 years to have a UK no. 1 with what song in 2000?

23 What is the biggest selling British female group of the 21st century?

24 What Cbeebies character took the no. 1 chart slot at Christmas 2000?

25 How many of the Spice Girls have had solo no. 1s?

26 What British singer won five Grammy Awards, including Best New Artist, in 2008?

27 What was the Red Hot Chilli Peppers' first album of the 21st century?

28 Robbie Williams sang top-10 duets with two Australians, in 2000 and 2001. Who were they?

29 Madonna's thirteenth no. 1 single, in 2008, was a duet with what American singer?

30 What two bands collaborated on a version of 'Walk This Way' for Comic Relief in 2007?

Quiz 91

1   What was played for the first time at an FA Cup final in April 1938?

2   In 1986, which Scottish footballer became the first to win 100 caps?

3   How many survivors of the 1958 Munich Air Disaster played in the side that won the European Cup 10 years later?

4   Who is England's most capped player of all time?

5   What was the first trophy Alex Ferguson won with Manchester United?

6   Who scored the winning goal in Spain's Euro 2008 victory?

7   What song did the England World Cup squad take to no. 1 in the summer of the Mexico World Cup in 1970?

8   What Dutch professional has had the longest name to be printed on the back of a shirt?

9   What former Real Madrid manager was appointed England manager at the end of 2007?

10   What is the venue for the 2010 World Cup?

11   What colour were the England team's shirts when they won the World Cup in 1966?

12   What two teams share Italy's San Siro Stadium?

13   Who were the only non-English side to win the FA Cup?

14   When did the First Division clubs break away from the Football League to form the Premier League?

15   What former Manchester United captain became the manager of Sunderland in 2006?

16 How many Englishmen have managed a Premier League-winning side?

17 What is the name of the Italian premier league?

18 How many times has Africa hosted the World Cup before 2010?

19 What side are ranked the world's richest in terms of income?

20 What year did Alex Ferguson steer Aberdeen to victory in the UEFA Cup?

21 What future Celtic manager was a member of Ferguson's 1983 cup-winning side?

22 What Spanish side are nicknamed Los Blancos?

23 Who is England's top goalscorer of all time?

24 What English side has the nickname of The Baggies?

25 What team has been the only university side ever to win the FA Cup?

26 What top Italian side plays in black-and-white vertical-striped shirts?

27 What Second Division team beat Don Revie's Leeds side to lift the FA Cup in 1973?

28 What UK professional football league was founded in 1992?

29 What former European Champions League winners play at the Estádio do Dragão (Stadium of the Dragon)?

30 What Scottish team have twice reached the final of the FA Cup and remain the only amateur side in the Scottish league?

Quiz 92

1   Which one grows up from a limestone cave floor, stalactites or stalagmites?

2   The Aswan Dam prevents flooding along which river?

3   In which country can you find the region of Patagonia?

4   Name one of the three Canadian territories.

5   Irian Jaya forms the western half of what Pacific island?

6   Mozambique is a former colony of which one-time European super-power?

7   It lies in the South China Sea, its population is under 2000 and its capital is Flying Fish Cove. What is it?

8   Which two countries lie on either side of the Gulf of Bothnia?

9   What group of islands in the Caribbean is owned by the Netherlands?

10 It used to be called Zaire, but what is it called now?

11 Is Uruguay on the east or west coast of South America?

12 Minsk is the capital of what country?

13 Which of the two Poles lies over land?

14 Which state lies to the north of California?

15 Castries is the largest town on which Caribbean island?

16   Off which landmass would you find the Amundsen Sea?

17   Spain has two city outposts adjoining Morocco on the south Mediterranean coast. Name one.

18   It used to be called Persia. What country is it now?

19   In what country would you find the city of Lima?

20   What is the only city which is in two continents?

21   On which Spanish costa is the city of Malaga?

22   They lie in the North Atlantic and their name translates as the Sheep Islands. What island group are they?

23   Which Canadian province lies north and west of the American state of Maine?

24   In what modern country is Timbuktu situated?

25   On which continent would you find the country of Guyana?

26   Which city is further north, Edinburgh or Glasgow?

27   Kansas City lies across two states. One is Kansas; what is the other?

28   In which group of islands would you find Graciosa, Pico and Flores?

29   Over what country does the Mistral wind blow?

30   How much of the earth's land surface area is desert – one tenth, one quarter or one third?

Quiz 93

1   What holiday is celebrated in the US on the fourth Thursday in November?

2   In German mythology, the Lorelei lived on a rock at the edge of the River Rhine. What did they do?

3   Which hero of Troy was killed by Achilles who then dragged his body behind his chariot under the Trojan walls?

4   In Celtic mythology, what kind of animal is a kelpie?

5   What Maori war dance do the New Zealand All Blacks perform before every rugby match?

6   The Celts knew this day as Samhain (pronounced sow-en); what popular festival has taken its place?

7   Where did the spirits of Viking warriors who died courageous deaths go?

8   When is the Mexican Dia de Los Muertos, or Day of the Dead?

9   If you are born in January, what precious stone is said to be your birthstone?

10   According to the Chinese calendar, 2009 is the year of what animal?

11   To the Greeks he was Pan, to the Romans Silvanus. What was he god of?

12   Who was the son of King Arthur who eventually betrayed his father?

13   What legendary Irish hero, child of the sun god Lug, turned into a frenzied one-eyed monster in battle?

14   Hallowe'en, or All Hallows' Eve, is on 31st October. What day is it the eve of?

15   If you were born on 17th March, what would your zodiac sign be?

16 What name is given to the day in December when the northern hemisphere is furthest from the sun?

17 What date in the old British calendar is Beltane?

18 The word Götterdämmerung, taken from Germanic mythology, indicates what?

19 Which of King Arthur's knights was the one who found the Holy Grail?

20 What name is given to the item which is used at séances and printed with numbers and letters at which a planchette points?

21 The French call it Poisson d'Avril. What do we know it as?

22 This god was Loki to the Norse, Vulcan to the Romans and Hephaestus to the Greeks. Of what element was he god?

23 On what date is Twelfth Night?

24 In Norse myth, Yggdrasil is the tree at the centre of the universe, supporting all the worlds. What type of tree is it?

25 In the language of flowers, what does a red rose represent?

26 What Neolithic burial mound on Orkney is aligned to be illuminated by the sun at the midwinter solstice?

27 What are the Six Celtic Nations?

28 Silver is a traditional gift for a 25th wedding anniversary. What is the gift for those married for 20 years?

29 What bird was considered a powerful omen of prophesy, war and death by the Ancient Britons?

30 What British hero was said to have defeated the invading Anglo-Saxons at Mons Badonicus, or Badon Hill, around 500 AD?

Quiz 94

Can you identify the voice artists from their roles listed below?

1   Fifi Forget-Me-Not in 'Fifi and the Flowertots'

2   Genie in 'Aladdin'

3   Narrator in 'The Little Princess'

4   Jessica Rabbit in 'Who Framed Roger Rabbit?'

5   Buzz Lightyear in 'Toy Story' and 'Toy Story 2'

6   Narrator in 'Roary the Racing Car'

7   Narrator in 'The Beeps'

8   Bugs Bunny

9   Puss in Boots in 'Shrek 2' & 'Shrek the Third'

10   Mr Fredrick Little in the 'Stuart Little' series

11   Scar in 'The Lion King'

12   Narrator in 'Thomas the Tank Engine' (1990s series)

13   Esmeralda in 'The Hunchback of Notre Dame'

14   Narrator in 'In The Night Garden'

15   Narrator in 'Pocoyo'

16 Mushu the Dragon in 'Mulan'

17 Mumble in 'Happy Feet'

18 Wiley the Sheep in 'Jakers!'

19 Homer in 'The Simpsons'

20 Yoda in the 'Star Wars' series

21 RJ in 'Over the Hedge'

22 Narrator in 'Roobarb & Custard Too'

23 Narrator in 'The Wombles'

24 Narrator in 'Camberwick Green', 'Trumpton' and 'Chigley'

25 Stinky Pete the Prospector in 'Toy Story 2'

26 Gollum in 'The Lord of the Rings' trilogy

27 Lightning McQueen in 'Cars'

28 Princess Fiona in the 'Shrek' series

29 Narrator in 'Fireman Sam' (original series)

30 Darth Vader in the 'Star Wars' series

Quiz 95

1   What English poet drowned in suspicious circumstances in the Mediterranean near Livorno in 1806?

2   The movie 'The Barretts of Wimpole Street' depicted the real-life romance between which two poets?

3   What Edward Lear couple 'went to sea in a beautiful pea-green boat'?

4   On what famous statue can you find inscribed lines from the sonnet, 'The New Colossus'?

5   What long-serving Poet Laureate was forced out of his position in 1689 because he was a Catholic?

6   'Season of mists and mellow fruitfulness! Close bosom-friend of the maturing sun' These are the opening lines of what poem?

7   Who wrote 'Anthem for Doomed Youth' in 1917 as a result of his experiences in the First World War?

8   Name the two Irish poets who won the Nobel Literature Prize for their efforts.

9   Clement Moore's poem, 'A Visit from St Nicholas', is better known as what?

10 In the epic poem 'Beowulf', who does the hero Beowulf set out to kill?

11 In 1814 Francis Scott Key wrote a poem that became a famous national anthem. What was the poem?

12 How many Circles of Hell are there in Dante's 'Divine Comedy'?

13 Which poet wrote the lines, 'How do I love thee? Let me count the ways.'

14 What hard-living poet's last words were, 'I've had eight straight whiskies, I think that's a record... after 39 years this is all I've done.'?

15 In the nursery rhyme 'Ding, Dong, Bell', who put pussy in the well?

16 According to poet John McCrae, where do '...the poppies blow Between the crosses, row on row'?

17 The first line of this sonnet is, 'Shall I compare thee to a summer's day?' Who wrote it?

18 'Rats! They fought the dogs and killed the cats, And bit the babies in the cradles'? From which Robert Browning poem do these lines come?

19 How many lines of poetry are in a sestet?

20 'Wee, sleekit, cow'rin, tim'rous beastie, O, what a panic's in thy breastie!' The first line of which Burns poem – 'To a Mouse', 'To a Louse' or 'To a Haggis'?

21 German writer Goethe's famous poem on the dangers of overreaching your abilities was immortalised in Disney's 'Fantasia'. What is it?

22 What do the initials in TS Eliot's name stand for?

23 What Conservative politician bought the Grantchester house that is the subject of a Rupert Brooke poem?

24 How many lines are there in a sonnet?

25 What Irish-born poet, whose son won a Best Actor Oscar in 2008, was made British poet laureate in 1968?

26 What 14th-century poet is said to have written the allegorical English poem 'Piers Plowman'?

27 Who wrote the nonsense poems, 'The Hunting of the Snark' and 'Jabberwocky'?

28 What poet was described as being 'mad, bad, and dangerous to know'?

29 Who was appointed British poet laureate in 1999 for ten years?

30 What 20th-century poet was described by WB Yeats as 'the handsomest young man in England'?

Quiz 96

1   What 19th-century Scots physicist established the presence of electromagnetic radiation?

2   Hungarian artist and journalist Lazlo Biro invented what in 1938?

3   In what century was gunpowder first used in China?

4   The quantum theory was developed by which German physicist?

5   What English doctor was a pioneer of antisepsis in the 19th century?

6   In what year did the Wright Brothers make their first powered aircraft flight?

7   Which signatory of the American Declaration of Independence proved that lightning is a form of electricity?

8   What English scientist devised the world-wide web?

9   In 1530 a Polish astronomer first claimed that planets move around the Sun, not the Earth as was thought. Who was he?

10   Charles Darwin's 'On The Origin Of Species By Natural Selection', containing his theories of evolution, was published in what year?

11   Radio transmissions were first sent across the Atlantic in 1901. What physicist first devised them?

12   Compasses were first used to navigate at sea by the Chinese and the Arabs. In which century?

13   What did Scottish inventor John Boyd Dunlop develop to cushion his son's bike ride on cobbled streets?

14   Which prolific American inventor devised the first successful lightbulb in 1879?

15   Which 19th-century French chemist devised a means of food preservation that killed off bacteria with heat?

16 When did the first home computer appear on the market?

17 Now an everyday process, it was first devised in 1451 and facilitated revolutionary advances. What is it?

18 Edward Jenner, an English doctor, devised the first vaccine and first used it in what year (to the nearest 10 years)?

19 The British inventor of the hovercraft died in 1999. What was his name?

20 The first car powered by internal combustion engine was devised in 1885. Who was its German inventor?

21 Iron smelting was first developed around how many years BC (to the nearest 500)?

22 What American inventor devised a system of communicating by sending coded dots and dashes by telegraph wire?

23 This famous 20th-century French marine explorer was co-inventor of scuba diving apparatus. Who was he?

24 Scots inventor Alexander Bain registered a design in 1843 for what machine still used in telecoms today?

25 English designer Harry Beck devised an item in 1933 that is a design classic and iconic symbol. What is it?

26 What everyday kitchen device did Englishman Kenneth Wood invent?

27 English citizens had close experience of the first rocket-propelled missile; what was it called?

28 This machine, first made in 1832, revolutionised gardening. What was it?

29 What English businessman created the world's first travel agency?

30 According to the inventor Thomas Edison, genius is 1% inspiration and 99% – what?

Quiz 97

1   What busy creatures does a melittologist study?

2   What does UEFA stand for?

3   Shiraz is a name commonly used in Australia for what type of grape?

4   How did Ancient Greek hero Theseus find his way out of the Labyrinth on Crete?

5   What did Nelson lose at the Battle of Santa Cruz de Tenerife in 1797?

6   Who is the only author to have his own number in the Dewey Decimal System of library-book classification?

7   What coloured headwear originally comes from a Hindu word meaning 'tie'?

8   What name is given to a group of identical cells that share their ancestry from a single common cell?

9   In Australia, what organisation is known as the ALP?

10   How many eighths are there in 0.50?

11   What is the only volcano on the Italian mainland?

12   Was Tin Pan Alley in New York a district with a concentration of music publishers, of beggars or of kitchenware manufacturers?

13   Which one is bigger, a gene or a chromosome?

14   Little Jackie Paper was the friend of what magical creature?

15   Malmo in Sweden is linked by rail to the capital of another country across the Strait of Øresund. What city is it?

16 What is the minimum legal maturation age for Scotch whisky?

17 What is the link between Robert Mugabe, Nicolae Ceaucescu, Benito Mussolini and Bob Geldof?

18 Which European country has abandoned the first two verses of its own national anthem?

19 What uniform colour is the Urdu word that means 'dusty'?

20 What golf-loving singer's last words were, 'That was a great game of golf, fellers!'?

21 What English king was believed to have hidden in an oak tree while on the run?

22 In the 'Teddy Bears' Picnic', what time to mummies and daddies take the teddy bears home to bed?

23 What European country has the longest-lived population on Earth?

24 How many banks are allowed to issue banknotes in the United Kingdom?

25 What colour is the number 0 on a European roulette wheel?

26 John Brown, inspiration for the 19th-century song 'John Brown's Body', was a political agitator in what cause?

27 A swastika became infamous as the symbol of Nazi Germany. But in Buddhism and Hinduism, what did it symbolise?

28 What year did the first motorway open in the UK?

29 In American politics, what is the GOP?

30 What work by the composer Handel features the 'Hallelujah' chorus?

Quiz 98

1   'I'd like to manage those four boys. It wouldn't take me more than two half days a week.' Who said this in 1961?

2   'I am become Death, the destroyer of worlds.' What scientist was quoting the Bhagavad-Gita in 1945?

3   'I think now would be a good time for a beer.' What did President Roosevelt want to celebrate with a drink in 1933?

4   'The only way to get rid of a temptation is to yield to it.' Famous advice from what noted wit?

5   Whose slogan in the 60s was, 'Hell, no, we won't go!'?

6   'I have played three presidents, three saints and two geniuses. If that doesn't create an ego problem, nothing does.' What actor's words are these?

7   What British novelist once described his Russian Roulette games as 'a gamble with a 16% chance of failure'?

8   'She gives him sex. He gives her class.' Which on-screen couple was actress Katherine Hepburn talking about here?

9   'I spent a lot of money on booze, birds and fast cars. The rest I just squandered.' Famous words attributed to what fast-living footballer?

10   In 'Twelfth Night', what did Shakespeare say was the 'food of love'?

11   According to Margaret Thatcher, what place 'is where you come when you have nothing better to do'?

12   What filmmaker said, 'There is no terror in a bang – only in the anticipation of it'?

13   Who once declared, while still an unknown, 'I want to be as famous as Persil Automatic'?

14   'It's just a job. Grass grows, birds fly, waves pound the sand. I beat people up.' These are the words of which famous champion?

15   What famous actress declared, '...I guess I am a fantasy'?

16 According to George Bernard Shaw, what 'is wasted on the young'?

17 '...they are lions led by donkeys.' Who was this general describing?

18 'For God's sake bring me a large Scotch. What a bloody awful country.' Home Secretary Reginald Maudling's assessment of what part of his beat in 1970?

19 'In our history, this is an unwritten and never-to-be-forgotten page of glory.' What was Heinrich Himmler talking about in 1943?

20 'His kind of music is deplorable, a rancid smelling aphrodisiac.' What fellow performer was Frank Sinatra talking about?

21 What Renaissance genius declared, 'The true work of art is but a shadow of the Divine perfection'?

22 Nigel Lawson, former Tory Chancellor, called this institution 'the English religion'. What was he talking about?

23 What famous Englishman declared that he wanted 'To blow you Scots back to your own native mountains!'?

24 'Have nothing in your houses that you do not know to be useful, or believe to be beautiful.' This was the advice of what still-popular Victorian designer?

25 'A single death is a tragedy, a million deaths is a statistic.' What 20th-century leader said this?

26 'I fear we have only awakened a sleeping giant, and his reaction will be terrible.' What prompted this Japanese admiral's remark in 1941?

27 'Television – teacher, mother, secret lover.' What TV character's words are these?

28 Who did Walt Disney say he loved 'more than any woman I've ever known'?

29 Who said of kissing Marilyn Monroe, 'It's like kissing Hitler'?

30 'I would have made a good Pope.' What US president said this?

Quiz 99

1 If you were watching the Magpies play at home, what ground would you be in?

2 James McAvoy played the role of Mr Tumnus, a faun, in what 2005 movie?

3 Who suffered a notorious 'wardrobe malfunction' during the live broadcast of the 2004 American Super Bowl?

4 Jermaine Jackson had a top 10 hit in the UK with 'Let's Get Serious'. What was the year?

5 The UK's best-selling single of 1980 was 'Don't Stand So Close To Me'. Who performed it?

6 Who founded the police force in Britain, giving his name to their nickname of 'bobbies'?

7 What song was DJ John Peel's favourite and was played at his funeral?

8 What band went on a 'Teenage Rampage' in 1974?

9 'A rose By any other name would smell as sweet' – lines by Shakespeare, but which work?

10 Juliet is a moon of which planet in the solar system?

11 On what futuristic TV show was the planet Uranus renamed 'Urectum', 'to end that stupid joke once and for all'?

12 Matt Groening, the creator of 'Futurama', is more famous for what other cartoon series?

13 What Simpson played Daisy Duke in 'The Dukes of Hazzard' movie in 2006?

14 In what 2005 blockbuster did Jessica Alba and Welsh actor Ioan Gruffudd appear as superheroes?

15 The classical four elements of nature are Earth, Air, Water and – what?

16 Which is hotter, a red fire or an orange fire?

17 The colour orange is associated with what European royal house?

18 What city is the capital of the Netherlands?

19 'The Diary of a Young Girl' was written by what Amsterdam citizen for over two years, from 1942 to 1944?

20 Anne Rice is author of the Gothic horror 'Vampire Chronicles' series, based in what American city?

21 What hurricane in 2005 flooded New Orleans, killing over 1500 people?

22 Are hurricanes areas of low or high atmospheric pressure?

23 The Negro spiritual 'Swing Low Sweet Chariot' is regularly sung by what sports fans?

24 What team won the Rugby World Cup in 2007?

25 What Spanish islands lie in the Atlantic less than 100 miles off the northwest coast of Africa?

26 The main airport of Tenerife in the Canary Islands is named after the Spanish queen. What is her name?

27 The city of Sofia is the capital of what Eastern European country?

28 Bulgaria's border with Romania to the north is marked by the Danube. What composer wrote the waltz, 'On the Beautiful Blue Danube'?

29 Inspired by the work of Johann Strauss II, what animated duo appeared in the cartoon 'Johann Mouse' in 1953, winning an Oscar in the process?

30 In the nursery rhyme 'Little Tommy Tucker', what does Tommy do to get his supper?

Quiz 100

1   What was the relationship between Mary, Queen of Scots and Queen Elizabeth of England?

2   Jon Voight starred in, among other movies, 'Deliverance' and 'Midnight Cowboy'. Who is his famous daughter?

3   The daughter of the prophet Mohammed shares a name with the location of a Portuguese shrine to the Virgin Mary. What is it?

4   Actor Martin Sheen has two sons who are both famous actors. One is Charlie Sheen; who is the other?

5   Paul Hill, one of the falsely accused Guildford Four, later married the daughter of which late American politician?

6   The father-in-law of Oscar winner Daniel Day Lewis is which late American playwright?

7   Zebedee the Galilean fisherman was father of two of Jesus's apostles. Who were they?

8   George V, king during the First World War, and Kaiser Wilhem II of Germany shared a grandparent. Who?

9   Carol Reed, director of the musical movie 'Oliver!', directed his nephew in the film. Who was he?

10 Which father-in-law of a British prime minister appeared in the 1970s 'Confessions of...' movie series?

11 Francis Ford Coppola directed his sister in 'The Godfather'. Who is she?

12 Which Nobel prizewinning playwright was the father-in-law of actor Charlie Chaplin?

13 Graham Hill won Motor Racing's Formula 1 championship twice in the 60s. What year did his son Damon win it?

14 Which Spinal Tap member is married to actress Jamie Lee Curtis?

15 Actor Gary Oldman is the brother of what 'EastEnders' actress?

16 The 'Carry On' actress Hattie Jacques was married to one of the 'Dad's Army' cast. Who was he?

17 What is the relationship between actor Warren Beatty and actress Shirley Maclaine?

18 Eddie Fisher's daughter, an actress, is best known for her role in a series of 70s and 80s movie blockbusters. Who is she?

19 Eric Clapton wrote the love song 'Wonderful Tonight' for the woman who later became his wife. Who is she?

20 What brothers did Fydor Dostoyevsky write about in 1880?

21 England centre-half Billy Wright was the first footballer to earn 100 caps. What famous singer was he married to?

22 'This Ole House' was a 1954 hit for Rosemary Clooney. Which movie heartthrob is her nephew?

23 Victorian Poet Christina Rossetti's brother was one of the most famous of the pre-Raphaelite painters. Who was he?

24 What brothers were stalwarts of the Manchester United defence throughout the 90s and into the 2000s?

25 Scots actor Denis Lawson played a rebel fighter in 'Star Wars'. His nephew later appeared in three 'Star Wars' movies. Who is he?

26 What one-time Chancellor of the Exchequer is the father of 'Domestic Goddess' Nigella Lawson?

27 The Wright Brothers were famous pioneers of flight. What were their first names?

28 What writing sisters lived in the parsonage at Haworth in Yorkshire?

29 This Nobel-prizewinning writer lost his son in the First World War, and his poem about his loss later became a play. Who was he?

30 The son of which Rat Pack member was kidnapped from Lake Tahoe, Nevada, in 1963?

Quiz 101

1   Who sang 'Save Your Love' in 1982?

2   What Bread song did Telly Savalas speak in 1975?

3   What did the Floaters want to do in 1977?

4   What Irish actor had a hit with 'MacArthur Park' in 1968?

5   What one-hit wonders had a novelty hit with the Hallowe'en anthem 'Monster Mash' in 1973?

6   Two of the cast from 'It Ain't Half Hot, Mum' took 'Whispering Grass' to no. 1 in 1975. Who were they?

7   He's the son of a Tremeloe and had his chart-topping moment with 'The One and Only'. Who is he?

8   What was the last order of Splodgenessabounds in 1980?

9   'Who Let the Dogs Out' – and what band sang this in 2000?

10 Matthews' Southern Comfort celebrated what central event of the flower-power era with their no. 1 hit in 1970?

11 Carl Douglas had a mega-hit with his song about what 70s craze?

12 Marrs took what house hit to no. 1 in 1987?

13 What did the Flying Lizards want in 1979?

14 1970 wasn't the only time 'Spirit in the Sky' was a hit, but it was the only time what singer had a hit with it?

15 Nena sang what Cold War hit in 1984?

16 Who claimed 'I'm the Urban Spaceman' in 1968?

17 Released in 1979, 'Rapper's Delight' was an early rap hit by what band?

18 What tear-jerking death song sung by Ricky Valance was his only hit in 1960?

19 What was Babylon Zoo's only hit in 1996?

20 What group of cartoon characters had their hit with 'Sugar Sugar' in 1969?

21 What comedians did 'The Stonk' in 1991?

22 Who had a no. 1 hit with 'Mambo No. 5 (A Little Bit of...)' in 1999?

23 What dance-floor favourite did Deee-Lite serve up in 1990?

24 Jilted John had a hit in 1978 about his girlfriend Julie dumping him for Gordon. What was the name of the song?

25 Who had a no. 1 hit in 1970 with 'Love Grows (Where My Rosemary Goes)?

26 Who had a hit in 1988 with 'John Kettley is a Weather Man'?

27 'Everybody's Free (to Wear Sunscreen)' was a 1999 hit for what film maker?

28 Whose advice in 1988 was 'Don't Worry Be Happy'?

29 The Crazy World of Arthur Brown had a crazy act that involved setting himself alight on stage. What song was his only hit?

30 What instrumental did B Bumble and the Stingers take into the charts in 1962 and again briefly 10 years later?

Quiz 102

1   Bucephalus was the horse of which legendary warrior?

2   What was the name of the dog in 'The Magic Roundabout' TV show?

3   What type of creature is an alewife?

4   Whose dog was Gnasher?

5   What do an Afrikaner, a Belted Galloway and a Droughtmaster have in common?

6   What is the common furniture beetle better known as?

7   In what year were dog licences abolished in Britain?

8   What kind of animal is the Looney Tunes character Speedy Gonzales?

9   How many toes has a normal cat?

10 What type of creature is a boomslang?

11 Who was the dog who looked after the Darling children in 'Peter Pan'?

12 What is the largest carnivore in Britain?

13 What do ungulates have that other mammals don't?

14 What is the world's most poisonous known fish?

15 What type of creature is a galliwasp?

16 What animal is used as the logo of the WWF?

17 Which creature changes its sex annually?

18 What name is used for a plantlike animal, such as coral?

19 What type of home does an eagle live in?

20 A leveret is a young what?

21 Which animal has a cry described as a 'laugh'?

22 In the US it's called a harvestman; what is it here?

23 Humans have unique fingerprints; which animal also has them?

24 How many noses has an ant?

25 What type of creature is a hairstreak?

26 What name is given to an otter's home?

27 The young of which creature is called a codling?

28 If dogs bark and cocks crow, what sound do deer make?

29 What is the legal minimum age for buying a pet in Britain?

30 Which one of Enid Blyton's Famous Five was the dog – Dick, Anne, Timmy, George or Julian?

Quiz 103

1   What movie was Elvis Presley filming when he was conscripted in 1958?

2   What director directed 'The Outlaw', showcasing the talents of Jane Russell?

3   What 1972 Jimmy Cliff film was instrumental in helping introduce reggae music to a worldwide audience?

4   The 1970s saw the birth of the blockbuster movie. What was the top-grossing blockbuster of that decade?

5   What movie scientist's car numberplate read 'OUTATIME'?

6   The biopic 'Coal Miner's Daughter' tells the story of which country singer?

7   In the film 'Casablanca', what is the surname of bar-owner Rick?

8   The movie, '10 Things I Hate About You', is based on which Shakespeare play?

9   In 'The Wizard of Oz', where does the Glinda, the Good Witch, come from?

10   The Palme d'Or top prize is awarded at what film festival?

11   What renowned Irish author opened Ireland's first cinema, the Volta in Dublin in 1909?

12   The Philip K Dick story 'Do Androids Dream of Electric Sheep?' was made into what dark near-future thriller?

13   The heroic defence of the mission station at Rorke's Drift in Natal in 1879 was immortalised in what 1964 film?

14   Who starred in 'Jerry Maguire', the 1996 comedy-drama movie about a sports agent?

15   What 1945 romantic movie, written by Noel Coward and directed by David Lean, epitomises the notion of the British stiff upper lip?

16   What classic movie depicted young Ralphie Parker's search for a BB gun for Christmas?

17   What American Civil War drama directed by Ang Lee features Toby Maguire, Jonathan Rhys Meyers and the singer Jewel?

18   She was in 'Top Gun' in 1986 and 'Courage Under Fire' in 1996. Who is she?

19   What organisation did Doctors Venkman, Stantz and Spengler set up in 1984?

20   The 1964 movie 'A Shot in the Dark' was the second outing for what immortal bumbling policeman?

21   In what 2001 movie do the children of retired two former secret agents end up saving their parents from the sinister Fegan Floop?

22   Who played both King Agamemnon and a firefighter in the 'The Time Bandits'?

23   Mel Gibson voiced Rocky the Rooster in what Oscar-winning Nick Park animation?

24   What Rowan Atkinson TV character made the jump to the big screen in 1997 in a movie directed by Mel Smith?

25   What special-effects wizard brought Greek mythology and Arabian Nights' stories to life with stop-motion animation?

26   George Bailey sees what life would be like without him in 'It's a Wonderful Life'. Who is the character who shows him?

27   What pig on Farmer Hoggett's farm thought he was a sheepdog in this 1995 movie of the same name?

28   What is the translation of the 1982 German war movie, 'Das Boot'?

29   His roles have included Romeo, Amsterdam Vallon and Jack Dawson. Who is he?

30   What actor was 'Down and Out in Beverly Hills' in 1986?

Quiz 104

1 How long ago, to the nearest thousand years, did Britain separate from Europe?

2 In what northern region of France did the Norse Vikings settle in the 10th century?

3 Which Roman emperor died in AD 14?

4 Who was the first Roman emperor to convert to Christianity?

5 What revered animal did the Ancient Egyptians call a 'miw'?

6 The new metalworking techniques of the Bronze Age allowed people to work successfully with what two types of metal?

7 What 4th century BC Greek king conquered most of the known world during his 13-year reign?

8 In what country was paper first developed, in the 2nd century BC?

9 What river in northern Italy did Julius Caesar cross with his army in 49 BC, signalling his challenge on Rome?

10 In what century did Tutankhamun rule Egypt?

11 The ancient city of Carthage is situated in what modern-day country?

12 In what century did the first coins appear in Britain?

13 What complete Neolithic village was uncovered during a storm on Orkney in 1850?

14 Who succeeded Julius Caesar as leader of Rome?

15 What holy site did the Vikings destroy on their first raid on England in 793 AD?

16 What Carthaginian general took his elephants across the Alps to crush the Romans at the battle of Cannae in 216 BC?

17 What year did the Romans finally pull out of Britain?

18 Who became the first king of the Israelites in 1020 BC?

19 What Roman emperor demanded that people worship him as a living god and wanted to make his horse a consul?

20 How long ago, to the nearest thousand years, was Stonehenge built?

21 The Greek philosopher Aristotle was tutor to what all-conquering Greek warrior?

22 What ancient king of the Israelites was depicted in stone by Michelangelo in the 16th century?

23 What two major Greek city states battled each other for dominance in the 5th century BC?

24 The city of Teotihuacan was the world's largest city around the 2nd century AD. What modern-day country is it in?

25 Who did Rome's Praetorian Guard guard?

26 What settlement did the Vikings found on Ireland's east coast in 998 AD?

27 What epic Old English poem, made into an animated movie in 2007, was written around the 8th century?

28 What small 4th century invention in China revolutionised mobility, travel and warfare?

29 The period of unprecedented peace and stability the Romans brought Europe in the first two centuries AD was known as what?

30 What major world religion was begun by its founder in southern Asia in the sixth century BC?

Quiz 105

1   In which book do a group of medieval pilgrims meet at the Tabard Inn in Southwark?

2   Who replaced Michael Morpurgo as Children's Laureate in 2005?

3   The title of Aldous Huxley's 'Brave New World' came from which Shakespeare play of discovery?

4   In which book are Amy, Beth, Jo and Meg March the main characters?

5   In 'The Lord of the Rings', who was maker of the One Ring?

6   What book is set on the fictional Hebridean islands of Great and Little Todday?

7   What French writer and author of 'Candide', was imprisoned in the Bastille for a year in 1717?

8   Previously the Whitbread Literary Awards, they are now called by what name?

9   In what classic modern novel would you find the characters Captain Yossarian and Major Major?

10   What Pulitzer prizewinning novel of race and injustice in the American South, published in 1960, became a classic of modern American fiction?

11   What was the name of Sherlock Holmes's housekeeper?

12   What is the first book of the New Testament?

13   What Stephen King story features a novelist held captive by a deranged fan?

14   'Schindler's List' was the 1993 movie based a Thomas Keneally book with a slightly different title. What was it called?

15   In which Dickens novel is Lady Dedlock a central character?

16 Who is the King of Rohan in Tolkien's 'Lord of the Rings'?

17 In the Sherlock Holmes stories, what is Dr Watson's first name?

18 In what war did George Orwell fight, later publishing his experiences in 'Homage to Catalonia'?

19 What 8th-century book, now at Dublin's Trinity College Library, is a supreme example of both illuminated manuscript and Celtic art?

20 Whose ghost returned from death to warn Scrooge?

21 Robert Louis Stevenson's 'Catriona' is a sequel to which of his other novels?

22 The characters in this comic fantasy novel include an angel, a demon, the Antichrist and the Four Horsemen of the Apocalypse. What's the book?

23 What competitive TV show awards a leather-bound copy of the Oxford English Dictionary to its champion in every series?

24 What compiler of the 'Guinness Book of Records' was assassinated by the Provisional IRA in 1975?

25 The bully of 'Tom Brown's Schooldays' was turned into an anti-hero in a series of novels by George Macdonald Fraser. Who was he?

26 What was the name of the evil, possessed car in the 1983 novel by Stephen King?

27 'A Warning to the Curious' and 'Casting the Runes' are stories by what classic English ghost-story writer?

28 What author, more famous for his other books, also wrote a compilation called 'The Father Christmas Letters' for his children?

29 The main character in this George Eliot novel is a miser who loses his gold but finds his real treasure in an unexpected place. Who is he?

30 The movie 'Trainspotting' was based on a novel of the same name by what author?

Quiz 106

1 You may find the coating polytetrafluoroethylene in any kitchen. What is it better known as?

2 Which of the Sun's rays does the ozone layer protect us from?

3 Almost 90% of water's weight comes from what?

4 A daguerreotype was an early form of what?

5 If someone has MRCVS or FRCVS after their name, what might you expect their profession to be?

6 What are the only two non-white metals?

7 Capsaicin is an irritant that produces a burning sensation in humans and other mammals. What foodstuff is it most commonly found in?

8 By roughly what percentage does water expand as it freezes – 5%, 10% or 20%?

9 What is the only planet in our solar system not to be named after a Greek or Roman god?

10 6 is the atomic number of what building-block of life?

11 What chemical element does the symbol Au represent?

12 What natural occurrence generates ozone every time it happens, helping to replenish the ozone layer?

13 In what year was Dolly the Sheep cloned?

14 What particle in an atom has no electric charge?

15 What gas is the least dense substance?

16 What is the best-known type of radiometric dating?

17 What does the acronym LED, as used in various light displays, stand for?

18 What was the name of the device in 'Back to the Future's De Lorean time machine that made time travel possible?

19 What name is given to the process of a liquid changing into a gas?

20 What branch of physics studies the origin and evolution of stars?

21 Tin is mixed with antimony what other chemical element to make pewter?

22 What instrument detects and measures radiation?

23 What moves at approximately 186,000 miles a second?

24 What process produces both energy for nuclear power and explosions in nuclear weapons?

25 Are molecules more tightly packed together in solids, liquids or gasses?

26 What scientist declared to President Truman after the development of the nuclear bomb, 'Mr President, I feel I have blood on my hands'?

27 What is the name given to any material that allows the transfer of heat?

28 What is the only letter of the alphabet that doesn't appear on the Periodic Table of Elements?

29 If a kilosecond is a thousand seconds, how many kiloseconds are in an hour?

30 The smallest particle of matter has a name that comes from the Greek word meaning 'indivisible'. What is it?

Quiz 107

1   Who was the WH who wrote the poem on which the film 'Four Weddings and a Funeral' was based?

2   His first names were Pelham Grenville and he immortalised the characters of Jeeves and Wooster. Who was he?

3   The initials of JFK, the iconic American president, are instantly recognisable. What do they stand for?

4   This US policeman founded the FBI, terrorised his staff, abused his powers and was rumoured to have unusual personal habits. Who was he?

5   What WH is a newsagent with a branch on every British High Street?

6   Joanne Kathleen is one of the best-selling authors of all time. What's the name she usually goes by?

7   What does the 'MC' in rap artist MC Hammer's name stand for?

8   This firm famously claimed to manufacture 57 varieties of food. Who are they?

9   British Victorian statesman WE Gladstone was prime minister four times, but what did his initials stand for?

10 What famously misanthropic actor said, 'I am free of all prejudices. I hate everyone equally'?

11 He was the author of 'Winnie-the-Pooh'; how did his name appear on the covers?

12 From TV's 'The A-Team', Mr T's alias of BA Baracus stood for – what?

13 What are the first names of Canadian singer k.d. lang?

14 This Oxford don wrote the Narnia books. Who was he?

15 The 'BB' in the name of blues singer and musician BB King stood for his nickname. What was it?

16 This US former sportsman was cleared of murdering his wife and her companion. He was known by his initials; who is he?

17 This American retailer who opened a chain of five-and-dime stores, and his shops still exist in Britain today. Who was he?

18 David Herbert wrote 'Lady Chatterley's Lover', but how did his name appear on the cover?

19 This Dutch artist's mathematically inspired work tried to depict infinity. His first names are rendered as initials. Who was he?

20 George W Bush, elected US president from 2001 to 2009, is distinguished from his father by his middle initial. What does it stand for?

21 What iconic American general commanded Confederate forces in the Civil War and delivered the South's surrender in 1865?

22 What JD wrote 'The Catcher in the Rye'?

23 His first names were Lafayette Ronald, he wrote on dianetics and he founded Scientology. Who was he?

24 What do English singer-songwriter PJ Harvey's initials stand for?

25 This radical American black leader was assassinated in 1965. His birth surname was Little; what was he known as?

26 HG Wells wrote 'War Of The Worlds'. What did 'HG' stand for?

27 What Irish-American author wrote 'The Ginger Man'?

28 Irish poet WB Yeats won the Nobel Prize in 1923. What do his initials stand for?

29 This British soldier was immortalised in the movie, 'Lawrence of Arabia'. Who was he?

30 This writer's first names are John Ronald Reuel though he's more famous under his initials. Who is he?

Quiz 108

1 This country was previously known as Rhodesia. What is it called now?

2 In what modern-day country is Timbuktu situated?

3 What country lies immediately west of Egypt?

4 What type of plant is the Tanzanian Peaberry?

5 What city does Table Mountain overlook?

6 Kilimanjaro is Africa's highest mountain, but what country is it in?

7 Africa accounts for almost 50% of the world's production of what valuable mineral?

8 What is the official language of Mozambique?

9 The Cape of Good Hope is not the southernmost point of Africa. What is?

10 Who were the first European settlers in the territory that is now South Africa, in 1652?

11 This Moroccan city's name is Spanish for 'white house'. What is it?

12 What city in Sierra Leone was established in the 18th century by slaves returning from the Americas?

13 How many African countries have a coast on the Mediterranean?

14 The dictator Idi Amin was the subject of the book and movie, 'The Last King of Scotland'. What country did he rule?

15 What ocean lies to the east of Africa?

16 The Bob Marley song 'Iron Lion Zion' refers to the revered Rastafarian leader Haile Selassie. Of what country was he emperor?

17 The most VCs ever awarded to one regiment for a single action was the result of what battle in Africa?

18 It's the biggest island in Africa and the title of a 2005 Walt Disney movie. What is it?

19 The world's second-largest lake is in Africa, was discovered by British explorer John Speke and is named after a British royal. What is it?

20 Africa is home to the world's largest living reptile. What is it?

21 What is Africa's most populous country?

22 What year did Nelson Mandela first become president of South Africa?

23 What African dweller is the largest of all living primates?

24 Two African countries' names begin with the letter 'Z'. Which ones?

25 What South African actress who won an Oscar in 2004 was the first from her country to win the award?

26 What language is spoken more than any other in Africa?

27 What British officer became famous for his last-stand and ultimately doomed defence of Khartoum against Sudanese rebels in 1885?

28 What body part on an African elephant is bigger than that on an Indian elephant?

29 What country shares a border with Egypt to the east?

30 What wars did the British fight with the descendants of the Dutch settlers in 1880-81 and again in 1899-1902?

Quiz 109

1   PT 109 was the number of which president's torpedo boat in the Second World War?

2   In 1881 the US had three presidents. Why?

3   The president lives at the White House in Washington DC. But where does the vice-president live?

4   Name one of the four presidents carved into the rock at Mount Rushmore, South Dakota.

5   What tune is played by the US Marine Band to announce the president's ceremonial entrance?

6   Which president has a memorial on the National Mall in Washington DC?

7   'A triumph of the embalmer's art.' Which president was Gore Vidal talking about?

8   A sign on the desk of President Harry S Truman read, 'The — stops here'. What's the missing word?

9   'This is the greatest thing in history!' Which president said this after the bombing of Hiroshima?

10 America's highest mountain is named after what US president?

11 What future president drafted the Declaration of Independence?

12 Who was the youngest president to be voted into office?

13 'He can't fart and chew gum at the same time.' Which president was Lyndon B Johnson talking about?

14 What made the presidency of Jefferson Davis unique?

15 What president served burgers cut in the shape of Texas to guests at his ranch?

16 Who resigned from presidential office rather than face impeachment?

17 'I'd much rather have that fellow inside my tent pissing out, than outside my tent, pissing in.' Which powerful American was President Johnson talking about?

18 Who was the first president of the United States?

19 Which president contracted a crippling disease in mid life but served out his time in office with his illness unsuspected by the public?

20 Rat Pack actor Peter Lawford was the brother-in-law of which president?

21 What president was the Teddy Bear named for?

22 Who was the only American president to serve more than two terms?

23 Lee Harvey Oswald was arrested for shooting President Kennedy. Who shot Lee Harvey Oswald on live TV?

24 Up to the presidential election of November 2008, how many presidents has America had?

25 In 1920 the US Congress passed into federal law the Prohibition of Alcohol despite the veto of the president. Who was he?

26 What president won a scholarship to Oxford University?

27 Who was the first president to be assassinated?

28 Who was born first, Ronald Reagan or John F Kennedy?

29 Who is the only Catholic ever to have been US president?

30 As the first president, George Washington is on the $1 bill. But who is on the $2?

Quiz 110

1   The first player to what score wins a game of lawn bowls?

2   What legendary New Zealand speedway rider became the first to win three consecutive world championships?

3   Who was the last British woman to win a Wimbledon singles title?

4   The Tote's Scoop6 bet is only run on which day of the week?

5   Which set of runners on a bobsleigh are used to steer – the front or back runners?

6   Football starts with a kick-off, but what game starts with a tip-off?

7   What is the number of the black ball in pool?

8   How many London bridges does the Boat Race pass under?

9   In what sport would you see a screw on a table?

10 What two things do amateur boxers wear in the ring that professional boxers don't?

11 Which is the most common bowls game – Lawn, Crown Green or Table?

12 What name is given to the style of start in motor racing where drivers run to their cars?

13 The American sport of softball is a gentler version of which sport?

14 What West Indian batsman, named one of the cricketers of the 20th century, also represented Antigua in World Cup qualifiers?

15 How many pins are in the back row in 10-pin bowling?

16 What ball game, originally from the Basque region, is played using baskets attached to the players' gloves?

17 What is the minimum number of points with which a player can win a six-game set of tennis?

18 The Canadian university town of Kingston, on the shores of Lake Ontario, is the birthplace of what team sport?

19 What was the birth name of Muhammad Ali?

20 What traditional song is the unofficial anthem of American baseball?

21 In what month is the Royal Ascot race meeting held?

22 What is Tiger Woods' real first name?

23 What trainer was known as the 'Queen of Aintree'?

24 Two sports take place on a piste. What are they?

25 Where is the Happy Valley racecourse?

26 When was betting tax abolished in the UK?

27 In badminton's new scoring format, the first player to how many points (by two clear points) wins the game?

28 How many rounds are usually in an amateur boxing contest?

29 What number lies to the left of (anti-clockwise from) 20 on a dartboard?

30 What jockey won the Derby at 19 at his first attempt, with Shergar in 1981?

Quiz 111

1 What is the maiden name of Harry Potter's mother?

2 Who is the keeper of keys and grounds at Hogwarts School?

3 What is the name of the wandmaker's shop in Diagon Alley?

4 What is special about the ceiling in the great hall at Hogwarts School?

5 What is the name of the house where the Weasley family live?

6 What was Lord Voldemort's name when he was a pupil at Hogwarts?

7 What is the only potion known to help werewolves?

8 What type of creatures run Gringotts, the wizarding bank?

9 In Hogwarts School there are four houses. What animal represents Hufflepuff house?

10 Quidditch is the wizarding world's favourite sport. What is the only thing that can end the game?

11 Who cast the spell that killed Albus Dumbledore in 'Harry Potter and the Half-Blood Prince'?

12 What family lives at 12 Grimmauld Place, London?

13 What is the only spell known to repel a dementor?

14 Who is Harry Potter's godfather?

15 Along with Hogwarts, what other two schools took part in the Triwizard Tournament in 'Harry Potter and the Goblet of Fire'?

16 What is the daily newspaper in the wizarding world?

17 What was the name of the gang formed by James Potter and his friends?

18 What was the name of the village where Harry lived with his parents when he was a baby?

19 Who is professor of Charms at Hogwarts school?

20 What is the name of the feared wizarding prison?

21 If you cast an Avada Kedavra spell on someone, what would happen to them?

22 What kind of creature is Buckbeak?

23 What is the main drawback of leprechaun gold?

24 What type of broom did Harry receive from a mystery benefactor in his third year?

25 Whose parents were named Lucius and Narcissa?

26 What company does Harry's Uncle Vernon work for?

27 What everyday activity do adult wizards need a licence to do?

28 Which King's Cross platform does the Hogwarts Express leave from?

29 What type of people can see the magical animals thestrals?

30 What is the name of the joke shop in Hogsmeade?

Quiz 112

Can you give the meanings of these foreign phrases that have made their way into English?

1   Hoi Polloi

2   Caveat Emptor

3   Amor Vincit Omnia

4   À Bon Marché

5   Requiescat In Pace

6   Sang Froid

7   Mazel Tov

8   Prét-à-Porter

9   Kia Ora

10   La Dolce Vita

11   Illegitimi Non Carborundum

12   E Pluribus Unum

13   Baksheesh

14   Billet-Doux

15   Ich Dien

16   Al Fresco

17   Carpe Diem

18   Sayonara

19   Post Meridiem

20   Jihad

21   In Flagrante Delicto

22   Wunderkind

23   Tabula Rasa

24   Schadenfreude

25   In Vitro

26   Sine Qua Non

27   A Capella

28   Ad Hoc

29   In Vino Veritas

30   Au Revoir

Quiz 113

1 What British playwright won the Nobel Prize for Literature in 2005?

2 Which Samuel Beckett play lasts 35 seconds, has no performers and is the world's shortest play?

3 What is memorable about a performance of 'Our American Cousin' at Ford's Theatre, Washington DC on 14 April 1865?

4 Henry VIII's Chancellor Thomas More was the subject of a play by Robert Bolt. What is it called?

5 The play, and later movie 'Amadeus' depicts the relationship of two composers: Mozart and his deadly rival. What was his rival's name?

6 What famous American playwright was the father-in-law of actor Daniel Day-Lewis?

7 The main character in this performance strangles his child, beats his wife to death and hangs his hangman. Who is he?

8 What Christopher Marlowe character sells his soul to Mephistopheles in return for 24 years of power?

9 'A Streetcar Named Desire' was a hit movie starring Marlon Brando, but who wrote the play on which it was based?

10 What play, performed in London, has the longest initial run of any play in the world?

11 'Juno and the Paycock', 'The Plough and the Stars' and 'Shadow of a Gunman' were all plays by what Irish playwright?

12 What play was translated to the big screen as the musical 'My Fair Lady'?

13 What American actor was appointed creative director of the Old Vic in 2003?

14 Where would you find the Globe, Lyric and Mermaid Theatres?

15 In what pantomime does Widow Twankey appear?

16 What name is given to the type of theatre where the stage is surrounded by the audience on all sides?

17 What world-famous English playwright and satirist of middle-class manners is associated with the Stephen Joseph Theatre in Scarborough?

18 In what Shakespeare play does the sprite Ariel appear?

19 Name the two Irish playwrights who won the Nobel Literature Prize for their work.

20 The word 'drama' is taken from a Greek word meaning what?

21 What Lerner-Loewe musical production was set in a Scottish village that only appears once every hundred years?

22 Why were England's theatres closed in 1642?

23 Theatre director Joan Littlewood was once married to what British folk singer?

24 What employee in a theatre team is responsible for overseeing the smooth running of all aspects of the show?

25 What three types of drama were composed and performed in Ancient Greece?

26 What name is given to furniture and other items on a stage that are used and not part of the scenery?

27 The song 'That's Your Funeral', as sung by two characters who are undertakers, did not transfer from the stage to the movie version of what musical?

28 Laetitia Prism was the governess in what famous 1895 comedy?

29 'Green Grow the Lilacs', by Lynn Riggs, was the basis for the libretto of what popular Rogers and Hammerstein musical?

30 What city holds the oldest fringe festival in the world?

Quiz 114

1   What was the currency in Germany before the Euro?

2   How much was a shilling worth in new money when Britain was decimalised?

3   'Can't Buy Me Love' was an early hit for the Beatles. In what year?

4   Which of Jesus's 12 Apostles was a tax collector?

5   Apart from the Queen, whose head features on the Bank of England £10 note?

6   What country would you be in if you were paying in dong?

7   Two of the classic English flat races feature money in their names. What are they?

8   'Money makes the world go round' is a familiar saying and formed the lyrics of the song 'Money Money', in which musical?

9   Who was the first English footballer to be sold for a million pounds?

10   How many pieces of gold were in Cortez's cursed chest in 'Pirates of the Caribbean: Curse Of The Black Pearl'?

11   How many pennies were in an old shilling?

12   How much is the top prize worth on 'Deal Or No Deal'?

13   If you bet a pony on a horse, how much would you be betting?

14   If you added together a nickel and a dime, how many cents would you have?

15   How many sides has a 50p piece?

16 How much was a bag of food for the birds in the movie 'Mary Poppins'?

17 How much money is left at the end of the legal case Jarndyce v Jarndyce in Charles Dickens' 'Bleak House'?

18 Which financial institution is known as The Old Lady of Thread-needle Street?

19 Who distributes Maundy Money on Maundy Thursday before Easter?

20 What country would you be in if you were spending drams?

21 £26 million pounds in gold bullion was stolen from Heathrow Airport in 1983 in what robbery?

22 Which coin was introduced into British currency in 1982?

23 What unit of currency is used in the British Overseas Territory the British Virgin Islands?

24 The US has more billionaires than any other country; which country is second?

25 How much was a guinea worth?

26 What was the first country to use paper money?

27 What song starts with the line, 'I work all night I work all day to pay the bills I have to pay'?

28 What unit of currency is used in South Africa?

29 On the edge of a British coin is the inscription, 'Standing on the shoulders of giants'. Which coin?

30 If someone gave you a monkey, how much would they give you?

Quiz 115

1 What are death caps and destroying angels?

2 Tarragon and fennel both share a similar flavour. What is it?

3 Hedera is the proper botanical name for which common climbing plant?

4 Which poisonous plant was believed to have a human-body-shaped root, and shriek when it was pulled up?

5 The African vegetable okra is known by what other name?

6 What colour are the berries on a mistletoe plant?

7 What substance in nettles causes their sting?

8 What was the first garden city in Britain?

9 Which edible plant was first called a love apple?

10 Which plant is used to produce the drug morphine?

11 What is a wild hyacinth better known as?

12 The French call it a fleur-de-lys; what is this plant called in Britain?

13 What plant is porridge made from?

14 Aspirin was originally derived from the bark of a tree. Which one?

15 Which country traditionally gifts London with a Christmas tree for Trafalgar Square?

16 Which writer is traditionally associated with a green carnation?

17 In the language of flowers, which herb is traditionally associated with Remembrance?

18 The Celts considered this tree to be magical; it's also associated with death. What is it?

19 What did the English celebrate on Oak Apple Day every 29th May?

20 Which organisation runs the Chelsea Flower Show each year?

21 Which celebrity gardener stepped down from hosting 'Gardeners' World' after illness in 2008?

22 What chemical substance makes plants green?

23 What name is given to plants that flower every two years?

24 What common plant has the botanical name 'ilex'?

25 In order to grow, a seed needs water, warmth and what element?

26 What type of wreath did Ancient heroes wear around their heads?

27 What plant was traditionally thought to give protection against vampires?

28 What red-flowered plant, native to Mexico and the Pacific US, is given as a traditional Christmas gift?

29 What colour is the edelweiss flower?

30 Succulents grow in areas with a lack of what?

Quiz 116

Can you identify the personalities behind these books?

1 'The Sound of Laughter'

2 'With Nails'

3 'As It Happens'

4 'The Good, the Bad And the Bubbly'

5 'Testament of Youth'

6 'Moab Is My Washpot'

7 'Just Williams'

8 'My Wicked Wicked Ways'

9 'Mein Kampf'

10 'Anything Goes'

11 'Humble Pie'

12 'It's Not About the Bike'

13 'Losing My Virginity'

14 'What's the Bleeding Time?'

15 'Scar Tissue'

Quiz 117

1 What 60s LA band took their name from the title of one of Aldous Huxley's books?

2 What song did Lulu sing when she represented Britain in the 1969 Eurovision Song Contest?

3 'Love is All Around' was a long-running hit for Wet Wet Wet in 1994. Who first recorded it in the 60s?

4 Britain first won the Eurovision Song Contest in 1967. What was the name of the song?

5 Who wrote Jimi Hendrix's classic hit 'All Along the Watchtower'?

6 What Newcastle band had a no. 1 hit in the UK and US with 'House of the Rising Sun'?

7 Pete Seeger wrote a song, later recorded by the Byrds, based on the words of the Bible's book of Ecclesiastes. What is it?

8 Who released the double album 'Blonde on Blonde' in 1966?

9 Which two original members of The Who have died?

10 They sang 'Dedicated to the One I Love', 'Monday Monday' and 'California Dreamin'. Who were they?

11 Folk-pop band The Seekers had hits throughout the 60s, including 'Morningtown Ride' and 'Georgy Girl'. Where were they from?

12 Eddie Cochran had a posthumous no. 1 hit in the UK in 1960. What was the name of the song?

13 A much-covered ska music hit by Millie in 1964 reached no. 2 in the UK charts and helped establish the Island record label. What was it?

14 What duo had a banned no. 1 hit with 'Je t'aime... moi non plus' in 1969?

15 What 1967 song by Scott McKenzie became the anthem of the 60s hippie counterculture?

16 What New York state concert in 1969 drew 400,000 people and was seen as the high point of the 60s hippie movement?

17 Written by The Big Bopper, this song about a pair of star-crossed Native American lovers reached no. 1 in the UK in 1960. What was it?

18 What famous record label was founded by Berry Gordy Jr in Detroit, Michigan and enjoyed great success in the 60s?

19 This 1968 death song by Bobby Goldsboro reached no. 2 in the UK and has since been voted the worst song of all time. What is it?

20 What founder member of the Rolling Stones drowned in his swimming pool in 1969?

21 Originally called The Drifters, they were Cliff Richard's backing band before gaining success in their own right. Who were they?

22 What group did Steve Marriot form after leaving the Small Faces?

23 The late-60s hit 'Abraham, Martin and John' was a tribute to four slain US leaders. Who were they?

24 The most successful female vocal act in history had their first British no. 1 with 'Baby Love'. Who were they?

25 What ex-'EastEnders' star sang on the 1962 hit 'Come Outside'?

26 What song was a hit in 1964 for Marianne Faithfull, later Mick Jagger's girlfriend, and then for the Rolling Stones in 1965?

27 What infamous California rock concert, marred by death and violence, was considered to mark the end of the 60s hippie era?

28 What 1966 release was a posthumous chart topper in the UK and US for country star Jim Reeves?

29 The lead singer of the Monkees was English and a former trainee jockey. Who is he?

30 A 1967 hit on both sides of the Atlantic related the suicide of Billie Joe McAllister off Mississippi's Tallahatchie Bridge. Who sang it?

Quiz 118

1 What is the longest picture ever to have won a Best Picture Oscar?

2 What 1999 movie shares first place in the Most-Nominated and Most Wins spots?

3 For what picture did Viggo Mortensen receive a Best Actor nomination?

4 What has been the permanent venue for the awards ceremony since 2002?

5 What musical has won most awards in Oscar history?

6 What year were the Oscars first presented?

7 In the 2001 Best Picture winner, what type of performer did Russell Crowe play?

8 How many directing Oscars did Francis Ford Coppola win for his 'Godfather' trilogy?

9 Which was the only one of 'The Lord of the Rings' trilogy to win the Best Picture award?

10 How did Mexican actor Emilio Fernández achieve Oscar immortality?

11 What Oscar first did Hattie McDaniel achieve in 1940 for her performance in 'Gone With the Wind'?

12 Jessica Tandy was the oldest winner of a competitive Oscar when she won with 'Driving Miss Daisy'. What age was she?

13 On what night of the week has the Oscar ceremony been held on since 1999?

14 What was the first-ever screen adaptation of a novel to win the Best Picture award?

15 What actor has the most Oscar nominations ever?

16 What was the first colour picture ever to win a Best Picture Oscar?

17 The 1993 Best Picture winner was shot almost completely in black and white. What was it?

18 What organisation presents the Oscars every year?

19 He was nominated eight times in his life for the Best Actor Oscar, but won only once, in 1987 for 'The Color of Money'. Who was he?

20 British actor John Mills won the 1971 Best Supporting Oscar for a part in which he didn't say a word. What was the movie?

21 What is the minimum length a picture has to be to qualify for a Best Picture nomination?

22 The youngest Oscar winner, Tatum O'Neal, was just 10 years and acting with her father when she won in 1973. What was the film?

23 How tall is the Oscar statuette?

24 What trilogy of films won the Best Visual Effects Oscar for three consecutive years?

25 Why were two separate awards made for Best Costume Design up until 1967?

26 The Oscar ceremony in 1929 was the first; what number is the 2010 ceremony?

27 Who is the actress with most Oscar nominations, but not Oscar wins, under her belt?

28 This actor became the first to be nominated for two consecutive posthumous awards, in 1956 and 1957. Who is he?

29 How many people are entitled to vote in the awarding of Oscars – around 400, around 1800 or around 6000?

30 What comedian has hosted the Oscar awards ceremony more times than anyone else?

Quiz 119

1   Who ruled England for only nine days?

2   What monarch began the tradition of Christmas Day broadcasts to the nation?

3   Who has ruled longer, Elizabeth I or Elizabeth II?

4   Who was the first Roman emperor?

5   Which British king was called 'the wisest fool in Christendom'?

6   In what century was Macbeth king in Scotland?

7   Which English king's nickname was 'Bluff Hal'?

8   Robert Bruce became King of Scots in 1306. His brother Edward was also a crowned king: of what country?

9   How many British monarchs were there in the 20th century?

10   Including Britain, how many EU countries have a monarch as head of state?

11   What age did Prince Charles reach in 2008?

12   What English king had the nickname 'Farmer George'?

13   Which royal family lives at the Amalienborg Palace?

14   What age was Queen Elizabeth, the Queen Mother, when she died?

15   Who was ruler of the Aztec people when the Spanish Conquistadores arrived in South America in the 16th century?

16 In what year did Queen Victoria die?

17 Who were the only two British rulers to have had a seat in the House of Commons?

18 What king was Spain's first monarch after the fall of fascism in 1975?

19 Who gave a special performance in Stockholm's Royal Opera House in 1976 to celebrate the marriage of King Carl Gustaf of Sweden?

20 Who was the last king of America?

21 Who is the longest-reigning British monarch?

22 Which two kings faced each other at the Battle of Bannockburn?

23 What country was King Zog king of?

24 Good King Wenceslas ruled over what country in the 10th century?

25 Who was the last tsar of Russia?

26 What yacht of the British royal family was decommissioned in 1997?

27 What English king who never enjoyed a good press, was known as Lackland for his lack of a proper inheritance?

28 Where is Princess Beatrice in order of succession to the throne?

29 What short-lived British ruler was nicknamed Tumbledown Dick and Queen Dick for his indecisiveness?

30 Who was the German Kaiser at the outbreak of the First World War?

Quiz 120

1   In which modern state is the Inca city of Machu Picchu?

2   What was the first name of South American revolutionary Che Guevara?

3   What town on Canada's Klondyke River was the scene of a gold rush in 1896, later giving its name to a TV western and a new word to the English language?

4   Who owned Florida before it passed to Britain in 1763?

5   What desert lies across the US-Mexico border?

6   In which South American country was a previously undiscovered tribe found in 2008?

7   Name one of the two capital cities that face each other across the River Plate estuary.

8   What is the only American state where you would feel a williwaw wind?

9   What Canadian province lies east of British Columbia?

10 What country is the world's largest coffee producer?

11 What is the capital of Canada's French-speaking province, Quebec?

12 What is the most northeasterly state in the US?

13 What is the language spoken by the Incas of South America?

14 Cape Horn lies off the southernmost point of which South American country?

15 The 20th century's deadliest volcano, which caused 30,000 deaths, is in what country?

16 What waterway at 9° N links the Atlantic and Pacific Oceans?

17 What modern-day city was once home to the Aztecs?

18 On what Caribbean island is the US detention camp at Guantanamo Bay?

19 What country are the Falkland Islands closest to?

20 What two South American countries have no coastline?

21 In 1973 General Pinochet overthrew the democratic government in what country?

22 What two countries have sovereignty over the Virgin Islands?

23 New Providence is the largest island of what Atlantic archipelago?

24 What State Route that follows the California coast, is one of the most scenic in America?

25 What two neighbouring countries have the largest indigenous populations in South America?

26 What does Rio de Janiero translate into English as?

27 What country has more borders with any other on the American continent?

28 Port Royal features in the 'Pirates of the Caribbean' movies. What island was the city on?

29 The world's highest capital city is in the Americas. What is it?

30 Bridgetown is the capital of what Caribbean island?

Quiz 121

Name the actor or actress who is famous in two roles.

1   Tucker Jenkins in 'Grange Hill' and Mark Fowler in 'EastEnders'

2   Audrey Fforbes-Hamilton in 'To The Manor Born' and Margo Leadbetter in 'The Good Life'

3   Bill Reynolds in 'Love Thy Neighbour' and Patrick Trueman in 'EastEnders'

4   Roy Figgis in 'Only When I Laugh' and Terry Collier in 'The Likely Lads'

5   Denise Bryson in 'Twin Peaks' and Fox Mulder in 'The X-Files'

6   Suzie Kettles in 'Tutti Frutti' and Harriet Pringle in 'Fortunes of War'

7   Angus Hudson in 'Upstairs, Downstairs' and George Cowley in 'The Professionals'

8   Eileen in 'Pennies from Heaven' and Vera Brittain in 'Testament of Youth'

9   Sir Godber Evans in 'Porterhouse Blue' and Francis Urquhart in 'House of Cards'

10 Brian Potter and Max the Doorman from 'Phoenix Nights'

11 Pop Larkin in 'The Darling Buds of May' and the narrator in 'Dangermouse'

12 Dolly in 'Dinnerladies' and Mavis Wilton in 'Coronation Street'

13 Lois Lane in 'Lois & Clark' and Susan Mayer in 'Desperate Housewives'

14 Martin Brice in 'Ever-Decreasing Circles' and Tom Good in 'The Good Life'

15 Chief Inspector Morse in 'Morse' and DI Jack Regan in 'The Sweeney'

16 Brother Cadfael in 'Cadfael' and Claudius in 'I, Claudius'

17 Arthur Dent in 'The Hitch-hiker's Guide to the Galaxy' and Bridey in 'Brideshead Revisited'

18 Freda Ashton in 'A Family at War' and Jill Swinburne in 'The Beiderbecke Affair'

19 Dr Joel Fleischman in 'Northern Exposure' and FBI Agent Don Eppes in 'Numb3rs'

20 Al Swearengen in 'Deadwood' and Judas Iscariot in 'Jesus of Nazareth'

21 Nora Batty in 'Last of the Summer Wine' and Doris Luke in 'Crossroads'

22 Chrissy Plummer in 'Man About the House' and Lilian in 'The Smoking Room'

23 Wolfie Smith in 'Citizen Smith' and Ben Harper in 'My Family'

24 Father Peter Clifford in 'Ballykissangel' and Danny Trevanion in 'Wild at Heart'

25 Dr Dan Clifford in 'Holby City' and Simon Pemberton in 'The Archers'

26 DCI William Bell in 'State of Play' and DCI Gene Hunt in 'Life on Mars'

27 Terry McCann in 'Minder' and Gerry Standing in 'New Tricks'

28 Jonathan Kent in 'Smallville' and Bo Duke in 'The Dukes of Hazzard'

29 Dr Caroline Todd in 'Green Wing' and Fran in 'Black Books'

30 Adam Parkinson in 'Butterflies' and Gary Sparrow in 'Goodnight Sweetheart'

Quiz 122

1   What is the UK's best-selling album of all time?

2   What singer-songwriter, famous for webcasting from her basement flat, had her first no. 1 with 'I Wish I Was a Punk Rocker with Flowers in my Hair'?

3   Who is the record holder for no. 1 hits in Britain?

4   In 2008, what British act became the first to reach the top of the US charts since the Spice Girls' 'Wannabe' in 1997?

5   Slade had two consecutive hits enter the chart at no. 1 in 1973. The second was 'Skweeze Me Pleeze Me'; what was the first?

6   'My Sweet Lord' by George Harrison was no. 1 in 1971. Years later it repeated the feat; what was the year?

7   What group has had more singles enter the chart at no. 1 than any other band?

8   What was Britain's top-selling no. 1 ever?

9   Billie Piper achieved fame as an actress with 'Doctor Who', but what was the no. 1 she had as a singer in 1998?

10   The hippie classic 'Something in the Air' reached no. 1 in 1969 and was the only hit for what band?

11   An unusual band took the Christmas no. 1 spot in 1984. Who were they and what was the song?

12   Two songs by what singer were consecutive no. 1s in 1982, weeks after his death?

13   'Young Love' was a no. 1 in 1957 for Tab Hunter. What teenybopper heartthrob took it to the top again in 1973?

14   'Bohemian Rhapsody' was no. 1 for Queen when Freddie Mercury died. In what year did they have a hit with it first time around?

15   What UK act had the most no. 1 albums ever?

16 The song was by Oasis; the video featured actor Patrick Macnee. It was no. 1 in 1996; what was it?

17 Aqua had a no. 1 hit in 1997 with what song featuring a child's toy?

18 The Vengaboys' 'We're Going to Ibiza' was based on what song that was a no. 1 from 1975?

19 Jamiroquai's only no. 1 came in 1998. What was it?

20 Cliff Richard had a no. 1 twice with 'Living Doll': first in 1959 with The Drifters and then in 1986 for Comic Relief with what comedy act?

21 What song by Aaliyah reached the no. 1 spot after her death?

22 Who had a no. 1 hit with 'Smile' in the summer of 2006?

23 'Band of Gold' was at the top for six weeks in 1970. Who sang it?

24 The first New Wave no. 1 came in 1978 from the Boomtown Rats. What was the song?

25 What band, fronted by Johnny Borrell, had a no. 1 with 'America' in 2006?

26 What former 'Neighbours' star had a hit with 'Kiss Kiss' in 2002?

27 In what year did Britney Spears have her first no. 1 with 'Baby One More Time'?

28 What novelty no. 1 did the Teletubbies have in 1997?

29 Robbie Williams and Nicole Kidman were at no. 1 in 2001 with 'Somethin' Stupid'. But what father-and-daughter duo took it to the top of the charts in 1967?

30 The Weather Girls had a no. 2 with this song in 1984, but in 2001 with Geri Halliwell it made no. 1. What was it?

Quiz 123

1   What is the state capital of Alaska?

2   Gaborone is the capital of which African nation?

3   In which American state does the Diablo wind blow?

4   Baffin, Victoria and Banks are all islands belonging to which country?

5   The north face of this mountain has the nickname 'Murder Wall'. Which mountain is it?

6   Dunkery Beacon is the highest point on which moorland between Somerset and Devon?

7   Name the three countries that the Atlas Mountains lie in.

8   Which type of clouds usually bring rain and snow?

9   What is the capital of Middle Eastern state Oman?

10   God is said to have given Moses the Ten Commandments on Mount Sinai. In which country is Mount Sinai?

11   What is the capital of the Australian state of Victoria?

12   What is the river that flows through York?

13   What name did the Romans give to Ireland?

14   When driving in Malta, which side of the road should you be on?

15   Continental, Cirque and Piedmont are all types of which geological feature?

16 Marrakesh is the former capital of Morocco. What is the current capital?

17 Andros, Paros and Mykonos are all members of which group of islands?

18 What mountain pass links the countries of Afghanistan and Pakistan?

19 In which ocean are the Cape Verde Islands?

20 Which sea surrounds Anglesey and the Isle of Man?

21 The Yarra River flows through which Australian city?

22 If you were to sail directly from Athens to Crete, what sea would you be on?

23 Entebbe used to be its capital; now it's Kampala. Which country is it?

24 Which country is bounded to the northwest by the Zuiderzee?

25 Which river with its source in the Appalachian Mountains, flows through the American capital?

26 Which nation announced in 2003 it was leaving the Commonwealth after being suspended by other members?

27 Which sea strait was said in ancient times to be bordered by the Pillars of Hercules?

28 What American city suffered a major earthquake that left over 3000 dead in 1906?

29 The mountain pass Little St Bernard links which two European countries?

30 The cities of Tanis, Sais and Zagazig lie on which river delta?

Quiz 124

1   Three of the four provinces in Ireland are Ulster, Leinster and Connacht. What's the fourth?

2   What rugby trophy did Munster lift in 2008?

3   As well as the Heineken Cup, what is the other major annual European club rugby trophy?

4   Football's European Cup was reorganised from a traditional knock-out to include a group stage in what season?

5   Which US building was attacked in 1993 when bombs went off in its underground garage?

6   An Oliver Stone movie, 'World Trade Center', dramatised the events of 9/11. Who was the lead actor?

7   Nicolas Cage is the nephew of which Oscar-winning director?

8   What was Coppola's next big movie after The Godfather Part II?

9   How many Horsemen of the Apocalypse were there?

10 What four-time Oscar winner works with Aardman Animations?

11 What London park is bounded by Piccadilly on its north side and has St James's Palace on its east?

12 What celebratory music by Handel was first performed in Green Park on 27 April 1749?

13 The most popular day for fireworks in Britain is 5th November, in memory of whose attempts to blow up the Houses of Parliament?

14 What graphic novel and movie features a rebel in a Guy Fawkes mask intent on freeing Britain from a fascist totalitarian government?

15 Alan Moore, author of 'V for Vendetta', also wrote 'The League of Extraordinary Gentlemen', with Allan Quatermain. In what H. Rider Haggard book did the character first appear?

16   What quality is normally attributed to King Solomon?

17   Athena is the Greek goddess of Wisdom. With what bird is she generally associated?

18   What is the collective term for a group of owls?

19   What country has the oldest existing national parliament in the world?

20   Of which European country was Iceland previously a dependency?

21   What is the name of the main peninsula of Denmark, that juts out northwards into the sea?

22   The Battle of Jutland was a major naval engagement between what two countries?

23   What is the capital of the German province of Bavaria?

24   The 2006 film 'Munich' dealt with the terrorist killings of competitors at the 1972 Olympics. Who directed the movie?

25   In what 1980 movie did Steven Spielberg appear five minutes before the end playing a clerk at the Cook County Assessor's Office?

26   John Landis directed 'The Blues Brothers'. He also directed a 14-minute music video that was the most successful ever. What was the song and who sang it?

27   Michael Jackson's one-time California home, Neverland, shared a name with the island home of what fictional character?

28   The success of 'Peter Pan' popularised what girl's name, unknown until it appeared in the book?

29   Wendy Richard was most famous for her role as Pauline Fowler in 'EastEnders'. But in what 70s sitcom did she play Miss Brahms?

30   Jeremy Lloyd and David Croft wrote 'Are You Being Served?'. What classic sitcom that began in 1968, did Croft write with Jimmy Perry?

Quiz 125

What names are these famous actors and actresses better known by?

1 Norma Jean Baker

2 Caryn Johnson

3 Thomas Mapother IV

4 Frederick Austerlitz

5 David McDonald

6 Jennifer Anastassakis

7 Percy James Patrick Kent-Smith

8 Joyce Frankenberger

9 Krishna Banji

10 Ilyena Mironoff

11 Marion Morrison

12 Barbara Deeks

13 Carlos Irwin Estevez

14 Maurice Micklewhite

15 Daniel Agraluscarsaca

16 Laurence Tureaud

17 Eric Bishop

18 Allan Stewart Konigsberg

19 Catherine Dorleac

20 Diana Fluck

21 Joaquin Raphael Bottom

22 Winona Horowitz

23 Diane Hall

24 Julia Elizabeth Wells

25 Natalie Hershlag

26 Kevin Fowler

27 Susan Tomalin

28 Roy Scherer

29 Michael Dumble-Smith

30 James Stewart

Quiz 126

1   Who wrote Sinead O'Connor's 1990 no. 1 hit, 'Nothing Compares 2U'?

2   Who had a hit in 1991 with 'Any Dream Will Do' from 'Joseph and the Amazing Technicolour Dreamcoat'?

3   Country singer Billy Ray Cyrus had his first hit in 1992. Now his daughter is arguably more famous. Why?

4   This famous family had a top 10 hit with 'Deep Deep Trouble' in 1991. Who are they?

5   What band did Robbie Williams leave to go solo in 1995?

6   Peter André had a top 10 hit with a song from Disney's 'The Little Mermaid'. What was it?

7   Who had a chart hit twice in the 90s with the theme from Friends, 'I'll be There for You'?

8   One country dominated Eurovision in the 90s, with four wins out of 10. Who was it?

9   Which former Spice Girl had a hit with Bryan Adams in 1998 with 'When You're Gone'?

10 Two versions of 'Wonderwall' got to no. 2 in 1995. Oasis's was one; whose was the other?

11 Hot Chocolate have released 'You Sexy Thing' three times. When was the most recent?

12 'Three Lions', released for the 1996 World Cup, was a hit for David Baddiel, Frank Skinner and the group they sang it with. Who were they?

13 Before her acting career, Billie Piper was a successful pop singer. How many no. 1 hits did she have?

14 The Simpsons had a no. 1 hit in 1991. What was the song?

15 Fatboy Slim's only no. 1 came in 1999. What was it?

16   Robbie Williams's first solo hit single came in 1996. What was it?

17   In 1995, who became the first British rock and pop star to be knighted?

18   The grunge anthem 'Smells Like Teen Spirit' was the biggest single for what influential Seattle band?

19   What two Irish boy bands are managed by impresario Louis Walsh?

20   'Under the Table and Dreaming' was the first album by which American jazz-rock outfit?

21   This song was a hit twice for D:Ream: first in 1994 and later when the Labour Party used it in its 1997 general election campaign. What was it?

22   Who disrupted Michael Jackson's performance of Earth Song at the 1996 BRIT Awards?

23   The Spice Girls' first single was 'Wannabe'. What was their second?

24   In 1991 a single became the first one ever to reach no. 1 for a second time. What was the song and its performer?

25   German electropop outfit Snap! had two UK no. 1s in the 90s. What were they?

26   Lulu's only no. 1 came in this decade, performed with which boy band?

27   'Common People' was one of the most popular hits for this Sheffield Britpop band. Who were they?

28   What band recorded the massive 1996 hit 'Can't Help Falling in Love With You'?

29   Siobhan Fahey, formerly of Bananarama, had a series of hits, including a 1991 no. 1, with her new act. What was the act called?

30   What band did Dave Grohl form after Nirvana ended?

Quiz 127

1   What was the name of the department store on the BBC sitcom, 'Are You Being Served'?

2   His TV roles included Thomas Banacek and 'The A-Team's Hannibal Smith. Who was he?

3   In the US teen show 'The OC', what do the initials stand for?

4   Which two members of 'The Young Ones' cast went on to star in 'Bottom'?

5   Which TV characters lived at 368 Nelson Mandela House, Dockside Estate, Peckham?

6   Which popular 90s US teen show featured a zip code in its title?

7   Robert Robinson was the first presenter of the long-running BBC show, 'Call My Bluff'. Who was the second?

8   What bar was Frasier Crane's favourite when he lived in Boston?

9   In 'Randall and Hopkirk (Deceased)', who was deceased – Jeff or Marty?

10 What town did the Home Guard platoon in 'Dad's Army' protect?

11 Which former England football manager was a writer on the 1970s TV series 'Hazell'?

12 The Lone Ranger's horse was called Silver, but what was the horse of his sidekick, Tonto?

13 Who was the second host of 'Countdown' after Richard Whiteley?

14 Soup Dragon, Iron Chicken and the Froglets shared a planet with the stars of this show. What was it?

15 This little-known and surreal cult series starred Robert Lindsay, David Threlfall and James Ellis as three nightwatchmen. What was it?

16 Which organisation's secret offices were behind Del Floria's Tailor Shop in this 1960s spy show?

17 On the Cbeebies show, 'Big Cook, Little Cook', what is Big Cook's name?

18 What illness did Dennis Potter's 'Singing Detective' have?

19 Which gangster's psychiatrist was Dr Jennifer Melfi?

20 What was the programme that first popularised TV snooker?

21 What colour is Gordon the Engine in 'Thomas the Tank Engine'?

22 In what city is 'Byker Grove' set?

23 The first programme to be shown on Channel 4 is still running today. What is it?

24 In what year did digital channel BBC 3 start broadcasting?

25 'QED' has been a popular quiz show. But what do its initials stand for?

26 What is the name of the BBC's teletext service?

27 Which children's TV show suffered from an urban myth that falsely claimed there were double entendres in the characters' names?

28 Which seminal 80s drama starring Jeremy Irons and Anthony Andrews was remade into a movie starring Emma Thompson and Michael Gambon in 2008?

29 This children's TV series was set in 2068 in an airborne head-quarters called Cloudbase. What was the series?

30 This son of a James Bond actor succeeded Michael Praed in the lead role in 'Robin of Sherwood'. Who is he?

Quiz 128

1   Up to the end of season 2007-08, only four teams had won the Premier League. Who are they?

2   What team, who started out with the name Odd, have won their national league a record 13 times?

3   What two countries were the first joint hosts of the World Cup?

4   Who is the all-time top scorer in the Premier League?

5   David Beckham wore the number 7 for Manchester United and England, and while at Real Madrid. What is his squad number at LA Galaxy?

6   What major side plays at the controversial and futuristic-looking Allianz Arena?

7   Who are the current holders of the Women's World Cup, having won the trophy in 2007?

8   The Irriducibili are the well known fans of what club?

9   What player and previous Golden Boot winner has scored most goals in European matches for a British side?

10   How many teams play in top-class English football?

11   Who were the last team to win the World Cup with a penalty shoot-out?

12   If you were watching the Black Cats play at home, what town would you be in?

13   Who was the first foreigner ever to manage England?

14   Who was the captain of the Manchester United side that lifted the European Cup in 1968?

15   When was the original Wembley Stadium demolished?

16 What country is the only one to top the FIFA World Ranking without ever having won the World Cup?

17 In what ground do France play their home matches?

18 How many teams have never been out of the Premier League since it was founded?

19 This team won every competition they entered in the 1966-67 season: Scottish League, Scottish Cup, Scottish League Cup, European Cup and Glasgow Cup. Who are they?

20 What team has the longest name in the eight top-class English or Scottish leagues?

21 What do Cardiff City, Wrexham and Swansea have in common?

22 Who became president of UEFA in 2007?

23 What two English sides won two consecutive European Cups in the four seasons from 1978 to 1981?

24 What side plays in the Estádio da Luz?

25 The Army team the Sappers won the FA Cup in 1870. What are they better known as?

26 Who played the fictional England manager Mike Bassett in the 2001 movie?

27 What is the westernmost team in the English league?

28 What top-class European league has the highest proportion of foreign players?

29 What two teams played in the first all-England European Champions League final?

30 What former Manchester City boss was appointed manager of Mexico in the summer of 2008?

Quiz 129

1   According to the poet Robert Burns, 'freedom and –' what go together?

2   When the US Congress fell out with France over the Iraq War in 2003, what did their canteen rename their French fries?

3   Which horseman of the Apocalypse rode a pale horse?

4   Where did Nellie the elephant meet the head of the herd?

5   'I have not failed. I've just found 10,000 ways that won't work.' These are the words of what successful American inventor?

6   How many inches longer than a yard is a metre?

7   What capital city stands on Zealand and Amager islands?

8   The Roman Emperor Caesar Augustus gave his name to what part of our calendar?

9   The poisonous gas carbon monoxide combines one carbon atom bonded to how many oxygen atoms?

10   'Reality is merely an illusion, albeit a very persistent one.' What scientist said this?

11   What country would you be in if the local beer was Red Stripe?

12   What herb would you use to make a pesto sauce?

13   What four creatures have been used to name road crossings in the UK?

14   How many numbers do you have to choose six from, on a normal National Lottery slip?

15   What was the name of Han Solo's ship in 'Star Wars'?

16 The company Bayerische Motoren Werke is better known as what?

17 To where would you ride a cock horse 'to see a fine lady upon a white horse'?

18 Cheese with holes generally comes from what country?

19 What would be the end result if you mixed a cocktail of charcoal, saltpetre and sulphur?

20 How many balls are on a snooker table at the start of the game?

21 What colour would you expect Chartreuse liqueur to be?

22 What three races make up the Triple Crown of British racing?

23 What direction is a ship turning in when it gives one short horn blast?

24 Michelangelo's 'David' statue carries his sling over what shoulder?

25 What was the name of Flash Gordon's girlfriend?

26 An excess of glucose in the urine suggests the possibility of what disease?

27 Does cork come from a plant, from a tree or from the ground?

28 What model did David Bowie marry in 1992?

29 What is the degrees longitude of the Prime Meridian?

30 How many furlongs is the minimum distance a horse race can be in Britain?

Quiz 130

1   What year did Disneyland in California open?

2   What is the name of Beauty in 'Beauty and the Beast'?

3   What famous Disney character did Clarence Nash voice for over 50 years?

4   Alfred Hitchcock once stated, 'Disney has the best casting. If he doesn't like an actor he just –' what?

5   What is the name of the Little Mermaid?

6   What full-length Disney animated movie was the first one ever to receive an Oscar nomination for Best Picture?

7   In what year did Walt Disney die?

8   What was the last Disney animated film to use hand-painted cels?

9   What was the first movie for which the Disney Studio hired real-life actors?

10   'Plane Crazy' was the first animated cartoon to feature what character?

11   What Walt Disney theme park ride was the inspiration for a series of successful movies that began in 2003?

12   In what Disney animated movie is Earth described as 'Section 17, Area 51'?

13   He was Oscar-nominated for his screenplay writing on 'Toy Story'. He later went on to produce 'Buffy the Vampire Slayer'. Who is he?

14   What animation studio, responsible for 'Toy Story', did the Walt Disney Company buy from Steve Jobs in 2006?

15   Who is the young hero of the 1994 award-winning animation 'The Lion King'?

16 What was Disney's first full-length animation?

17 Who was the wicked vizier to the sultan in 'Aladdin'?

18 What actor was offered an original Picasso painting by the Walt Disney Company as an apology after a public falling-out?

19 Spaceship Earth is centrepiece and icon of what part of Walt Disney World in Florida?

20 In what country is 'Beauty and the Beast' set?

21 What English actor played Emelius Brown in 'Bedknobs and Broomsticks' and George Banks in 'Mary Poppins'?

22 What song from 'Aladdin' won a Best Original Song Oscar for Alan Menken and Tim Rice?

23 'The Love Bug' was the first in a series of movies featuring an unusual Volkswagen Beetle called – what?

24 Under what company name does Disney release its movies aimed at an older market?

25 Sulley and Mike are the main characters in what 2001 animated movie?

26 How many Disney Resorts are there outside the US?

27 What TV movie became the Disney Channel's most successful ever when it was first shown in 2006?

28 Randy Newman was nominated for an Oscar for Best Original Song for 'Toy Story'. What was the song?

29 'He's dying to become a chef' – the tagline of what 2007 Pixar-produced Oscar-winning animation?

30 Who steals 99 puppies in the movie '101 Dalmatians'?

Quiz 131

1   British pop star Pete Best was actually born in which country?

2   What band had their only top 20 hit when 'Brimful of Asha' went to no. 1 in 1998?

3   'If Not for You' was Olivia Newton-John's first UK hit, in 1971. Who wrote it?

4   What male duo dressed as the women from Abba for a video of their 1992 cover of 'Take a Chance on Me'?

5   What five famous musicians made up the Travelling Wilburys?

6   What type of music is j-pop?

7   Who won three consecutive BRIT Awards for Best Single by a British Artist from 1999 to 2001?

8   What Welsh singer was 'Holding Out for a Hero' in 1984?

9   Whose breakthrough album, 'Voice of an Angel', was the top UK classical crossover album of 1998?

10 What rapper was bottled off the stage at the Reading Festival in 2005?

11 Which former Eurythmic won a Best Original Song Oscar in 2003 for her theme for 'The Lord of the Rings: The Return of the King'?

12 Who had three no. 1 hits in the 70s with 'Tiger Feet', 'Lonely This Christmas' and 'Oh Boy'?

13 What award-winning band was originally called Tony Flow and the Miraculously Majestic Masters of Mayhem?

14 In 1974, 'Long Live Love' by Olivia Newton John came fourth for the UK in the Eurovision song contest. What was that year's winner?

15 What Canadian band had their first hit in the UK with 'How You Remind Me'?

16 What long-established American punk band played themselves in 'The Simpsons Movie' in 2007, singing its theme song?

17 What Canadian pop star took the picture of the Queen that is used on official Canadian stamps?

18 Two bands alternated the BRIT Award for Best British Group from 2000 to 2003. Coldplay was one. Who was the other?

19 What was Bruce Springsteen's first UK top 20 hit?

20 Who controversially became the first hip hop act to headline at Glastonbury in 2008?

21 What reformed four-piece act took the BRIT Award for Best Live Act at the 2008 awards?

22 What band did Pete Doherty join after leaving The Libertines?

23 Who wrote the lyrics for The Smiths?

24 What 1969 release was Fleetwood Mac's first UK no. 1?

25 A defining 80s video showcased what no. 1 single taken from Robert Palmer's 'Riptide' album?

26 What band predicted a riot in 2004?

27 What BRIT Award winners, with UK no. 1 hit albums 'Hot Fuss' and 'Sam's Town', have been called the 'best British band to come out of America'?

28 Who had a no. 1 UK hit in 2006 after a 29-year gap since his last one?

29 What is Ozzy Osbourne's real first name?

30 Who played the lead singer of the Weird Sisters in 'Harry Potter and the Goblet of Fire', performing 'Do the Hippogriff'?

Quiz 132

Can you name the source TV show for each of these spinoffs?

1 'Angel: the Series'

2 'Frasier'

3 'Count Duckula'

4 'Torchwood'

5 'The Lone Gunmen'

6 'The Pebbles and Bamm-Bamm Show'

7 'Ashes to Ashes'

8 'Scooby and Scrappy-Doo'

9 'Max and Paddy's Road to Nowhere'

10 'Softly, Softly'

11 'Going Straight'

12 'Joey'

13 'Boston Legal'

14 'Dastardly and Muttley'

15 'The Roly Mo Show'

16 'Stargate Atlantis'

17 'NCIS'

18 'Grace and Favour'

19 'Laverne & Shirley'

20 'Whatever Happened to the Likely Lads?'

21 'The Bionic Woman'

22 'George and Mildred'

23 'The Colbys'

24 'Lewis'

25 'Holby Blue'

26 'Melrose Place'

27 'The Sarah Jane Adventures'

28 'Xena: Warrior Princess'

29 'Bindi the Jungle Girl'

30 'Knots Landing'

Quiz 133

1   How many Minor Arcana cards are in a Tarot deck?

2   In what numerical line-up did Sloth replace Sadness?

3   What is the first astrological sign of the 12 signs of the zodiac?

4   How many people are seated at the table in the da Vinci painting of 'The Last Supper'?

5   What name is given to the branch of mathematics that studies systems of numbers?

6   How many monkeys were in the title of the 1995 Terry Gilliam film that starred Bruce Willis and Brad Pitt?

7   How much is a score?

8   Between what two British cities does the M8 run?

9   If you're playing bingo, what number should you cover when Kelly's Eye is called?

10 What is the normal age for retirement in the UK?

11 How many lines are in a limerick?

12 If you suffer from triskaidekaphobia, what would you be afraid of?

13 How many of each creature did Noah take into the ark to escape the Flood?

14 Instead of diamonds, hearts, clubs and spades, what are the four suits in a Spanish deck of cards?

15 How many squares are on a sudoku grid?

16 What number do mystics consider to represent spiritual perfection?

17 How many years have you been married when you celebrate your crystal wedding anniversary?

18 How many items would you find in a brace?

19 Who is the only woman in the Fantastic Four?

20 How many cards are there in a normal deck?

21 In cricket, if a batsman knocks the ball over the boundary without it touching the ground, how many runs does he earn?

22 How many plagues were visited on the Ancient Egyptians?

23 What number is not used by cars in Formula 1 races?

24 What number does the Roman numeral MM represent?

25 How many human blood groups are there?

26 Name the Seven Deadly Sins.

27 From what city do the American football team known as the 49ers come?

28 The directions north, south, east and west are known as the four what directions?

29 Ministering to prisoners and burying the dead are just two of what seven virtues?

30 How many years of solitude did Gabriel García Márquez write about in his 1967 novel?

Quiz 134

1   In which Beatles movie does the song 'All My Loving' appear?

2   The theme from the movie 'Breakfast At Tiffany's' became an easy-listening classic. What is it?

3   What song did Sam play for Rick and Elsa in 'Casablanca'?

4   The 'EastEnders' theme music was used in a song recorded by Anita Dobson. What was it?

5   What Canadian composer has written the scores of several major movies, winning three Oscars for his work on 'The Lord of the Rings' trilogy?

6   The Bob Dylan song, 'Knockin' on Heaven's Door', was the theme of which Sam Peckinpah movie?

7   'Good Morning, Starshine', 'Aquarius' and 'Ain't Got No... I Got Life', all come from which musical?

8   Elvis Presley sang the song 'Wooden Heart' in which one of his movies?

9   What traditional English song provided the music for the classic BBC cop show 'Z Cars'?

10   Which Monty Python member composed and sang the theme for the BBC comedy 'One Foot In The Grave'?

11   Who had a top 10 hit with his cover of 'The Snowman' theme, 'Walking In The Air'?

12   'Suicide is Painless' was the theme tune to which TV show?

13   'My Heart Belongs to Daddy' comes from the musical, 'Let's Make Love'. Who sang the song in the film?

14   Who sings the 'Dad's Army' theme, 'Who Do You Think You Are Kidding, Mr Hitler'?

15   Tony Christie's 'Avenues and Alleyways' was the theme of a 1970s hit TV series starring Roger Moore and Tony Curtis. What was it?

16 'Duelling Banjos' was the theme of which John Boorman thriller?

17 'Don't Cry For Me, Argentina', from the hit show and musical 'Evita', was a hit for several people. Who wrote it?

18 The song 'Secret Love' first featured in which 1950s cross-dressing musical Western?

19 Which song was the theme tune for 'The Office'?

20 'The Soprano's theme, 'Woke Up This Morning', was performed by what British group?

21 Which classic children's animated series had the jaunty sea shanty 'The Hornblower' as its theme?

22 In which Astaire-Rogers movie was the Irving Berlin song, 'Cheek to Cheek' performed?

23 What Oscar-winning song played in 'Forrest Gump' and 'Spider-Man 2' but was first heard 'Butch Cassidy and the Sundance Kid'?

24 What BBC composer wrote many themes, including 'Only Fools and Horses', 'The Two Ronnies' and' Last of the Summer Wine'?

25 The theme for 80s and 90s series 'Minder' was recorded by one of its stars. What is the song called?

26 Who wrote and sang the theme for the 70s show, 'The Wombles'?

27 What American composer wrote the themes for 'Hill Street Blues', 'The A-Team' and 'Quantum Leap' and had a song written for him on the Who's 'Endless Wire' album?

28 This band, successful in their own right, performed the 'Father Ted' theme as well as songs from the series. Who are they?

29 What theme spelled out the main character's name in a code, with other characters' names also coded in the score?

30 What composer wrote the score for 'Men in Black', 'Spider-Man', 'Sleepy Hollow' and others, and most famously for 'The Simpsons'?

Quiz 135

Can you identify the movie these last words come from?

1 'Louis, I think this is the beginning of a beautiful friendship.'

2 'The greatest trick the Devil ever pulled was convincing the world he didn't exist. And like that, he's gone.'

3 'In spite of everything, I still believe that people are really good at heart.'

4 'May the Force be with you.'

5 'Mr. Hammond, after careful consideration, I've decided not to endorse your park.' 'So have I.'

6 'Love means never having to say you're sorry.'

7 '...but I never got it. I never let it in.'

8 'Look, Daddy. Teacher says, every time a bell rings, an angel gets his wings.' 'That's right, that's right. Attaboy, Clarence.'

9 'God bless our ships and all who sail in them.'

10 'Oh, good. For a minute, I thought we were in trouble.'

11 'As you wish.'

12 The old man was right – only the farmers won. We lost. We'll always lose.'

13 'I'm the boss, I'm the boss, I'm the boss, I'm the boss, I'm the boss... boss, boss, boss, boss, boss, boss.'

14 'Don Corleone.'

15 'I'll go home, and I'll think of some way to get him back. After all, tomorrow is another day!'

16 'Well, nobody's perfect.'

17 'I love this town!'

18 'I used to hate the water.' 'I can't imagine why.'

19 'I'm not even gonna swat that fly. I hope they are watching. They'll see. They'll see and they'll know and they'll say, "Why, she wouldn't even harm a fly".'

20 'Eliza? Where the devil are my slippers?'

21 'Let's go home, Debbie.'

22 'I look up at the Moon, and wonder: when will we be going back? And who will that be?'

23 'To God, there is no zero. I still exist!'

24 'Auntie Em, there's no place like home!'

25 'Merry Christmas!'

26 'Greetings, programs!'

27 'And I felt His voice take the sword out of my hand.'

28 'Roads? Where we're going, we don't need roads.'

29 'And here is your receipt.'

30 'We're devils and blacksheep and really bad eggs! Drink up, me hearties, yo ho!'

Answers

Quiz 1

1 Rogers & Hammerstein **2** 'Carousel' **3** Ben Elton **4** Cole Porter
5 'The Little Shop of Horrors' **6** 'Fiddler on the Roof' **7** 'Rent'
8 Jeremy Brett **9** 'Yankee Doodle Dandy' **10** 'Cabaret' **11** 'Cats'
12 'Tommy' **13** 'Oh! What a Lovely War' **14** 'The Wizard of Oz'
15 'Jesus Christ Superstar' **16** 'The Blues Brothers' **17** 'The Producers'
18 'Bugsy Malone' **19** 'The Rocky Horror Picture Show' **20** John
Travolta **21** Siam **22** 'Grease' **23** Björn Ulvaeus & Benny Andersson
24 'West Side Story' **25** 'High School Musical' **26** The Scarecrow, the
Cowardly Lion, the Tin Man **27** 'Oliver!' **28** 'Can You Feel the Love
Tonight' **29** David Soul **30** 'Joseph and the Amazing Technicolor
Dreamcoat'

Quiz 2

1 Billy Idol **2** Spike **3** 'Tom & Jerry' **4** A pig **5** 'Animal Farm'
6 Eric Arthur Blair **7** 1994 **8** South Africa **9** 6 **10** Revelation
11 Watergate **12** Traitor's Gate **13** Barcelona **14** Freddie Mercury
15 Venus **16** Florence **17** Crimean War **18** Queen Victoria **19** British
Columbia **20** 'Discovery' **21** Captain Scott **22** Major **23** Orion (the
Hunter) **24** Superman **25** Clark Kent **26** Canterbury **27** Geoffrey
Chaucer **28** Geoffrey Rush **29** Canada **30** 1982

Quiz 3

1 Conservatives (1979) **2** Access credit card **3** Kentucky Fried Chicken
4 News of the World **5** John Lewis Partnership **6** Hoover vacuum
cleaner **7** Frosties **8** Martini **9** Lilt **10** Irn Bru **11** Heinz Baked Beans
12 Standard Fireworks **13** Rice Krispies **14** Schweppes **15** Renault Clio
16 Nimble Bread **17** Castlemaine XXXX (fourex) **18** Fry's Five Boys
Chocolate **19** Cresta **20** Kia-Ora **21** Fry's Turkish Delight **22** Ferrero
Rocher **23** Ready Brek **24** Um Bongo **25** Mars Bar **26** Brut After
Shave **27** Cadbury's Creme Egg **28** Maynard's Wine Gums **29** Audi
30 Pepsi

Quiz 4

1 Billy the Kid **2** Rupert Brooke **3** She threw herself in front of the
king's horse at the Derby **4** Alexander the Great **5** Buddy Holly, Ritchie
Valens, the Big Bopper **6** Jesse James **7** 'Mama' Cass Elliot, Keith
Moon **8** The eruption of Vesuvius **9** Mark Antony **10** Virgina Woolf
11 He shot himself **12** Mark Rothko **13** WB Yeats **14** Christopher
Marlowe **15** Their ashes were blasted into space **16** Lord Admiral
Horatio Nelson **17** Che Guevara **18** Rudyard Kipling **19** Danton
20 Thermopylae **21** Captain Smith of the 'Titanic' **22** Socrates
23 Dorothy Parker **24** A tortoise **25** Eddie Cochran **26** Tupac Shakur
27 Jimi Hendrix, Janis Joplin, Jim Morrison **28** Christopher Wren
29 Errol Flynn **30** Mel Blanc

Quiz 5

1 Time And Relative Dimension(s) In Space **2** Terry Nation **3** Colin Baker **4** John Simm **5** Sarah Jane Smith **6** Gallifrey **7** Lalla Ward **8** 10 **9** UNIT (United Nations Intelligence Taskforce) **10** Peter Purves **11** Derek Jacobi **12** Russell T Davies **13** The Timelords **14** K-9 **15** Christopher Eccleston **16** Captain Jack Harkness **17** Steven Moffat **18** First Doctor **19** Tenth Doctor **20** Donna Noble **21** 12 (allowing 13 incarnations) **22** Forwards **23** Sonic screwdriver **24** Douglas Adams **25** The Slitheen **26** Davros **27** Romana **28** Cardiff **29** Paul McGann **30** 'Torchwood'

Quiz 6

1 Asia **2** Tropic of Capricorn **3** The Andes **4** Gain **5** 24,902 miles **6** Caspian Sea **7** Anticlockwise **8** 3% **9** Suriname **10** A circle quartered by a cross **11** 22 April **12** Tokyo **13** Blue Moon (it's the second one) **14** Dead Sea **15** Marianas (or Mariana) Trench **16** Ayers Rock **17** About the same **18** 65,868 mph **19** Pacific **20** Madrid **21** 8 **22** 14 °C **23** Cheetah **24** It's the world's largest volcano **25** Sahara **26** Midnight **27** 4.6 billion **28** Yellowstone **29** The original single continent **30** 'The Hitch-hiker's Guide to the Galaxy'

Quiz 7

1 Battle of Britain **2** Bolsheviks **3** Neville Chamberlain **4** Suffragettes **5** 1922 **6** Unilateral Declaration of Independence **7** Israel **8** 1990 **9** Union of Soviet Socialist Republics **10** USA **11** Bertrand Russell **12** Cultural Revolution **13** Robert Baden-Powell **14** Franz Ferdinand **15** Australia & New Zealand **16** Smoking in enclosed public places **17** Japanese attack on Pearl Harbor **18** St Petersburg **19** Ireland **20** 1982 **21** The Allied crossing point between West and East Berlin **22** Alcohol **23** (Boxing Day) Tsunami **24** The 9/11 attacks **25** Charles & Diana and Andrew & Sarah **26** 2004 **27** The Dambusters **28** Assassination of JFK **29** Benazir Bhutto **30** 2007

Quiz 8

1 'Trumpton' **2** 'Ashes To Ashes' **3** 1961 **4** 'Mr Benn' **5** 'Daktari' **6** Looby Loo & Teddy **7** The Wombles **8** 1969 **9** 'Blue Peter' **10** Bagpuss **11** They all presented 'Play School' **12** Basil Brush **13** 5 of the US Mercury astronauts, the first to fly in space **14** 'Crackerjack' **15** 'Play Away' **16** A dragon **17** Thomas the Tank Engine **18** The Tomorrow People **19** 'White Horses' **20** Joan Collins **21** 'Wacky Races' **22** The Double-Deckers **23** 'Do Not Adjust Your Set' **24** Bizzy Lizzy **25** Yogi Bear **26** The Flintstones **27** Catweazle **28** '(Hergé's Adventures of) Tintin' **29** The Mystery Machine **30** 'Grange Hill'

Quiz 9

1 Colin McRae **2** The NFL (America's National Football League)
3 Muhammad Ali **4** World Cup (football) **5** Her mother (the Princess
Royal) **6** New Delhi **7** A period of play (7.5 minutes) **8** 12 **9** Played
the hole 3 under par **10** Lance Armstrong **11** Glamorganshire
12 Hurling **13** Grand champion **14** Gold **15** 6 **16** Bowling crease
17 The race is being ended prematurely **18** New York Knickerbockers
19 Yachting (or Sailing) **20** Tug o' War, Rowing, Back-stroke swimming
21 High-jump event **22** Dick Fosbury **23** 30 **24** Spider **25** Strike
another player's ball with yours **26** The horse's saddle, bridle and bit
27 An over in which a wicket is taken but no runs scored **28** Jockeys
29 She was the first woman cox **30** Curling (it's a brush)

Quiz 10

1 Gossip **2** Avocado **3** Beggar **4** Flatterer **5** Estate agent **6** Garage
7 Grill **8** Hot-dog sausage **9** Ice lolly **10** Jam **11** Dual carriageway
12 Noughts and Crosses **13** Open-air stands **14** Pedestrian crossing
15 Pushchair **16** Queue **17** Receptionist **18** Swiss roll **19** Tap
20 Tram **21** Trousers **22** Waistcoat **23** Wallet **24** Saloon car
25 Roundabout **26** Spanner **27** Candy floss **28** Dummy **29** Docker
30 Flyover

Quiz 11

1 Huey, Dewey & Louie **2** Mel Blanc **3** Bluto (aka Brutus & Bruno)
4 'Spirited Away' **5** 'The Snowman' **6** He was bitten by a radioactive
spider **7** Krypton **8** Frank Miller **9** Stan Lee **10** 1954 **11** Marvel
Comics **12** 'Bugs Bunny' **13** 13 Charlie Brown's **14** 'Tin Toy' **15** Rex
16 'Maus' **17** 9/11 **18** Officer (Charlie) Dibble **19** Scott Adams
20 Neil Gaiman **21** 'Punch' **22** Robin Williams **23** Pluto
24 Beanotown **25** 'The Dandy' **26** Beavis & Butt-Head **27** 'From
Hell' **28** 'Pinky and the Brain' **29** Courage the Cowardly Dog
30 'Billy's Boots'

Quiz 12

1 German Invasion Of USSR, 1941 **2** Grenadier, Coldstream, Scots, Irish,
Welsh **3** They are the only private army allowed in the UK **4** Culloden
(1746) **5** The Royal Flying Corps **6** Allied Invasion Of Normandy (1944)
7 Household Cavalry **8** The British Civil Wars (also known as the
English Civil Wars) **9** Delta Force **10** Reveille **11** Admiral of the Fleet
12 Appomattox **13** Rome & Carthage **14** Cranwell **15** The Queen
16 French Foreign Legion **17** HMS 'Dreadnought' **18** Navy, Army And
Air Forces Institutes **19** Wars of the Roses **20** Peter de la Billière
21 Montgomery & Rommel **22** The Phoney War **23** The Hundred
Years War **24** D-Day landing beaches in Normandy **25** Boxer Rebellion
26 American War of Independence **27** Victoria Cross **28** Charge of
the Light Brigade **29** Second Battle of Ypres (1915) **30** Dwight D
Eisenhower

Quiz 13

1 Radio Telefis Éireann **2** 1989 **3** Ford **4** Chicago **5** A quarter **6** They were all unmarried **7** He was married **8** International Committee of the Red Cross **9** 4.30 **10** N & D (Nuclear Disarmament) **11** Roger Bacon **12** Ulysses **13** Japan **14** Barnes Wallis **15** A public limited company **16** Liebraumilch **17** Japan **18** Pineapple **19** The NHS **20** Horatio **21** Gambia **22** Mark Antony **23** Oxford (University) **24** Flags **25** Oldest continuously published newspaper in the UK (first published 1665) **26** St Paul's **27** Euston **28** Salvation Army **29** Train à Grande Vitesse (trans: High-Speed Train) **30** Equilateral triangle

Quiz 14

1 Oxygen **2** Red **3** Carbon **4** 120 mph or 195 kph **5** 212 °F **6** Nucleus **7** Silver **8** Mercury, Caesium, Gallium **9** James Joyce (in 'Finnegans Wake') **10** Seismologist **11** Newton's Third Law of Motion **12** 3500 million **13** Hydrogen **14** An insulator **15** RAdio Detection And Ranging **16** Igneous **17** Solid, liquid, gas **18** Clouds **19** Gamma rays **20** Quaternary **21** The Curie family (1903, 1911, 1935) **22** Carbon Dioxide **23** San Andreas Fault **24** Bombing of Hiroshima & Nagasaki (1945) **25** Edwin Hubble **26** Aluminium **27** Glass **28** The neutron **29** Salt **30** The epicentre

Quiz 15

1 'Four Weddings and a Funeral' 2 'Rocky 3' 3 'Robin Hood: Prince of Thieves' 4 'Titanic' 5 'Austin Powers: The Spy Who Shagged Me' 6 'Dangerous Minds' 7 'Mannequin' 8 'Days of Thunder' 9 'Saturday Night Fever' 10 'Reservoir Dogs' 11 'The Jewel of the Nile' 12 'Armageddon' 13 'There's Something About Mary' 14 'Top Gun' 15 'Do the Right Thing' 16 'Peter's Friends' 17 'The Bodyguard' 18 'Grease' 19 'Moulin Rouge' 20 'The Lion King' 21 'An Officer and a Gentleman' 22 'Aladdin' 23 'The Beach' 24 'The Full Monty' 25 '8 Mile' 26 'Karate Kid 2' 27 'Back to the Future' 28 'Madagascar' 29 'Dirty Dancing' 30 'When Harry Met Sally'

Quiz 16

1 Jerusalem 2 Panchen Lama 3 By white smoke from the Vatican chimney 4 Thomas à Becket 5 Francis of Assisi 6 Quakers 7 West Bank 8 David 9 The first 10 A Jesuit 11 Augustine (of Canterbury) 12 Martin Luther 13 5 14 St Matthew 15 Genesis 16 Talk 17 Damascus 18 Carpenter 19 John Calvin 20 Pope 21 Minaret 22 Exodus 23 Menorah 24 'Oh Come All Ye Faithful' 25 Mary Baker Eddy 26 Passover 27 Holy Week 28 Church of Jesus Christ of the Latter-day Saints 29 Hinduism 30 Ramadan

Quiz 17

1 Volkswagen (Beetle) **2** Los Angeles International **3** On the water (it's a Venetian water bus) **4** Waterloo **5** Queensland And Northern Territory Aerial Service **6** 1937 **7** 'Tam o' Shanter' **8** York **9** The ship's compass **10** The Mini car **11** Charles Lindbergh **12** Glasgow, Liverpool, Newcastle **13** Israeli **14** The General Lee **15** 1969 **16** 1918 **17** The 'Golden Hind' **18** Greenpeace **19** Rail (it's the French national railway) **20** Tax discs **21** John Lennon Airport **22** 1958 **23** 'Calypso' **24** Ford's Model T **25** The M4 **26** 'Gypsy Moth IV' **27** Green **28** The 'Beagle' **29** Boston **30** White Star

Quiz 18

1 Fresco **2** Bauhaus **3** Light and Dark **4** The Tate **5** (Hans) Holbein the Younger **6** da Vinci & Michelangelo **7** 'The Scream' **8** Surrealism **9** 'The Angel of the North' **10** It was the only one he sold in his lifetime **11** The Hermitage in St Petersburg **12** Whistler's Mother **13** Milan **14** Michelangelo **15** LS Lowry **16** Claude Monet **17** Banksy **18** Salvador Dali **19** 'Fiddler on the Roof' **20** God's **21** Tracey Emin **22** Gesso **23** Jackson Pollock **24** 'Guernica' **25** Gilbert & George **26** 'The Hay Wain' **27** National Gallery **28** (Henri de) Toulouse-Lautrec **29** JMM Turner **30** Damien Hirst

Quiz 19

1 'Peter Pan' (JM Barrie) **2** 'Pride and Prejudice' (Jane Austen) **3** 'Jaws' (Peter Benchley) **4** 'The Da Vinci Code' (Dan Brown) **5** 'Charlie and the Chocolate Factory' (Roald Dahl) **6** 'A Christmas Carol' (Charles Dickens) **7** 'Rebecca' (Daphne du Maurier) **8** 'The Wind in the Willows' (Kenneth Grahame) **9** 'The Old Man and the Sea' (Ernest Hemingway) **10** 'Redwall' (Brian Jacques) **11** 'The Trial' (Franz Kafka) **12** 'The Lion, the Witch and the Wardrobe' (CS Lewis) **13** 'Moby Dick' (Herman Melville) **14** 'Harry Potter and the Philosopher's Stone' (JK Rowling) **15** The Godfather' (Mario Puzo) **16** The Bible **17** 'Anne of Green Gables' (LM Montgomery) **18** '1984' (George Orwell) **19** 'Gone With The Wind' (Margaret Mitchell) **20** 'The Hitch-Hiker's Guide to the Galaxy' (Douglas Adams) **21** 'Around The World In 80 Days' (Jules Verne) **22** 'Macbeth' (William Shakespeare) **23** 'Anthem for Doomed Youth' (Wilfred Owen) **24** 'The Crow Road' (Iain Banks) **25** 'Five on a Treasure Island' (Enid Blyton) **26** 'The Diary of A Young Girl' (Anne Frank) **27** 'Northern Lights' (Philip Pullman) **28** 'Stormbreaker' (Anthony Horowitz) **29** 'Mary Poppins' (PL Travers) **30** 'The Gruffalo' (Julia Donaldson)

Quiz 20

1 Knight of the Order of the Thistle **2** Hyper Text Transfer Protocol
3 Mumps, Measles & Rubella **4** Ministry of Transport **5** National
Association for the Advancement of Coloured People **6** Critically ill
patients (it's an Intensive Care Unit) **7** First Aid Nursing Yeomanry
8 Light Amplification by Stimulated Emission of Radiation **9** Double
Income No Kids Yet **10** Iesus Nazarenus Rex Iudaeorum (Jesus of
Nazareth King of the Jews) **11** Mothers Against Drunk Driving
12 A Doctor (or Physician) **13** Gaelic Athletic Association **14** Aide-de-
Camp **15** Hard Black **16** Attention Deficit Hyperactivity Disorder
17 American Standard Code for Information Interchange **18** British
Expeditionary Force **19** Financial Times Stock Exchange **20** Because
one is a Master of Foxhounds and the other in the League Against Cruel
Sports **21** Bovine Spongiform Encephalopathy **22** Bicycle Motocross
23 Methicillin-Resistant Staphylococcus Aureus **24** Peninsular &
Oriental **25** Self-Contained Underwater Breathing Apparatus **26** Nota
Bene (Latin for 'note well') **27** Parsec **28** PVC **29** Air-Raid
Precaution **30** International Standard Book Number

Quiz 21

1 'Star Wars' **2** 'The Simpsons Movie' **3** 'Monsters, Inc.' **4** 'The Blues Brothers' **5** 'Ghostbusters' **6** 'Jaws 2' **7** 'The Amityville Horror' **8** 'Titanic' **9** 'RoboCop' **10** 'The Exorcist' **11** 'Toy Story 2' **12** 'Back to the Future' **13** '300' **14** 'Friday the 13th' **15** 'Sex and the City' **16** 'Crocodile Dundee' **17** 'Spider-Man' **18** 'The Da Vinci Code' **19** 'Deliverance' **20** 'The Matrix' **21** 'The Sting' **22** 'Pirates of the Caribbean: At World's End' **23** 'Night at the Museum' **24** 'Halloween' **25** 'Transformers' **26** 'Die Hard' **27** 'The Life of Brian' **28** 'I Am Legend' **29** 'The Lord of the Rings: The Fellowship of the Ring' **30** 'Independence Day'

Quiz 22

1 John Lennon **2** Henry Kissinger **3** JK Rowling **4** Richard Nixon **5** The Queen **6** Margaret Thatcher **7** Charlie Chaplin **8** Ronnie Kray **9** Enoch Powell **10** French President Charles de Gaulle **11** Dylan Thomas **12** Neville Chamberlain **13** Martin Luther King Jr **14** Cecil Rhodes **15** Winston Churchill **16** Quentin Crisp (attributed) **17** Al Capone **18** Margaret Thatcher **19** Jean-Paul Sartre **20** William Shakespeare (Polonius in 'Hamlet') **21** Harold Wilson **22** Muhammad Ali **23** Timothy Leary **24** Edward Heath **25** Harold Macmillan **26** Albert Einstein **27** General Douglas Haig (Commander of British forces 1915-18) **28** Banksy **29** Tony Blair **30** Andy Warhol

Quiz 23

1 'Casablanca' **2** 'The Lord Of The Rings' (specifically in 'The Fellowship of the Ring' & 'The Return of the King') **3** 'Friends' **4** 'Star Wars' **5** 'EastEnders' **6** 'The Simpsons' **7** 'Frasier' **8** 'Harry Potter' series (specifically 'Order Of The Phoenix') **9** 'The Sopranos' **10** 'Ashes to Ashes' **11** 'Star Trek: The Next Generation' **12** 'Coronation Street' **13** 'Neighbours' **14** 'Buffy the Vampire Slayer' **15** 'Back To The Future' **16** 'Emmerdale' **17** 'Balamory' **18** 'The Godfather' **19** ''Allo! 'Allo!' **20** 'Life on Mars' **21** 'Blackadder the Third' **22** 'Harry Potter' series **23** 'Treasure Island' **24** 'Hollyoaks' **25** 'Ballykissangel' **26** 'The Archers' **27** 'Cabaret' **28** 'Only Fools and Horses' **29** 'The Young Ones' **30** 'Deadwood'

Quiz 24

1 Kublai Khan **2** A stately pleasure-dome **3** Tony Blair **4** 'Vision On' **5** Lourdes **6** Madonna **7** Britney Spears's 'Baby One More Time' **8** Stephen Hawking **9** Merlin **10** Arthur **11** The Holy Grail **12** 'The Da Vinci Code' **13** Enigma **14** Alan Turing **15** Steve Coogan **16** Apple Inc. **17** The Beatles **18** 'Love Me Do' **19** War **20** 1984 **21** Big Brother **22** Jimmy Dean **23** Ronald Reagan **24** Jodie Foster **25** Gloucester **26** The Severn **27** Into Wales **28** 1969 **29** Woodstock **30** 'Peanuts'

Quiz 25

1 Gary Sobers **2** 9 **3** Manchester United **4** IBF, WBA, WBC, WBO
(in full: International Boxing Federation, World Boxing Association,
World Boxing Council, World Boxing Organisation) **5** 11 **6** New Zealand
7 Benson & Hedges Cup **8** 5 years **9** Stirling Moss **10** Tom Morris
(Old & Young) **11** Johnny Weismuller **12** 9 **13** South Korea **14** Shooting, Fencing, Swimming, Riding and Cross-country running **15** Boston
Red Sox **16** The County Championship officially began that year
17 Blackpool **18** 3 **19** The US Masters **20** Viv Anderson
21 Fairyhouse **22** The player playing with White **23** Wigan
24 The race is 500 miles long **25** Jack Nicklaus **26** Floor, Vault,
Beam, Asymmetric (or Uneven) Bars **27** America's Cup **28** 4
29 They are all Formula 1 race circuits **30** Tour of Italy, Tour of Spain

Quiz 26

1 Red **2** Boris Johnson **3** Highgate Hill **4** 11th **5** The Great Fire of
1666 **6** Mary & Elizabeth **7** The London Eye **8** 42 **9** Bethlehem Royal
(or Bedlam) **10** St Paul's **11** Crystal Palace **12** Paddington
13 221B Baker Street **14** William Wordsworth **15** Justice **16** Big Ben
17 St Pancras **18** Canary Wharf Tower **19** St Mary le Bow **20** 12
21 The Kinks **22** St Bartholomew's (or Barts) **23** Sam Wanamaker
24 5 **25** Winchester **26** National Portrait Gallery **27** Carnaby Street
28 Charles Dickens **29** Victoria & Albert Museum (or The V&A)
30 Buckingham Palace

Quiz 27

1 'Yesterday' **2** 'Ob-La-Di, Ob-La-Da' **3** On the set of 'A Hard Day's Night' **4** Ravi Shankar **5** Ringo Starr **6** Julian Lennon (John's son) **7** 'Let It Be' **8** Michael Jackson **9** George Martin **10** 1969 **11** Mary Hopkin **12** 'A World Without Love' **13** 11 **14** 'Penny Lane' & 'Strawberry Fields Forever' **15** 'I Wanna Be Your Man' **16** Elton John **17** 1971 **18** John Lennon **19** Brian Epstein (their manager) **20** 'My Sweet Lord' **21** 11 (George 1, Ringo 3, John 2, Paul 5) **22** Mike McGear (Mike McCartney) **23** John Fred and his Playboy Band **24** Barbara Bach **25** Apple Records **26** Ringo Starr **27** George Harrison **28** 'It Don't Come Easy' **29** Diana Dors **30** Paul McCartney

Quiz 28

1 Donegal **2** Belfast **3** 'The Soldier's Song' **4** Harp **5** St James's Gate Brewery **6** 3 **7** Mary **8** County Cork **9** 'Angela's Ashes' **10** Belfast **11** County Down **12** Potato **13** Trinity **14** Shamrock **15** Newgrange **16** 6 **17** David Trimble **18** The Royal Canal **19** 'A Nation Once Again' **20** Shannon **21** 'Ireland's Call' **22** The GPO **23** Sinn Fein **24** Dáil Éireann **25** Arthur Griffith & Michael Collins **26** 1949 **27** Constance Markievicz **28** The Troubles **29** Good Friday Agreement **30** Linen

Quiz 29

1 A black dog **2** A winged horse **3** Polar bear **4** Snakes **5** Snowy
6 Stag **7** Lion **8** Shergar **9** Laika **10** Mrs Norris **11** 160 million
12 Ox & Ass **13** Bear **14** Snakes **15** Parrot **16** 'Alice's Adventures In
Wonderland' (or 'Alice In Wonderland') **17** Cerberus **18** Rat fleas
19 Jeremy Clarkson **20** Shadowfax **21** Cat **22** 'Aesop's Fables'
23 Fry **24** Squirrel **25** 'Animal Farm' **26** Dragon **27** Stoat
28 People for the Ethical Treatment of Animals **29** On its legs (they're
hairs) **30** Lion & Unicorn

Quiz 30

1 Mont Blanc **2** Banana spider **3** The Beatles **4** Hamlet **5** Theodore
Roosevelt **6** China **7** 'Titanic' **8** The car industry **9** Ceylon (now Sri
Lanka) **10** Josef Bican **11** Maize **12** John Glenn **13** Tottenham
Hotspur **14** Indian Cobra **15** USA **16** Hydrogen **17** Toyota **18** Rome
19 Ashmolean Museum, Oxford **20** USA **21** Wal-Mart Stores
22 Pablo Picasso **23** Joe Louis **24** Finland **25** Indonesia
26 Cotton **27** Mexico **28** Tiger Woods **29** The UK **30** India

Quiz 31

1 Snoop Dogg **2** Charles Dickens **3** The Penguin **4** Agatha Christie **5** Badly Drawn Boy **6** Ultimate Warrior **7** Boy George **8** Captain Marvel **9** Jeremy Brett **10** Gerald Ford **11** John Lydon **12** Kemal Ataturk **13** Bruce Lee **14** Pink **15** Pelé **16** Captain Scarlet **17** The Rock **18** Maria Callas **19** Eminem **20** Haile Selassie **21** Joe Strummer **22** John Ford **23** Jordan **24** Magnus Magnusson **25** Audrey Hepburn **26** Buddha **27** Bono **28** Lenin **29** Freddie Mercury **30** Lassie

Quiz 32

1 European Economic Community **2** Arc de Triomphe **3** Switzerland **4** Wisent (or European Bison) **5** Malta **6** 1 January 2002 **7** France **8** Madrid **9** 6 **10** Ireland **11** 1973 **12** Greenland **13** Portugal **14** Cyprus **15** Napoleon Bonaparte **16** Gulf Stream (or North Atlantic Drift) **17** Belgium, France, Italy, Germany, Luxembourg, Netherlands **18** Slovakia **19** USA, Canada, Turkey **20** Hagia Sophia (or St Sophia) **21** Bonn **22** Richard Rogers **23** Brussels & Strasbourg **24** Capri **25** Netherlands **26** Peter Mandelson **27** Stockholm **28** Florence **29** Norway **30** Guggenheim Museum, Bilbao

Quiz 33

1 10,000 **2** 5 **3** Richter Scale **4** Diamond **5** Trapezoid **6** The area **7** Gregorian **8** 23 mph **9** A Joule **10** Time **11** Library books **12** Scalene Triangle **13** 60 mph **14** 4 inches **15** 130 dB **16** 10 **17** North Star (or Pole Star) **18** Trafalgar Square **19** East **20** 15 **21** A Newton **22** Isobars **23** 10 **24** Barometer **25** An earthquake's intensity on the Earth's surface **26** 24 **27** Beginning **28** A Watt **29** 35 (159 litres) **30** 100

Quiz 34

1 Biba **2** Babouche **3** Red **4** Braces **5** 1860 **6** Over head and shoulders **7** It has a zig-zag edge **8** Hardy Amies **9** Muumuu **10** Puttees **11** Ralph Lauren **12** Clog **13** Yarmulka **14** Yves St Laurent **15** Sou'wester **16** Christian Dior **17** Coco Chanel **18** Head (or head and neck) **19** Pashmina **20** Ruff **21** Silk **22** 'Casablanca' **23** Fez **24** Diane von Furstenberg **25** Around his neck **26** Jean Paul Gaultier **27** Vivienne Westwood **28** Chloé **29** Yves St Laurent **30** Quentin Crisp

Quiz 35

1 ABC 2 Clare Grogan 3 Aneka 4 Genesis 5 'I Should be so Lucky'
6 'There's No-one Quite Like Grandma' 7 Enya 8 Duran Duran
9 'Another Brick in the Wall (Part II)' (by Pink Floyd) 10 'Walking on
Sunshine' 11 The Proclaimers 12 Eurythmics 13 Bananarama
14 The Jam 15 Big Audio Dynamite 16 'Belfast Child' 17 'Panic' (by
The Smiths) 18 Depeche Mode 19 'Shaddap You Face' (by Joe Dolce)
20 Julian Cope 21 'Relax' (by Frankie Goes to Hollywood)
22 Madonna (the Eurythmics reached no. 3) 23 Paul McCartney &
Stevie Wonder 24 Cait O'Riordan 25 Kirsty MacColl 26 US soldiers
fighting in Vietnam 27 4 28 Roger Whittaker & Des O'Connor
29 Vanessa Paradis 30 Paul Weller formed both

Quiz 36

1 Doctor of Philosophy 2 Pawn & knight 3 California 4 When
reversing 5 Chile 6 With ice cream 7 'EastEnders', Christmas Day
1986 (or when Den Watts serves Angie with divorce papers)
8 Blackpool 9 Portugal (Douro Valley) 10 Irish 11 Blue 12 12
13 New York 14 Moulin Rouge 15 Mozarella 16 (South) America
17 Alabama 18 Argentina 19 Indirect 20 Lord Provost 21 Knitting
22 Jehovah's Witnesses 23 Bordeaux 24 Sleepy Hollow
25 Territorial Army 26 8 27 Single Transferable Vote 28 House of
Representatives 29 Dreams 30 Newfoundland & Labrador

Quiz 37

1 March **2** Procrastination **3** 9 **4** Faith **5** Light **6** Sweet **7** A day
8 The pen **9** 9 **10** Good intentions **11** Endured **12** Healer
13 Necessity **14** Live **15** The tune **16** Skin a cat **17** Gossip **18** Sow
19 Blood **20** The tree **21** Silence **22** Rome **23** Rats **24** Practice
25 Gold **26** Variety **27** Please **28** Death **29** Honesty **30** God

Quiz 38

1 30% **2** Canada **3** Oxbow lake **4** Victoria **5** Lundy **6** The Shannon
7 First Watch **8** Twilight Zone **9** The Nile **10** Cook Strait **11** Gravity of
Moon & Sun **12** Seaweed **13** La Manche **14** Europe & Asia
15 Superior **16** The Congo **17** Antarctic Ice Sheet **18** Bermuda Triangle
(or Devil's Triangle) **19** Iceland & Greenland **20** 70% **21** Atlantic &
Arctic Oceans **22** Between the Australian mainland & Tasmania **23** 0°
(or the Equator) **24** Atlantic Ocean **25** Spring Tide **26** 'The Blue
Planet' **27** 'EastEnders' **28** Great Barrier Reef **29** Venezuela
30 Galleon

Quiz 39

1 'Oklahoma!' **2** 'Body Heat' **3** 'Robin Hood: Prince of Thieves'
4 'The Lord of the Rings: The Return of the King' **5** 'The Godfather'
6 'Braveheart' **7** 'Silence Of The Lambs' **8** 'Heathers' **9** 'Shirley
Valentine' **10** 'Back to the Future' **11** 'Dirty Harry' **12** 'The Terminator'
13 'Jerry Maguire' **14** 'Jaws' **15** 'Brokeback Mountain' **16** 'The Sixth
Sense' **17** 'The Wizard of Oz' **18** 'The Godfather' **19** 'The Big Sleep'
20 'High Noon' **21** 'Toy Story' **22** 'X-Men' **23** 'The Lord of the
Rings: The Fellowship of the Ring' **24** 'Gladiator' **25** Monty Python's
'Life of Brian' **26** 'The Italian Job' **27** 'Bridge on the River Kwai'
28 'The Adventures of Robin Hood' **29** 'The Simpsons Movie'
30 'Carry on Cleo'

Quiz 40

1 'Toy Story' **2** Telstar **3** Altair **4** 8 **5** Uniform Resource Locator
6 16 : 9 **7** Pixel **8** 1982 **9** Trojan Horse **10** Apple Computer **11** 1992
12 Phishing **13** 'Tron' **14** Jonathan Ive **15** (dot) dk **16** A 404
17 Apple **18** North **19** IBM **20** Malware **21** Northern Ireland **22** 4
23 Deep Thought **24** Beta **25** Infrared Light **26** Cybersquatters
27 Maximum Image **28** Redmond, Washington **29** Easter Egg
30 Modem

Quiz 41

1 Verona **2** 'Romeo and Juliet' **3** David & Victoria Beckham **4** 1995
5 Oklahoma **6** Tornado Alley **7** 'The Wizard of Oz' **8** The Scarecrow
9 Jon Pertwee **10** The Third **11** 'Rock DJ' **12** Chris Evans **13** Pam St
Clement **14** 'Oranges & Lemons' **15** Vitamin C **16** Liver **17** George
Best **18** Belfast **19** Alex 'Hurricane' Higgins **20** 'My Fair Lady'
21 'Pygmalion' **22** George Bernard Shaw **23** Ford Capri **24** Bay of
Naples **25** Eruption of Mount Vesuvius **26** Vulcan **27** 'Star Trek'
28 (Episode IV) A New Hope **29** Faith & Love (or Charity) **30** Robert
Burns

Quiz 42

1 Chicane **2** Missing the ball completely **3** The stick used to hit the ball
4 Straw or Mini-fly **5** Cape **6** 1981 **7** Cliff Thorburn **8** A beginners'
slope **9** Black-and-white hoops **10** Nadia Comaneci **11** 4 **12** 12 August
(Glorious Twelfth) **13** Croquet **14** Body only **15** Freestyle, Greco-
Roman **16** Greyhound racing **17** Swimming **18** Rafael Nadal
19 Clean and Jerk, Snatch **20** Alfred Lyttelton **21** Billiards & Snooker
22 Polo **23** Motor racing **24** Arthur Ashe **25** Italy **26** Federation
Cup **27** Beth Tweddle **28** Calcutta Cup **29** 7 **30** Australian

Quiz 43

1 Charlie Higson **2** Quentin Blake **3** Noddy **4** Narnia **5** Belfast
6 Mr Bump **7** Prince Edward Island **8** 'Harry Potter and the Sorcerer's
Stone' **9** 'Treasure Island' **10** The Gruffalo **11** 'His Dark Materials'
12 Winnie-the-Pooh **13** Big Friendly Giant **14** 'The Cat in the Hat'
15 'Lord of the Flies' **16** Little Wolf **17** Madonna **18** Blue **19** Horrid
Henry **20** 'The Tinder Box' **21** St Custard's **22** 'Hansel and Gretel'
23 Michael Rosen **24** Lemony Snicket **25** Terry Jones
26 Paddington Station **27** 'Stormbreaker' **28** 'The Demon
Headmaster' **29** Asterix & Obelix **30** Brown

Quiz 44

1 Jane Asher, Gerald Scarfe **2** Victoria Beckham **3** Actor Jason Robards
4 Lee Majors & Ryan O'Neal **5** Gary Kemp (of Spandau Ballet) **6** Greg
Allman **7** Jonny Lee Miller, Billy Bob Thornton **8** Seal **9** Richie
Sambora (of Bon Jovi) **10** Maurice Gibb **11** Octavia (sister of Emperor
Caesar Augustus) **12** Jeff Banks **13** George Lazenby **14** Sting **15** Gary
Oldman **16** Richard Dawkins **17** Coleen **18** Dario Franchitti **19** Carla
Bruni **20** Tony Parker **21** Kenneth Branagh **22** Gwyneth Paltrow
23 Catherine Zeta Jones **24** Brian May **25** Mimi Rogers, Nicole
Kidman **26** Elizabeth Hurley **27** John F Kennedy, Aristotle Onassis
28 Nicole Appleton **29** Michael Jackson, Nicolas Cage **30** Anne of
Cleves & Catherine Parr

Quiz 45

1 Billy the Kid **2** Gary Gilmore **3** California **4** 1965 **5** 1998 **6** All were suspected of being Jack the Ripper **7** Johnny Cash **8** 1868 **9** Fydor Dostoevsky **10** Hung, drawn & quartered **11** Oliver Cromwell **12** Charles Manson **13** Dick Turpin **14** 1964 **15** 'Prison Break' **16** The Great Train Robbery **17** Agatha Christie **18** Ruth Ellis (in 1955) **19** Hugh Grant **20** Lord Haw-Haw (William Joyce) **21** Edward I **22** Colin Dexter **23** Saudi Arabia **24** Derek Bentley **25** Ronnie Biggs **26** Trial by fire **27** Lord Lucan **28** Mince pies **29** Oklahoma bombing **30** (John) Rebus

Quiz 46

1 India, Pakistan, Bangladesh **2** France **3** Singapore **4** Thailand **5** 1948 **6** Peking **7** Cambodia **8** Petra **9** China **10** Peter the Great **11** Nepal **12** 12 **13** Tokyo **14** Ho Chi Minh City **15** Ankara **16** United Arab Emirates **17** Bay of Bengal **18** 1997 **19** Coffee **20** East Timor **21** Bengal **22** Bombay **23** Taiwan **24** Cambodia **25** Bombay (or Mumbai) **26** Khyber Pass **27** Indian National Congress **28** Mongolia **29** Philippines **30** Raffles

Quiz 47

1 Baccarat **2** Strand, Fleet Street, Trafalgar Square **3** 28 **4** 64
5 Dr Black **6** 22 **7** Royal Flush **8** 15 **9** 37 (0–36; 38 on American)
10 Q & Z **11** 22 **12** 'Jumanji' **13** Snap-dragon **14** Backgammon
15 'The Seventh Seal' **16** Mario **17** 4 **18** Twister **19** 22 **20** Tetris
21 Tic-Tac-Toe **22** The Sims **23** Donkey Kong **24** 12 **25** Old Kent
Road **26** Dungeons & Dragons **27** Sega **28** 5 **29** 2002 **30** Red,
orange, yellow, green, blue, white

Quiz 48

1 Set sail **2** Maple leaf **3** Lebanon **4** Bhutan **5** Blue & Yellow
6 White **7** Hawaii **8** Rwanda **9** 12 **10** Cyprus **11** Switzerland **12** 5
13 Ensign **14** Outer edge furthest from the flagpole **15** Bunting
16 Alaska **17** Jolly Roger **18** Brazil **19** Blue **20** Australia & New
Zealand **21** Libya **22** Brunei Darussalam (hands) **23** Liberia
24 White, Blue, Red **25** Nepal **26** Yellow & White **27** California
Republic **28** 5 **29** 1991 **30** Royal Standard

Quiz 49

1 Pharos of Alexandria & Great Pyramid at Giza **2** 'The Mummy' **3** 65
4 Artemis & Apollo **5** Janus **6** Papyrus **7** Gamma **8** Alexander the
Great **9** Lion **10** Helen **11** Egyptian, Greek, Roman **12** Anubis
13 'The Iliad' & 'The Odyssey' **14** Howard Carter & Lord Carnarvon
15 Antonine Wall **16** Victory **17** The dead person's internal organs
18 River Styx **19** Claudius **20** The Acropolis (in Athens)
21 The 'Argo' **22** Thermopylae **23** Cupid **24** Via Appia **25** Theseus
26 Apollo **27** Re (or Ra) **28** Rosetta Stone **29** Sparta **30** Cleopatra

Quiz 50

1 Hippocratic Oath **2** Ibuprofen **3** 1967 **4** Prozac **5** Joseph Lister
6 FG Banting, CH Best, JJR Macleod **7** Arthur Conan Doyle
8 Haematologists **9** Aspirin **10** Low blood pressure **11** Eyes **12** 'Peter
Pan' **13** 1948 **14** London **15** Florence Nightingale **16** Medécins Sans
Frontières **17** Netherlands **18** Measles **19** Penicillin **20** Keyhole
surgery **21** Epidural **22** Blood poisoning **23** Hearing **24** Jonas Salk
25 Diabetes **26** Dead On Arrival **27** Your mouth (they're a dentist)
28 Nose **29** Diarrhoea **30** Mosquito

Quiz 51

1 The Jordanaires **2** Switzerland **3** Eddie Fisher **4** 1952 **5** 'Rudolph the Red-Nosed Reindeer' **6** The Beverley Sisters **7** Shirley Bassey **8** 'Secret Love', 'Whatever Will Be, Will Be (Que Sera, Sera)' **9** Eddie Cochran **10** 'I Taut I Taw a Puddy Tat' **11** Jimmy Young **12** Sheet music **13** 'Back in the USA' **14** 'Smoke Gets in Your Eyes' **15** 'Heartbreak Hotel' **16** 'Love Potion No. 9' **17** The Everly Brothers **18** 'Hoots Mon' **19** 'Lady and the Tramp' **20** 'La Bamba' **21** Bobby Day **22** Nina Simone **23** 'Johnny B. Goode' **24** 'Be-Bop-A-Lula' **25** Revolutions per minute **26** Fats Domino **27** Bill Haley and His Comets **28** 'Sixteen Tons' **29** 'Love Me Tender' **30** Little Richard

Quiz 52

1 Judi Dench **2** 12 **3** Chris Cornell **4** 'From Russia With Love' **5** 'GoldenEye' **6** 'Diamonds Are Forever' **7** 'On Her Majesty's Secret Service' **8** 'The Spy Who Loved Me' **9** Venice **10** Tom Jones **11** Francisco Scaramanga **12** 6 **13** SPecial Executive for Counter-intelligence, Terrorism, Revenge and Extortion **14** Blofeld **15** Christopher Walken **16** Aston Martin **17** Lotte Lenya **18** Sean Bean **19** Teri Hatcher appears in both **20** 2 **21** 'Octopussy' **22** John Barry **23** 'Live And Let Die' **24** 'Tomorrow Never Dies' **25** 'Casino Royale' **26** 'Casino Royale' **27** 'Nobody Does It Better' **28** Roald Dahl **29** Oddjob **30** 22

Quiz 53

1 Peasants' Revolt **2** Edward I **3** Harold II **4** Armada **5** Manhattan Island **6** Lancaster **7** The Crusades **8** 1492 **9** William Wallace **10** Bayeux Tapestry **11** Henry VIII **12** King Charles I **13** The Pale **14** Samuel Pepys **15** Richard III **16** II (Second) **17** Magna Carta **18** Owain Glyndwr **19** Mary, Queen of Scots **20** Wessex **21** Alhambra **22** Hundred Years War **23** Mongol Empire **24** Bologna **25** Oliver Cromwell **26** It was the first book printed in England **27** Domesday Book **28** Knights Templar **29** Richard Cromwell **30** Salem

Quiz 54

1 Indonesia **2** Croque Madame **3** Deep-fried seafood **4** Garlic **5** Champagne **6** 190 ºC **7** A bloater is smoked whole while a kipper is split and gutted **8** At the start (they are appetisers) **9** Derbyshire, Leicestershire & Nottinghamshire **10** Tomato **11** Steak Tartare **12** Hummus **13** Dry Martini **14** Byron **15** Skye **16** Coriander **17** Blackcurrants **18** Lassi **19** The stomach lining of an animal (usually sheep or cow) **20** Nettles **21** Aniseed (or Anise) **22** Butterfly-shaped (or bow-tie) **23** Chewing gum **24** Darjeeling **25** Prunes wrapped in bacon **26** Port **27** Frogs' legs **28** Blue Curaçao **29** Honey **30** Apple

Quiz 55

1 US Open, Australian Open, French Open 2 Gordon Ramsay 3 14
4 Linfield 5 England 6 Angling (they're knots) 7 Badminton
8 The Mavericks 9 Christopher Chataway 10 60 11 22 12 Lee Trevino
13 Dallas Cowboys 14 80 (in 1889) 15 Basketball 16 Snooker
17 Presidents Cup 18 Brian Lara 19 Durham 20 5 feet 21 Chicago
Bulls 22 1 (Wimbledon) 23 Jonah Lomu (8 tries, 1999) 24 San
Marino 25 Lord's Cricket Ground 26 Synchronised Swimming
27 White 28 Margaret Court 29 Rod Laver (1969) 30 Ferrari

Quiz 56

1 Horse 2 Dolphin 3 Spiders 4 Killer whale 5 Lion 6 Horse 7 Shark
8 Rat 9 Otter 10 Kangaroo 11 Kestrel 12 Orang-Utan 13 Mouse
14 Leopard 15 Duck 16 Dog 17 Chimpanzee 18 Horse 19 Dog
20 Pig 21 Snake 22 Mice 23 Rabbits 24 Dinosaurs 25 Mice
26 Dogs 27 Penguin 28 Bear 29 Pig 30 Rat

Quiz 57

1 (African) Elephant 2 30 3 (Fruit) Bat 4 Potato 5 Mauritius
6 Bamboo 7 Hard wood 8 Mute swan 9 Basalt 10 Sheep
11 Jurassic 12 It moves from water to land 13 Elk 14 Cullinan Diamond
15 Yellow 16 Marsupials 17 Diamond 18 Prehistoric life through
fossils 19 Met Office (Meteorological Office) 20 Duck 21 Cricket
22 Brain 23 Diamonds 24 Hummingbird 25 USA 26 Less than 1%
27 They absorb water 28 Skuas 29 6 30 Australia

Quiz 58

1 Alcohol 2 Wounded Knee 3 Donkey 4 Gold had been found there
5 New Hampshire 6 Alaska & Hawaii 7 Harvard 8 Jamestown
9 Delaware 10 4th of July 11 Native Americans 12 US Flag
13 Death Valley, California 14 Charleston 15 Wild Bill Hickok
16 Albany 17 'Mayflower' 18 Montana 19 Underground Railroad
20 California 21 Yankee Doodle 22 Queens, Bronx, Brooklyn, Staten
Island 23 11 24 Hawaii 25 Uncle Sam 26 President 27 50
28 Bald eagle 29 Vietnam Veterans Memorial 30 Rhode Island

Quiz 59

1 Canopus **2** (Pronghorn) Antelope **3** Liver **4** USSR **5** University of London **6** Cumbria **7** Japan **8** Ben Macdhui **9** Second Woman PM **10** Jordan **11** 'Quotations from the Works of Chairman Mao Tse-Tung' ('The Little Red Book') **12** Monaco **13** John Landy **14** Bertha von Suttner (1905; for Peace) **15** UK **16** Venus **17** India **18** Islam **19** Band Aid (1984), 'Do They Know It's Christmas?' **20** Tibia (Shin-bone) **21** Exodus **22** New Guinea **23** Dwight Eisenhower **24** Alain Prost **25** Patrick Troughton **26** Bengali **27** Germany **28** Manchester United **29** 'Little Red Rooster' **30** Pat Eddery

Quiz 60

1 Soil **2** A sheep **3** Spelunker **4** Magic, especially sleight of hand **5** Navigators who built canals in the 18th century **6** Books, especially Bibles **7** 28 **8** A tightrope **9** Flowers **10** Teaching **11** Wine **12** Machiavelli **13** Your wife would be sitting at the table **14** Father **15** Arrows **16** Flags **17** Bumps on the human head **18** Rolling On the Floor Laughing **19** E **20** Their spelling **21** Black **22** Fish **23** Alpha & Beta **24** Moose **25** A cat **26** Papa **27** Nostrils **28** E **29** Words **30** Omega

Quiz 61

1 'One Foot In The Grave' (Victor Meldrew) **2** 'Who Wants To Be A Millionaire?' (Chris Tarrant) **3** 'Little Britain' (Andy) **4** 'The Simple Life' (Paris Hilton) **5** Hill Street Blues' (Sergeant Esterhaus) **6** 'The Basil Brush Show' (Basil Brush) **7** 'King Of The Hill' (Hank Hill) **8** 'The Sopranos' (Tony Soprano) **9** 'South Park' (Stan or Kyle) **10** 'In The Night Garden' (Narrator) **11** 'Paul Daniels Magic Show' (Paul Daniels) **12** 'Star Trek: The Next Generation' (Jean Luc Picard) **13** 'The Simpsons' (Bart Simpson) **14** 'Chucklevision' (The Chuckle Brothers) **15** 'Coronation Street' (Vera Duckworth) **16** 'The Apprentice' (Alan Sugar) **17** 'Pinky & The Brain' (The Brain) **18** 'Dad's Army' (Corporal Jones) **19** 'The Flintstones' (Fred Flintstone) **20** 'Dexter's Laboratory' (Dee Dee) **21** 'The League Of Gentlemen' (Tubbs) **22** 'Da Ali G Show' (Ali G) **23** 'Blackadder' series (Baldrick) **24** 'Father Ted' (Father Jack Hackett) **25** 'Only Fools and Horses' (Del Boy) **26** 'The Fast Show' (Suit You tailors Ken & Kenneth) **27** 'Bugs Bunny' **28** 'Are You Being Served?' (Mr Humphries) **29** 'Mastermind' (originally Magnus Magnusson) **30** Harry Hill's TV Burp' (Harry Hill)

Quiz 62

1 2 (0 & 1) **2** Factor **3** 7 **4** 40 **5** 17 **6** 20 **7** 44 **8** 3 **9** Acute **10** 22 **11** 24 **12** 42 **13** 12 **14** Googol **15** 'Numb3rs' **16** Sector **17** 72 **18** 90 **19** 7 **20** Pythagoras' Theorem **21** 5 **22** 14 cm **23** Prime number **24** 9 **25** 21 **26** 40 **27** 55 **28** 46 **29** 19 (they are prime numbers) **30** 7 (I, V, X, L, C, D, M)

Quiz 63

1 Pete Seeger **2** Steeleye Span **3** The Punjab **4** Phil Coulter **5** Portugal **6** Ronnie Drew **7** 'Green Grow the Rushes, O' **8** Brendan & Dominic Behan **9** 'God Bless Africa' **10** Bob Dylan **11** The Clancy Brothers **12** 'Happy Days Are Here Again' **13** 'The Irish Rover' **14** Dropkick Murphys **15** American Civil War **16** Ewan MacColl **17** The Corries **18** Woody Guthrie **19** Henry VIII **20** Victor Jara **21** 'Summer Is Icumen In' **22** Rufus & Martha Wainwright **23** Christina Rossetti **24** Tommy Makem **25** Dominic Behan **26** 'Letter from America' **27** Athy **28** 'All Through the Night' **29** 'God Bless America' **30** Alan Stivell

Quiz 64

1 Norman Foster **2** Church of the Holy Family (Sagrada Familia) **3** Capability Brown **4** Nicholas Hawksmoor **5** A lighthouse **6** Le Corbusier (aka Charles-Édouard Jeanneret-Gris) **7** Charles Rennie Mackintosh **8** Richard Rogers **9** Frank Lloyd Wright **10** Pritzker Architecture Prize **11** Sydney Opera House **12** Basil Spence **13** Eiffel Tower **14** East **15** Taipei 101, Taiwan **16** Sacré Coeur Basilica **17** The Colosseum **18** The congregation **19** Motte & Bailey **20** Prince Charles **21** Assisi **22** 30 St Mary Axe **23** Khufu (or Cheops) **24** Inigo Jones **25** To house the Great Exhibition **26** The latrine or toilet **27** Versailles **28** Buckingham Palace **29** London Bridge **30** Houses of Parliament (Palace of Westminster)

Quiz 65

1 Muhammad Ali (or Cassius Clay) **2** Johnny Cash **3** Calamity Jane **4** Louis Armstrong **5** Edward I **6** Hippocrates **7** Twiggy **8** Eric Liddell **9** The Red Baron **10** Charles II **11** The Great White Shark **12** Richard Nixon **13** Lord Haw Haw **14** Lucky **15** Margaret Thatcher **16** William Shakespeare **17** Edith Piaf **18** Ronald Reagan **19** Joan of Arc **20** Gandhi **21** Robespierre **22** Brian Lara **23** George Washington **24** Cliff Thorburn **25** William the Conqueror (or William I) **26** For his work in abolishing the slave trade in Britain **27** Stanley Matthews **28** Oliver Cromwell **29** The Lionheart **30** Frank Sinatra

Quiz 66

1 Clark Kent / Superman **2** George **3** The Angels ('Captain Scarlet') **4** The Champions **5** Summers **6** His wife Chrissie murdered him with a doorstop **7** Dougal **8** Winnie-the-Pooh **9** Frasier's **10** 'Casualty' **11** 'Black Books' **12** 'The X-Files' **13** Lurcio **14** 'Doctor Who' **15** Bishop Len Brennan **16** 'Shameless' **17** Mary Alice Young **18** Will & Grace **19** The Jetsons **20** 6 **21** (Dr) David Banner **22** 'ER' **23** 'Homicide: Life on the Street' **24** Crime Scene Investigation **25** 'Brookside' **26** 'Life on Mars' & 'Ashes to Ashes' **27** Erinsborough **28** Colorado **29** '24' **30** 4

Quiz 67

1 False **2** True **3** False (it's in Antarctica) **4** True (he drinks it more than any other drink throughout the novels) **5** False (he never set foot on continental America) **6** True (on the blank tile) **7** True (he rewrote it from memory) **8** False (they considered but turned down the NIPS in favour of the PSNI – Police Service of Northern Ireland) **9** True **10** False (they were founded in Dublin) **11** True **12** False (he won in 1921) **13** True **14** True (he won the Young Player award) **15** False (it's inland) **16** False (all mammals sleep) **17** True **18** False (it's home to Middlesex CCC) **19** True **20** True **21** True (peahens do) **22** False (the Spanish has no lyrics) **23** True **24** False **25** True **26** False (it's in Pakistan) **27** False (it's worse flying west to east) **28** True **29** True **30** False (all are in Asia)

Quiz 68

1 Murder **2** The Knesset **3** Fjords **4** Gunfight at the OK Corral **5** 25 **6** Kinshasa, Zaire **7** Anger **8** TV's Inspector Morse **9** Pontoon **10** Lisbon **11** Stormont **12** By crossed swords **13** Six degrees of separation **14** Archaeoastronomy **15** Edmund Hillary **16** Neville Chamberlain (1938) **17** Franklin D Roosevelt **18** Earth **19** 'Noddy' **20** Once a year **21** Eddie Dickens **22** Rear **23** Chestnut **24** Adriatic **25** Red **26** Romania **27** Dodge City **28** Its tongue **29** Anorexia **30** Paddington Bear

Quiz 69

1 'The Man Who Sold the World' **2** The Goodies **3** (Sergei) Prokofiev
4 Tom Robinson **5** Mike Reid **6** 10cc **7** 'Hot Love' **8** Sex Pistols
9 Boomtown Rats **10** Blondie **11** Ian Dury & the Blockheads **12** 'Coz I
Luv You' **13** 'American Pie' **14** Ray Stevens **15** 'Ring Ring' **16** David
Bowie **17** 'Ernie (The Fastest Milkman in the West)' **18** Their League
Cup Final appearance **19** The Osmonds **20** The Jam **21** Indian,
Cowboy, Construction Worker, Cop (or Admiral), Soldier (or Sailor),
Leatherman **22** 'Lola' **23** 'I Just Want to be Your Everything'
24 Sid Vicious **25** A golden fiddle **26** 'Van der Valk' **27** The Buggles'
'Video Killed the Radio Star' **28** Stiff Little Fingers **29** 'Mull of
Kintyre' **30** The Buzzcocks

Quiz 70

1 'Ice Age' **2** 'Men In Black' **3** 'Mission: Impossible' **4** 'Dirty Harry'
5 'High Noon' **6** 'The Fly' **7** 'Pulp Fiction' **8** 'Speed' **9** 'Wayne's
World' **10** 'Interview with the Vampire' **11** '10 Things I Hate About You'
12 'The Usual Suspects' **13** 'Lock, Stock & Two Smoking Barrels'
14 'Alien' **15** 'Trading Places' **16** 'The Lion King' **17** 'The Outlaw'
18 'Braveheart' **19** 'The Incredible Hulk' **20** 'Rent' **21** 'Austin Powers:
International Man of Mystery' **22** 'Sleepy Hollow' **23** 'Mean Girls'
24 'Scream' **25** 'Hairspray' **26** 'Dirty Dancing' **27** 'Rocky'
28 'Goodbye Lenin' **29** 'Little Shop of Horrors' **30** 'High School
Musical'

Quiz 71

1 Hydrogen **2** 28 days **3** Ursa Major or the Great Bear **4** Phoenix
5 Neptune **6** Galileo **7** Vostok 1 **8** Challenger **9** Nitrogen **10** James
Lovell, Jack Swigert, Fred Haise **11** 1980s **12** 6 **13** Jupiter
14 Southern Fish **15** Pluto **16** Apollo 8 **17** 15 billion **18** Uranus
19 Supernova **20** Castor & Pollux **21** 1990 **22** The stratosphere
23 Venus **24** Helen Sharman **25** 1972 **26** Wormhole **27** First
tourist in space **28** Black hole **29** Uranus **30** First American to walk
in space

Quiz 72

1 'Macbeth' **2** 'Richard III' **3** Anne Hathaway **4** 'Titus Andronicus'
5 154 **6** Stratford-upon-Avon **7** Julius Caesar's **8** Cyprus **9** 3
10 'Romeo & Juliet' **11** 'Hamlet' **12** The Lord Chamberlain's Men (later
The King's Men) **13** The Globe **14** None; he did not go to university
15 13 **16** 'Macbeth' **17** Comedy **18** Naples **19** Joseph Fiennes
20 'Macbeth' **21** St George's Day **22** James VI (of Scots) and I (of
England) **23** Iambic penameter **24** Tom Stoppard **25** We are
26 The Avon **27** Kenneth Branagh & Emma Thompson
28 Excommunication from the Church **29** 'Hamlet' **30** Brutus

Quiz 73

1 Michael Caine **2** USA (Hawaii) **3** William **4** Mimi Rogers **5** Chris Martin **6** Jane Asher **7** Hear'Say **8** Luciano Pavarotti **9** Edwin **10** Kate Winslet **11** Gavin Henson **12** Tracey Ullman **13** Imran Khan **14** Irish **15** Belgium **16** Nadine Coyle **17** Wayne Rooney **18** Angelina Jolie & Brad Pitt **19** Kylie Minogue **20** Naomi Campbell **21** The Beckhams **22** Oprah Winfrey **23** Kirsty Gallacher **24** Nelson Mandela **25** Greg Norman & Chris Evert **26** Richie Sambora & Tommy Lee **27** Cat Deeley **28** Peter André & Katie Price (Jordan) **29** Cyd Charisse **30** Penélope Cruz

Quiz 74

1 Botany Bay **2** Jeremy Clarkson **3** Western Australia **4** Melbourne **5** Papua New Guinea **6** The Gold Coast **7** 'Down Under' **8** Uluru or Ayres Rock **9** Peter Jackson **10** Wellington **11** Southern Cross **12** Gallipoli **13** Tasmania **14** Crocodile Dundee **15** Kiwi **16** Oval **17** Australian Capital Territory **18** Kiri Te Kanawa **19** North Island **20** Darwin **21** Christchurch **22** All Blacks **23** Russell Crowe **24** Alice Springs **25** Joey **26** Queensland **27** Tasmania **28** 'The Lord of the Rings' **29** Cate Blanchett **30** Tasman Sea

Quiz 75

1 Belgium **2** 1715, 1745 **3** Canada **4** France **5** Canada **6** Britain
7 Trafalgar Day **8** London's sewage system **9** California **10** Steam engine **11** Thomas Telford **12** Friedrich Nietzsche **13** Napoleon
14 The Chartists **15** The General Strike **16** Britain **17** Guiseppe
Garibaldi **18** William Blake **19** George Stephenson **20** Manchester
21 Andrew Carnegie **22** John Cadbury **23** Denmark **24** France
became a republic **25** Impressionism **26** Bismarck **27** Sigmund Freud
28 Charles Stewart Parnell **29** Abraham Lincoln **30** Isambard
Kingdom Brunel

Quiz 76

1 Tuberculosis **2** The retina **3** Horses **4** Folic acid **5** The big toe
6 Chickenpox **7** The liver **8** 23 seconds **9** Hydrochloric **10** 3
11 Blood pressure **12** Blackheads **13** It protects your windpipe during
swallowing (by closing) **14** 20 **15** Red blood cells **16** In your mouth
(it's your tongue) **17** 12 **18** Neurons **19** To keep sweat out of the eyes
20 100,000 **21** 37 °C **22** DNA **23** Shinbone **24** 33 **25** Pancreas
26 Fingers & toes **27** Gallbladder **28** 280 days **29** Skin **30** A girl

Quiz 77

1 Apollo XIII suffers serious damage, 1970 **2** Nelson Mandela's release, 1990 (South African citizen) **3** Trains come to a halt after a snowfall that BR can't clear **4** Marriage of Charles & Diana (Diana) **5** Watergate investigation (President Nixon) **6** Profumo Affair (a Cabinet member) **7** Discovery of DNA structure (Crick & Watson) **8** Arrest of Adolf Eichmann, 1960 **9** Britain's proposed EEC entry (Labour leader Hugh Gaitskell) **10** Battle of the Somme preparations (Earl Haig) **11** 'Titanic' sinking (survivor) **12** VE Day (US newspaper) **13** Burning of banned books in Germany, 1933 **14** Apollo XI Moon Landing, 1969 **15** England winning the World Cup final, 1966 (Kenneth Wolstenholme) **16** Britain re-establishes its presence in the Falkland Islands, 1982 (Margaret Thatcher) **17** Challenger Space Shuttle explosion, 1986 **18** Lisbon Treaty for 'closer EU integration', 2007 (former French President Giscard d'Estaing) **19** Normandy Landings, 1944 (US soldier) **20** First manned space flight (Yuri Gagarin) **21** Trial to ban 'Lady Chatterley's Lover', 1960 (Prosecution) **22** Celtic win the European Cup, 1967 (Jock Stein) **23** Queen Anne Boleyn's execution, 1536 **24** Scott's Antarctic expedition (Captain Oates sacrifices himself) **25** July 1944 Bomb Plot (Hitler) **26** Death of Marilyn Monroe (Jean Cocteau quote) **27** Conquering Everest (Edmund Hillary) **28** Queen Catherine Howard's execution, 1542 **29** Opening of Tutankhamun's tomb (Howard Carter) **30** Britain in the Second World War, 1940 (Churchill's first speech as PM)

Quiz 78

1 Both died in the bathroom **2** John Peel **3** Heart disease **4** 'The Crow' **5** Spike Milligan **6** Spanish Flu outbreak **7** Killed by a poison umbrella tip **8** Marvin Gaye **9** 'Celebrity Deathmatch' **10** Terracotta Army **11** Queen Victoria **12** Pompeii & Herculaneum **13** Humphrey Bogart **14** Joe Orton **15** Joe di Maggio (her ex-husband) **16** Tutankhamun **17** Rasputin **18** Mosquito **19** Oscar Wilde **20** Isadora Duncan **21** Under 10 **22** Andrew Johnson **23** Tennessee Williams **24** James Dean **25** 155,000 **26** George Sanders **27** Sonny Bono **28** 79 (or 78.7) **29** Hades **30** Ned Kelly

Quiz 79

1 Michael Parkinson **2** Radio 4, Radio 3, Radio 2 **3** 'The Archers' **4** Alistair Cooke **5** 1967 **6** Classic FM, Virgin Radio, talkSPORT **7** 'I'm Sorry I Haven't a Clue' **8** John Peel **9** 'Brain of Britain' **10** Brookfield **11** USA **12** 'War of the Worlds' **13** Broadcasting House **14** Tony Blackburn **15** 1992 **16** 'The Lone Ranger' **17** 1973 **18** Shock jocks **19** Al Gross **20** FM **21** 'Gunsmoke' **22** 1939 **23** Piccadilly Radio **24** Alan Freed **25** 'The Mighty Boosh' **26** Heinrich Hertz **27** 'Just a Minute' **28** Brian Johnston **29** Richard Dimbleby **30** 'Hancock's Half Hour'

Quiz 80

1 Citius, Altius, Fortius (Faster, Higher, Stronger) **2** Greece **3** 1948
4 Zeus **5** Olympia **6** Seoul **7** Blue, Black, Red, Yellow, Green
8 Munich (1974) **9** 1984 (Los Angeles) **10** USA **11** Africa **12** 1 day
13 France **14** Norway **15** 1896 **16** Mark Spitz **17** Allan Wells **18** Kelly
Holmes **19** Pole Vault & Hammer Throw **20** He revived the Games
(after a 1503-year absence) **21** Tibet **22** USA **23** Pentathlon **24** 3
25 Victory **26** France **27** British Olympic Association **28** Australia,
France, Great Britain, Greece, Switzerland **29** Steve Redgrave, Rowing
30 30

Quiz 81

1 Santa's Little Helper **2** 'Krusty the Clown Show' **3** Mrs (Edna)
Krabappel **4** Rod & Todd **5** Kwik-E-Mart **6** Springfield Retirement
Castle **7** Abe (Abraham J) Simpson **8** Springfield Nuclear Power Plant
9 Jebediah Springfield **10** 9 **11** Lard Lad **12** Comic-book Guy
13 Shelbyville **14** Vermont **15** Mayor 'Diamond' Joe (Joseph Fitzpatrick
Fitzgerald Fitzhenry) Quimby **16** Groundskeeper Willie **17** Patty &
Selma Bouvier **18** Sideshow Bob **19** 1989 **20** Barney Gumble **21** Duff
22 Saxophone **23** Mr Burns **24** Ralph **25** Troy McClure **26** Yeardley
Smith **27** The First Church of Springfield **28** Hallowe'en **29** Principal
of Springfield Elementary School **30** 742 Evergreen Terrace, Springfield

Quiz 82

1 'Life on Mars' **2** Sailors **3** England expects that every man will do his duty **4** West Germany (not 'Germany') **5** 1990 **6** In the new Channel Tunnel **7** Strait of Gibraltar **8** Atlantic Ocean and the Mediterranean Sea **9** 21 **10** Blackjack or Pontoon **11** James Bond **12** 'From Russia with Love' **13** White, blue and red **14** Yellow **15** The current world champion **16** Bobby Fischer **17** Los Angeles **18** Sydney **19** Brisbane **20** Bee Gees **21** 'Saturday Night Fever' **22** Romeo and Juliet **23** Elizabeth I **24** 1996 **25** 'Our Friends in the North' **26** 10 **27** Decimal **28** 12 **29** Henry Fonda **30** Ted Turner

Quiz 83

1 Baseball **2** Football **3** Boxing **4** Horse racing **5** Cycling **6** Pool **7** Mountaineering **8** Bobsleighing **9** Boxing **10** Ice hockey **11** Football **12** Kungfu **13** Tennis **14** Running **15** (NASCAR) Car racing **16** Football **17** Surfing **18** American football **19** Skiing **20** American football **21** Basketball **22** Football **23** Boxing **24** Car racing **25** Baseball **26** Gymnastics **27** Horse racing **28** Pool **29** Cycling **30** Golf

Quiz 84

1 'Gloriana' **2** (Niccolò) Paganini **3** 'The Barber Of Seville' **4** Luciano Pavarotti, Plácido Domingo, José Carreras **5** She is stabbed (by Don José) **6** Libretto **7** 'Water Music' **8** The Rhinemaidens **9** Leonard Bernstein **10** Pluck It (it's a 4-string guitar) **11** They're all types of dance **12** 'La Marseillaise' **13** (Sergei) Prokofiev **14** 'Rule, Britannia' **15** George Gershwin **16** 'Diva' **17** 'Danny Boy' **18** 'The Threepenny Opera' **19** 'Romeo And Juliet' **20** They are all organ stops **21** Scaramouche **22** 'Madame Butterfly' **23** Peter Maxwell Davies **24** (Ludwig van) Beethoven **25** (Gioachino) Rossini (Tournedos Rossini) **26** Very soft **27** Felix Mendelssohn **28** Simon Rattle **29** (Karlheinz) Stockhausen **30** The Proms (or The Promenade Concerts or The BBC Proms)

Quiz 85

1 (John) Alcock & (Arthur Whitton) Brown **2** Henry the Navigator The **3** Wright Brothers **4** 'Santa Maria' **5** Dr David Livingstone **6** Captain Cook **7** Richard Burton **8** 1958 **9** Leif Ericson **10** Roald Amundsen **11** Ferdinand Magellan **12** (Hernán) Cortés **13** Francis Drake **14** Columba (or Columbkille) **15** Edmund Hillary **16** Ranulph Fiennes **17** Mary Slessor **18** Canada **19** Greenland **20** 1912 **21** Charles Lindbergh **22** Julius Caesar **23** St Brendan **24** Portugal **25** Tasmania (or Van Diemen's Land) **26** Roald Amundsen **27** Francis Chichester **28** Holland **29** Amelia Earhart **30** Amerigo Vespucci

Quiz 86

1 Ice Cream **2** Crocus **3** Easter eggs **4** Elvis Presley **5** Hunger
6 Avocados **7** Yeast **8** Cactus **9** Simnel cake **10** Potato
11 Delia Smith **12** Pasteurisation **13** Absinthe **14** Anchovies **15** Hot
cross buns **16** Apple **17** Strawberry **18** 1 **19** Czech Republic **20** 8
21 Soup **22** Groundskeeper Willie ('The Simpsons') **23** Lemon
24 Hungary **25** Choux pastry **26** Eating bread and honey
27 Louisiana **28** Cheese (or curd cheese) **29** Orange **30** They're
types of potato

Quiz 87

1 Peak District **2** Dover **3** Macleod **4** Winston Churchill **5** Isambard
Kingdom Brunel **6** Red **7** Forth Bridge **8** Scotland (November)
9 Caerphilly **10** Isle of Man **11** Richard III of England **12** Wales
Millennium Centre **13** One Canada Square, London **14** Falkland Islands
15 Aberdeen **16** Windsor Castle **17** 1880s (in 1880) **18** Loch Lomond
19 George Cross **20** Andrew, George and Patrick **21** Golden Eagle
22 The Humber **23** Spain **24** GB is England, Scotland, Wales and
their islands; UK is GB plus Northern Ireland **25** A thistle **26** Black
Rod **27** Prime Minister **28** Cambridge **29** M25 **30** Daffodil

Quiz 88

1 'Private Eye' **2** Lemuel Gulliver **3** The Reform Club **4** 'Viz' **5** Arthur C Clarke **6** Stephen King **7** 'Utopia' **8** Rip Van Winkle **9** 'One for all, and all for one' **10** Boromir & Faramir **11** The Knight **12** Discworld **13** Sherlock Holmes **14** Understand other languages **15** 'Sunday Times' **16** 'Frankenstein' **17** Dean Koontz **18** Jean-Paul Sartre **19** Sherlock Holmes & Dr Watson **20** '1984' **21** Salman Rushdie **22** L Ron Hubbard **23** '84 Charing Cross Road' **24** Grimm **25** 4 **26** 'The Lord of the Rings' **27** Yorkshire **28** Ben Gunn **29** 'Ulysses' **30** Hercule Poirot

Quiz 89

1 British Gas (privatisation) **2** Milky Way **3** Coca-Cola **4** Playtex **5** Hamlet **6** Polo Mints **7** Heineken **8** Murray Mints **9** Duracell batteries **10** Topic **11** Kit-e-cat **12** Yorkie Chocolate Bar **13** Anadin **14** The Co-op **15** Swan Vesta **16** Opal Fruits **17** Nike **18** Esso Petrol **19** Terry's Chocolate Orange **20** L'Oréal **21** Yellow Pages **22** Remington **23** Disprin **24** Woolworth's **25** Smarties **26** Rowntree's Lion Bar **27** Nicotinel **28** Orange **29** Pal (dogfood) **30** British Airways

Quiz 90

1 Element 4 **2** White Stripes **3** Audio Bullys **4** 'Back to the Future'
5 Pink **6** The Tweenies **7** Girls Aloud **8** Take That **9** 'The United
States of Whatever' **10** Comic Relief **11** Manic Street Preachers
12 Electric 6 **13** Mick Jones **14** George Michael **15** Download chart
16 Elvis Presley & Cliff Richard **17** 'Lose Yourself' **18** 'Babylon'
19 Jack Black **20** The Scissor Sisters **21** 'I Have a Dream' & 'Seasons
in the Sun' **22** 'Don't Call Me Baby' **23** Sugababes **24** Bob the
Builder **25** 4 (Victoria's highest chart position was 2) **26** Amy
Winehouse **27** 'By the Way' **28** Kylie Minogue & Nicole Kidman
29 Justin Timberlake **30** Sugababes & Girls Aloud

Quiz 91

1 Extra time **2** Kenny Dalglish **3** 2 **4** Peter Shilton **5** FA Cup (season
1989-90) **6** Fernando Torres **7** 'Back Home' **8** Vennegoor of
Hesselink (20 letters) **9** Fabio Capello **10** South Africa **11** Red
12 AC Milan & Internazionale **13** Cardiff City (1927) **14** 1992
15 Roy Keane **16** None (up to the start of season 2008-09) **17** Serie A
18 None **19** Real Madrid (figures to end of season 2006-07) **20** 1983
21 Gordon Strachan **22** Real Madrid **23** Bobby Charlton **24** West
Bromwich Albion **25** Oxford University (1874) **26** Juventus
27 Sunderland **28** Welsh Premier League **29** FC Porto **30** Queen's
Park

Quiz 92

1 Stalagmites **2** The Nile **3** Argentina **4** Yukon, Nunavut, Northwest Territories **5** New Guinea **6** Portugal **7** Christmas Island **8** Sweden & Finland **9** Netherlands Antilles **10** Democratic Republic of Congo **11** East **12** Belarus **13** South Pole **14** Oregon **15** St Lucia **16** Antarctica **17** Ceuta, Melilla **18** Iran **19** Peru **20** Istanbul **21** Costa del Sol **22** Faeroe Islands **23** Quebec **24** Mali **25** South America **26** Edinburgh **27** Missouri **28** Azores **29** France **30** One third

Quiz 93

1 Thanksgiving **2** Lured sailors to their doom by singing **3** Hector **4** Horse (water horse) **5** The Haka **6** Hallowe'en **7** Valhalla **8** 2nd November **9** Garnet **10** Ox **11** Woods **12** Mordred **13** Cuchulainn **14** All Saints' Day **15** Pisces **16** Winter Solstice **17** 1st of May **18** A disastrous end (literally Twilight of the Gods) **19** Galahad **20** Ouija board **21** April Fool's Day **22** Fire **23** 5th January **24** Ash **25** True love **26** Maes Howe **27** Ireland, Wales, Scotland, Isle of Man, Cornwall, Brittany **28** China **29** Raven **30** King Arthur

Quiz 94

1 Jane Horrocks **2** Robin Williams **3** Julian Clary **4** Kathleen Turner
5 Tim Allen **6** Stirling Moss **7** Tom Baker **8** Mel Blanc **9** Antonio
Banderas **10** Hugh Laurie **11** Jeremy Irons **12** Michael Angelis
13 Demi Moore **14** Derek Jacobi **15** Stephen Fry **16** Eddie Murphy
17 Elijah Wood **18** Mel Brooks **19** Dan Castellaneta **20** Frank Oz
21 Bruce Willis **22** Richard Briers **23** Bernard Cribbins **24** Brian Cant
25 Kelsey Grammer **26** Andy Serkis **27** Owen Wilson **28** Cameron
Diaz **29** John Alderton **30** James Earl Jones

Quiz 95

1 (Percy Bysshe) Shelley **2** Elizabeth Barrett & Robert Browning
3 The Owl and the Pussycat **4** The Statue of Liberty **5** John Dryden
6 'Ode to Autumn' **7** Wilfred Owen **8** William Butler Yeats, Seamus
Heaney **9** 'The Night Before Christmas' **10** Grendel **11** 'The Star-
Spangled Banner' **12** 9 **13** Elizabeth Barrett Browning **14** Dylan
Thomas **15** Little Johnny Green **16** 'In Flanders Fields' **17** William
Shakespeare **18** 'The Pied Piper of Hamelin' **19** 6 **20** 'To a Mouse'
21 'The Sorcerer's Apprentice' **22** Thomas Stearns **23** Jeffrey Archer
24 14 **25** Cecil Day-Lewis **26** William Langland **27** Lewis Carroll
28 Lord Byron **29** Andrew Motion **30** Rupert Brooke

Quiz 96

1 James Clerk Maxwell **2** The ballpoint pen **3** 10th **4** Max Planck
5 Joseph Lister **6** 1903 **7** Benjamin Franklin **8** Tim Berners-Lee
9 Copernicus **10** 1859 **11** Guglielmo Marconi **12** 11th **13** The pneu-
matic tyre **14** Thomas Edison **15** Louis Pasteur **16** 1975 **17** Printing
18 1796 **19** Christopher Cockerell **20** Karl Benz **21** 1500 **22** Samuel
Morse **23** Jacques Cousteau **24** Fax machine **25** London
Underground map **26** The food mixer **27** V2 rocket (1944)
28 The lawn mower **29** Thomas Cook **30** Perspiration

Quiz 97

1 Bees **2** Union of European Football Associations **3** Syrah **4** He
followed a trail of string he had left coming in **5** His arm **6** William
Shakespeare **7** Bandana **8** Clone **9** Australian Labor Party **10** 4
11 Vesuvius **12** Music publishers **13** Chromosome **14** Puff the Magic
Dragon **15** Copenhaen **16** 3 years **17** All received honorary knight-
hoods **18** Germany **19** Khaki **20** Bing Crosby **21** Charles II
22 6 o' clock **23** Andorra **24** 8 **25** Green **26** Abolition of slavery
27 Good luck **28** 1958 **29** Grand Old Party (or Republican Party)
30 'Messiah'

Quiz 98

1 Brian Epstein **2** J Robert Oppenheimer **3** The ending of Prohibition in the US **4** Oscar Wilde **5** US anti-draft protesters during Vietnam War **6** Charlton Heston **7** Graham Greene **8** Fred Astaire & Ginger Rogers **9** George Best **10** Music **11** Home **12** Alfred Hitchcock **13** Victoria Adams (or Victoria Beckham) **14** Muhammad Ali **15** Marilyn Monroe **16** Youth **17** British troops in the First World War (the speaker was German) **18** Northern Ireland **19** The proposed Final Solution **20** Elvis Presley **21** Michelangelo **22** The NHS **23** Guy Fawkes **24** William Morris **25** Joseph Stalin **26** Bombing of Pearl Harbor **27** Homer Simpson **28** Mickey Mouse **29** Tony Curtis **30** Richard Nixon

Quiz 99

1 St James's Park **2** 'The Lion, the Witch and the Wardrobe' **3** Janet Jackson **4** 1980 **5** The Police **6** Robert Peel **7** The Undertones' 'Teenage Kicks' **8** The Sweet **9** 'Romeo & Juliet' **10** Uranus **11** 'Futurama' **12** 'The Simpsons' **13** Jessica Simpson **14** 'The Fantastic Four' **15** Fire **16** An orange fire **17** Netherlands **18** Amsterdam **19** Anne Frank **20** New Orleans **21** Hurricane Katrina **22** Low atmospheric pressure **23** England rugby fans **24** South Africa **25** Canary Islands **26** Queen Sofía (or Reina Sofía) **27** Bulgaria **28** Johann Strauss II (or the Younger) **29** Tom & Jerry **30** Sings

Quiz 100

1 They were cousins **2** Angelina Jolie **3** Fatima **4** Emilio Estevez **5** Robert Kennedy **6** Arthur Miller **7** James and John **8** Queen Victoria **9** Oliver Reed **10** Tony Booth **11** Talia Shire **12** Eugene O'Neill **13** 1996 **14** Christopher Guest (Nigel Tufnel in Spinal Tap) **15** Laila Morse (Mo Harris) **16** John Le Mesurier **17** Brother and sister **18** Carrie Fisher (Princess Leia) **19** Patti Boyd **20** The Brothers Karamazov **21** Joy Beverley **22** George Clooney **23** Dante Gabriel Rossetti **24** Gary & Phil Neville **25** Ewan McGregor **26** Nigel Lawson **27** Orville & Wilbur **28** The Brontës **29** Rudyard Kipling **30** Frank Sinatra

Quiz 101

1 Renée & Renato **2** 'If' **3** 'Float On' **4** Richard Harris **5** Boris Pickett & the Crypt Kickers **6** Windsor Davies & Don Estelle **7** Chesney Hawkes **8** 'Two Pints of Lager and a Packet of Crisps, Please' **9** Baha Men **10** 'Woodstock' **11** 'Kung Fu Fighting' **12** 'Pump up the Volume' **13** 'Money' **14** Norman Greenbaum **15** '99 Red Balloons' **16** Bonzo Dog Doo-Dah Band **17** Sugarhill Gang **18** 'Tell Laura I Love Her' **19** 'Spaceman' **20** The Archies **21** Hale & Pace **22** Lou Bega **23** 'Groove Is in the Heart' **24** 'Jilted John' **25** Edison Lighthouse **26** Tribe of Toffs **27** Baz Luhrmann **28** Bobby McFerrin **29** 'Fire' **30** 'Nut Rocker'

Quiz 102

1 Alexander the Great **2** Dougal **3** A fish **4** Dennis the Menace
5 They're all types of cattle **6** Woodworm **7** 1988 **8** A mouse
9 18 (5 front paw and 4 back) **10** A snake **11** Nana **12** A badger
13 Hooves **14** Stonefish **15** A lizard **16** A giant panda **17** An oyster
18 Zoophyte **19** An eyrie **20** Hare **21** Hyena **22** Cranefly or Daddy
Longlegs **23** Koala **24** 5 **25** Butterfly **26** A holt **27** A cod **28** Bell
29 12 **30** Timmy

Quiz 103

1 'King Creole' **2** Howard Hughes **3** 'The Harder They Come' **4** 'Star
Wars' **5** Doc Brown ('Back to the Future') **6** Loretta Lynn **7** Blaine
8 'The Taming of the Shrew' **9** The North **10** Cannes **11** James Joyce
12 'Blade Runner' **13** 'Zulu' **14** Tom Cruise **15** 'Brief Encounter'
16 'A Christmas Story' **17** 'Ride With the Devil' **18** Meg Ryan
19 'Ghostbusters' **20** Inspector Clouseau **21** 'Spy Kids' **22** Sean
Connery **23** 'Chicken Run' **24** Mr Bean **25** Ray Harryhausen
26 Clarence the Angel **27** 'Babe' **28** The Boat **29** Leonardo DiCaprio
30 Nick Nolte

Quiz 104

1 8000 years **2** Normandy **3** Augustus **4** Constantine **5** Cat
6 Copper & Tin **7** Alexander the Great **8** China **9** The Rubicon
10 14th century BC **11** Tunisia **12** 1st century BC **13** Skara Brae
14 Caesar Augustus (or Octavian) **15** Lindisfarne **16** Hannibal
17 410 AD **18** Saul **19** Caligula **20** 4000 years **21** Alexander the
Great **22** David **23** Athens & Sparta **24** Mexico **25** The Emperor
26 Dublin **27** 'Beowulf' **28** The stirrup **29** Pax Romana
30 Buddhism

Quiz 105

1 'The Canterbury Tales' **2** Jacqueline Wilson **3** 'The Tempest'
4 'Little Women' **5** Sauron **6** 'Whisky Galore' **7** Voltaire **8** Costa
Book Awards **9** 'Catch-22' **10** 'To Kill a Mockingbird' **11** Mrs Hudson
12 Gospel of Matthew **13** 'Misery' **14** 'Schindler's Ark' **15** 'Bleak
House' **16** Théoden **17** John **18** Spanish Civil War **19** 'Book of Kells'
20 Jacob Marley **21** 'Kidnapped' **22** 'Good Omens' **23** 'Countdown'
24 Ross McWhirter **25** 'Flashman' **26** 'Christine' **27** MR James
28 JRR Tolkien **29** Silas Marner **30** Irvine Welsh

Quiz 106

1 Teflon **2** Ultraviolet light rays **3** Oxygen **4** Photograph **5** Vet
6 Gold & Copper **7** Chilis **8** 10% **9** Earth **10** Carbon **11** Gold
12 A bolt of lightning **13** 1997 **14** The neutron **15** Hydrogen
16 Radiocarbon Dating **17** Light-Emitting Diode **18** Flux capacitor
19 Vaporisation **20** Astrophysics **21** Copper **22** Geiger counter
23 Light **24** Nuclear fission **25** Solids **26** J Robert Oppenheimer
27 Conductor **28** J **29** 3.6 **30** Atom

Quiz 107

1 WH Auden **2** PG Wodehouse **3** John Fitzgerald Kennedy **4** J Edgar
Hoover **5** WH Smith **6** JK Rowling **7** Master of Ceremonies
8 HJ Heinz **9** William Ewart **10** WC Fields **11** AA Milne **12** Bad
Attitude **13** Kathryn Dawn **14** CS Lewis **15** Blues Boy **16** OJ Simpson
(Orenthal James) **17** FW Woolworth **18** DH Lawrence **19** MC Escher
20 Walker **21** Robert E Lee **22** JD Salinger **23** L Ron Hubbard
24 Polly Jean **25** Malcolm X **26** Herbert George **27** JP Donleavy
28 William Butler **29** TE Lawrence **30** JRR Tolkien

Quiz 108

1 Zimbabwe **2** Mali **3** Algeria **4** Coffee **5** Cape Town **6** Tanzania **7** Diamonds **8** Portuguese **9** Cape of Agulhas **10** The Dutch **11** Casablanca **12** Freetown **13** 5 **14** Uganda **15** Indian Ocean **16** Ethiopia **17** Rorke's Drift **18** Madagascar **19** Lake Victoria **20** Nile crocodile **21** Nigeria **22** 1994 **23** Gorilla **24** Zimbabwe & Zambia **25** Charlize Theron **26** Arabic **27** General Gordon **28** Its ears **29** Israel **30** Boer Wars

Quiz 109

1 John F Kennedy **2** The first left office, the second was assassinated and the third was his replacement (Hayes, Garfield, Arthur) **3** Admiralty Building, Washington **4** George Washington, Thomas Jefferson, Theodore Roosevelt, Abraham Lincoln **5** 'Hail to the Chief' **6** Abraham Lincoln **7** Ronald Reagan **8** Buck **9** Harry S Truman **10** (William) McKinley **11** Thomas Jefferson **12** John F Kennedy **13** Gerald Ford **14** He was the only president of the Confederate States of America **15** Lyndon B Johnson **16** Richard Nixon **17** J Edgar Hoover, FBI Director **18** George Washington **19** Franklin D Roosevelt **20** John F Kennedy **21** Theodore Rooseveldt **22** Franklin D Roosevelt **23** Jack Ruby **24** 43 **25** Woodrow Wilson **26** Bill Clinton **27** Abraham Lincoln **28** Ronald Reagan **29** John F Kennedy **30** Thomas Jefferson

Quiz 110

1 21 **2** Ivan Mauger **3** Virginia Wade **4** Saturday **5** Front **6** Basketball **7** 8 **8** 2 **9** Snooker **10** Vests & Headguards **11** Lawn **12** Le Mans start **13** Baseball **14** Viv Richards **15** 4 **16** Jai Alai **17** 24 **18** Ice Hockey **19** Cassius Clay **20** 'Take Me Out to the Ball Game' **21** June **22** Eldrick **23** Jenny Pitman **24** Skiing & Fencing **25** Hong Kong **26** 2001 **27** 21 **28** 4 **29** 5 **30** Walter Swinburn

Quiz 111

1 Evans **2** Rubeus Hagrid **3** Olivander's **4** It is enchanted to look like the sky outside **5** The Burrow **6** Tom Riddle **7** Wolfsbane **8** Goblins **9** A badger **10** When a seeker catches the golden snitch **11** Severus Snape **12** The Black family **13** The Patronus Charm (or Expecto Patronum) **14** Sirius Black **15** Durmstrang & Beauxbatons **16** 'The Daily Prophet' **17** The Marauders **18** Godric's Hollow **19** Professor Flitwick **20** Azkaban **21** They would die **22** Hippogriff **23** It disappears **24** A Firebolt **25** Draco Malfoy **26** Grunnings (drill makers) **27** Apparate **28** $9^3/_4$ **29** Those who have seen death **30** Zonko's

Quiz 112

1 The Common People, the Rabble **2** Let the Buyer Beware
3 Love Conquers All **4** Cheap, A Good Bargain (literally: good market)
5 May He/She Rest in Peace **6** Composure in the Face Of Danger
(literally: cold blood) **7** Congratulations, Good Luck (Modern Hebrew)
8 Ready-To-Wear, Off-The-Peg **9** Good Luck (Maori) **10** The Sweet
Life, The Good Life **11** Don't Let the Bastards Grind You Down (mock
Latin) **12** One Out of Many or Out of Many, One **13** Gratuity, Tip
14 Love Letter (literally: sweet letter) **15** I Serve **16** In the Open Air
17 Seize the Day, Enjoy the Day **18** Goodbye (Japanese)
19 Afternoon, After Midday **20** Struggle, Strive (Arabic) **21** In the
Act of a Crime (literally: as the crime is blazing); it has come to mean
caught in the act of sexual intercourse **22** Prodigy, Very Talented Child
23 Clean Slate **24** Pleasure in Another's Misfortune **25** In a Test
Tube (literally: in glass) **26** An Essential Requirement (literally: without
which nothing) **27** Singing Without Instrumental Accompaniment
28 For This Particular Purpose **29** Truth in Drunkenness (or Wine);
Drunks Speak the Truth **30** Till We Meet Again, Till We See Each Other
Again

Quiz 113

1 Harold Pinter **2** 'Breath' **3** President Lincoln was shot attending it
4 'A Man For All Seasons' **5** (Antonio) Salieri **6** Arthur Miller **7** Punch
(from 'Punch & Judy' shows) **8** 'Doctor Faustus' **9** Tennessee Williams
10 'The Mousetrap' **11** Sean O'Casey **12** 'Pygmalion' **13** Kevin Spacey
14 London **15** 'Aladdin' **16** Theatre in the round **17** Alan Ayckbourn
18 'The Tempest' **19** George Bernard Shaw, Samuel Beckett **20** Action
21 'Brigadoon' **22** The puritanical Parliament disapproved of them
23 Ewan MacColl **24** Stage manager **25** Tragedy, Comedy & Satire
26 Props **27** 'Oliver!' **28** 'The Importance of Being Earnest'
29 'Oklahoma!' **30** Edinburgh

Quiz 114

1 Mark or Deutschmark **2** 5p **3** 1964 **4** Matthew **5** Charles Darwin
6 Vietnam **7** 1000 Guineas & 2000 Guineas **8** 'Cabaret' **9** Trevor
Francis **10** 882 **11** 12 **12** £250,000 **13** £25 **14** 15 **15** 7 **16** Tuppence
17 None **18** The Bank of England **19** The Queen **20** Armenia
21 The Brinks-Mat Robbery **22** The 20p **23** US dollar **24** Russia
25 21 shillings (today = £1.05) **26** China **27** 'Money, Money, Money'
(Abba) **28** Rand **29** £2 **30** £500

Quiz 115

1 Poisonous toadstools **2** Aniseed or Anise **3** Ivy **4** Mandrake
5 Gumbo or Ladies' Fingers **6** White **7** Formic acid **8** Letchworth in
Hertfordshire (1903) **9** Tomato **10** Opium poppy **11** Bluebell **12** Iris
13 Oats **14** Willow **15** Norway **16** Oscar Wilde **17** Rosemary **18** Yew
19 The restoration of the monarchy in 1660 **20** The RHS (Royal
Horticultural Society) **21** Monty Don **22** Chlorophyll **23** Biennials
24 Holly **25** Oxygen **26** Laurel or Bay **27** Garlic **28** Poinsettia
29 White **30** Water

Quiz 116

1 Peter Kay **2** Richard E Grant **3** Jimmy Saville **4** George Best **5** Vera
Brittain **6** Stephen Fry **7** Kenneth Williams **8** Errol Flynn **9** Adolf
Hitler **10** John Barrowman **11** Gordon Ramsay **12** Lance Armstrong
13 Richard Branson **14** James Robertson Justice **15** Anthony Kiedis
16 Simon Cowell **17** Adam Ant **18** Graeme Obree **19** George Orwell
20 Quentin Crisp **21** Ernest Shackleton **22** Roald Dahl **23** Jane
Goodall **24** Margaret Thatcher **25** Alex Higgins **26** Steve Irwin
27 Arnold Schwarzenegger **28** Madonna **29** Russell Brand
30 Ronnie Corbett

Quiz 117

1 The Doors ('Doors of Perception') **2** 'Boom Bang-a-Bang'
3 The Troggs **4** 'Puppet on a String' **5** Bob Dylan **6** The Animals
7 'Turn! Turn! Turn!' **8** Bob Dylan **9** Keith Moon & John Entwistle
10 The Mamas and the Papas **11** Australia (Melbourne) **12** 'Three
Steps to Heaven' **13** 'My Boy Lollipop' **14** Jane Birkin & Serge
Gainsbourg **15** 'San Francisco (Be Sure to Wear Flowers in your Hair)'
16 Woodstock **17** 'Running Bear' **18** Motown **19** 'Honey' **20** Brian
Jones **21** The Shadows **22** Humble Pie **23** Abraham Lincoln, Martin
Luther King Jr, John and Robert F Kennedy **24** The Supremes
25 Wendy Richard **26** 'As Tears Go By' **27** Altamont **28** 'Distant
Drums' **29** Davy Jones **30** Bobbie Gentry

Quiz 118

1 'Gone With the Wind' **2** 'Titanic' **3** 'Eastern Promises' **4** Kodak
Theatre, Hollywood **5** 'West Side Story' **6** 1929 **7** A gladiator **8** 1
9 'The Return of the King' **10** He was the model for the Oscar statuette
11 First black woman to win **12** 80 **13** Sunday **14** 'All Quiet on the
Western Front' **15** Jack Nicholson **16** 'Gone With the Wind'
17 'Schindler's List' **18** The Academy of Motion Picture Arts & Sciences
19 Paul Newman **20** 'Ryan's Daughter' **21** 40 minutes **22** 'Paper
Moon' **23** 13.5 inches (34cm) **24** 'The Lord of the Rings' **25** One was
given for black-and-white films and one for colour **26** 81st **27** Meryl
Streep **28** James Dean **29** Around 6000 **30** Bob Hope

Quiz 119

1 Lady Jane Grey **2** George V **3** Elizabeth II **4** Caesar Augustus
5 James VI and I (VI of Scotland & I of England) **6** 11th **7** Henry VIII
8 Ireland **9** 6 **10** 7 **11** 60 **12** George III **13** Danish **14** 101
15 Montezuma **16** 1901 **17** Oliver & Richard Cromwell **18** Juan Carlos
19 Abba **20** George III **21** Queen Victoria **22** Edward II of England
and Robert I, King of Scots **23** Albania **24** Bohemia **25** Nicholas II
26 'Britannia' **27** King John **28** Fifth **29** Richard Cromwell
30 Wilhelm II

Quiz 120

1 Peru **2** Ernesto **3** Bonanza **4** Spain **5** Sonoran Desert **6** Peru
7 Montevideo & Buenos Aires **8** Alaska **9** Alberta **10** Brazil
11 Quebec City **12** Maine **13** Quechua **14** Chile **15** Martinique (Mont
Pelée) **16** Panama Canal **17** Mexico City **18** Cuba **19** Argentina
20 Bolivia & Paraguay **21** Chile **22** UK & USA **23** The Bahamas
24 State Route 1 **25** Peru & Boliva **26** River of January **27** Brazil
28 Jamaica **29** La Paz (Bolivia) **30** Barbados

Quiz 121

1 Todd Carty **2** Penelope Keith **3** Rudolph Walker **4** James Bolam **5** David Duchovny **6** Emma Thompson **7** Gordon Jackson **8** Cheryl Campbell **9** Ian Richardson **10** Peter Kay (he also plays Safety Officer Keith Lard and DJ Paul le Roy on the show) **11** David Jason **12** Thelma Barlow **13** Teri Hatcher **14** Richard Briers **15** John Thaw **16** Derek Jacobi **17** Simon Jones **18** Barbara Flynn **19** Rob Morrow **20** Ian McShane **21** Kathy Staff **22** Paula Wilcox **23** Robert Lindsay **24** Stephen Tompkinson **25** Peter Wingfield **26** Philip Glenister **27** Dennis Waterman **28** John Schneider **29** Tamsin Greig **30** Nicholas Lyndhurst

Quiz 122

1 'Queen's Greatest Hits (volume 1)' **2** Sandi Thom **3** Elvis Presley **4** Coldplay **5** 'Cum on Feel the Noize' **6** 2002 **7** Westlife **8** 'Candle in the Wind 97' by Elton John **9** 'Because We Want To' **10** Thunderclap Newman **11** Band Aid, 'Do They Know it's Christmas?' **12** John Lennon **13** Donny Osmond **14** 1975 **15** The Beatles **16** 'Don't Look Back in Anger' **17** 'Barbie Girl' **18** 'Barbados' (by Typically Tropical) **19** 'Deeper Underground' **20** The Young Ones **21** 'More than a Woman' **22** Lily Allen **23** Freda Payne **24** 'Rat Trap' **25** Razorlight **26** Holly Valance **27** 1999 **28** 'Teletubbies Say Eh-oh!' **29** Frank & Nancy Sinatra **30** 'It's Raining Men'

Quiz 123

1 Juneau **2** Botswana **3** California **4** Canada **5** The Eiger **6** Exmoor
7 Morocco, Algeria, Tunisia **8** Nimbostratus **9** Muscat **10** Egypt
11 Melbourne **12** The Ouse **13** Hibernia **14** Left **15** Glaciers **16** Rabat
17 Cyclades **18** The Khyber Pass **19** Atlantic **20** The Irish Sea
21 Melbourne **22** The Aegean **23** Uganda **24** The Netherlands
25 The Potomac **26** Zimbabwe **27** Gibraltar **28** San Francisco
29 Italy & France **30** The Nile

Quiz 124

1 Munster **2** Heineken Cup **3** European Challenge Cup **4** 1992-93
5 The World Trade Center (Tower 1) **6** Nicolas Cage **7** Francis Ford
Coppola **8** 'Apocalypse Now' **9** 4 **10** Nick Park **11** Green Park
12 Fireworks Music (or Music for the Royal Fireworks) **13** Guy Fawkes
14 'V for Vendetta' **15** King Solomon's Mines **16** Wisdom **17** Owl
18 Parliament **19** Iceland (founded 930) **20** Denmark **21** Jutland
22 Britain & Germany **23** Munich **24** Steven Spielberg **25** 'The
Blues Brothers' **26** 'Thriller' by Michael Jackson **27** Peter Pan
28 Wendy **29** 'Are You Being Served?' **30** 'Dad's Army'

Quiz 125

1 Marilyn Monroe **2** Whoopi Goldberg **3** Tom Cruise **4** Fred Astaire **5** David Tennant **6** Jennifer Aniston **7** Sylvester McCoy **8** Jane Seymour **9** Ben Kingsley **10** Helen Mirren **11** John Wayne **12** Barbara Windsor **13** Charlie Sheen **14** Michael Caine **15** Dan Ackroyd **16** Mr T **17** Jamie Foxx **18** Woody Allen **19** Catherine Deneuve **20** Diana Dors **21** Joaquin Phoenix **22** Winona Ryder **23** Diane Keaton **24** Julie Andrews **25** Natalie Portman **26** Kevin Spacey **27** Susan Sarandon **28** Rock Hudson **29** Michael Crawford **30** Stewart Granger

Quiz 126

1 Prince **2** Jason Donovan **3** She stars in Disney's 'Hannah Montana' **4** The Simpsons **5** Take That **6** 'Kiss the Girl' **7** The Rembrandts **8** Ireland **9** Melanie Chisholm or Sporty Spice **10** Mike Flowers Pops **11** 1997 **12** Lightning Seeds **13** 3 **14** 'Do the Bartman' **15** 'Praise You' **16** 'Freedom' **17** Cliff Richard **18** Nirvana **19** Boyzone, Westlife **20** Dave Matthews Band **21** 'Things Can Only Get Better' **22** Jarvis Cocker **23** 'Say You'll Be There' **24** 'Bohemian Rhapsody', Queen **25** 'The Power', 'Rhythm is a Dancer' **26** Take That **27** Pulp **28** UB40 **29** Shakespears Sister **30** The Foo Fighters

Quiz 127

1 Grace Brothers **2** George Peppard **3** Orange County **4** Rik Mayall & Adrian Edmondson **5** The Trotters (from 'Only Fools & Horses') **6** 'Beverly Hills 90210' **7** Bob Holness **8** 'Cheers' **9** Marty **10** Walmington-on-Sea **11** Terry Venables **12** Scout **13** Des Lynam **14** 'The Clangers' **15** 'Nightingales' **16** UNCLE **17** Ben **18** Psoraisis **19** Tony Soprano **20** 'Pot Black' **21** Green **22** Newcastle-upon-Tyne **23** 'Countdown' **24** 2003 **25** Quod Erat Demonstrandum (which was to be proved) **26** Ceefax **27** 'Captain Pugwash' **28** 'Brideshead Revisited' **29** 'Captain Scarlet' **30** Jason Connery

Quiz 128

1 Manchester United, Arsenal, Chelsea, Blackburn Rovers **2** Rosenborg **3** South Korea & Japan (2002) **4** Alan Shearer **5** 23 **6** Bayern Munich **7** Germany **8** Lazio **9** Henrik Larsson **10** 92 **11** Italy (2006) **12** Sunderland **13** Sven-Göran Eriksson **14** Bobby Charlton **15** 2003 **16** Spain **17** Stade de France **18** 7 (up to the start of season 2008-09) **19** Celtic **20** Inverness Caledonian Thistle **21** They are Welsh teams playing in the English football league **22** Michel Platini **23** Liverpool & Nottingham Forest **24** Benfica **25** Royal Engineers **26** Ricky Tomlinson **27** Plymouth Argyle **28** England's Premier League **29** Manchester United & Chelsea **30** Sven-Göran Eriksson

Quiz 129

1 Whisky **2** Freedom fries **3** Death **4** On the road to Mandalay
5 Thomas Edison **6** 3 **7** Copenhagen **8** The month of August **9** 1
10 Albert Einstein **11** Jamaica **12** Basil **13** Zebra, Panda, Pelican, Puffin
14 49 **15** Millennium Falcon **16** BMW **17** Banbury Cross
18 Switzerland **19** Gunpowder **20** 22 **21** Green **22** Derby, 2000
Guineas, St Leger **23** Starboard **24** Left **25** Dale Arden **26** Diabetes
27 A tree (cork oak) **28** Iman **29** 0º **30** 5 furlongs

Quiz 130

1 1955 **2** Belle **3** Donald Duck **4** Tears him up **5** Ariel **6** 'Beauty and
the Beast' **7** 1966 **8** 'The Little Mermaid' **9** 'Song of the South'
10 Mickey Mouse **11** Pirates of the Caribbean **12** 'Lilo & Stitch'
13 Joss Whedon **14** Pixar **15** Simba **16** 'Snow White & the Seven
Dwarfs' **17** Jafar **18** Robin Williams **19** Epcot **20** France **21** David
Tomlinson **22** 'A Whole New World' **23** Herbie **24** Touchstone
Pictures **25** Monsters, Inc. **26** 3 (Paris, Tokyo, Hong Kong) **27** 'High
School Musical' **28** 'You've Got a Friend in Me' **29** 'Ratatouille'
30 Cruella De Vil

Quiz 131

1 India **2** Cornershop **3** Bob Dylan **4** Erasure **5** Roy Orbison, Tom Petty, George Harrison, Geoff Lynne, Bob Dylan **6** Japanese pop music **7** Robbie Williams **8** Bonnie Tyler **9** Charlotte Church **10** 50 Cent **11** Annie Lennox **12** Mud **13** Red Hot Chili Peppers **14** 'Waterloo' by Abba **15** Nickelback **16** Green Day **17** Bryan Adams **18** Travis **19** 'Born to Run' **20** Jay-Z **21** Take That **22** Babyshambles **23** Morrissey **24** 'Albatross' **25** 'Addicted to Love' **26** Kaiser Chiefs **27** The Killers **28** Leo Sayer **29** John **30** Jarvis Cocker

Quiz 132

1 'Buffy the Vampire Slayer' **2** 'Cheers' **3** 'Dangermouse' **4** 'Doctor Who' **5** 'The X-Files' **6** 'The Flintstones' **7** 'Life on Mars' **8** 'Scooby Doo, Where Are You!' **9** 'Phoenix Nights' **10** 'Z-Cars' **11** 'Porridge' **12** 'Friends' **13** 'The Practice' **14** 'Wacky Races' **15** 'Fimbles' **16** 'Stargate SG-1' **17** 'JAG' **18** 'Are You Being Served?' **19** 'Happy Days' **20** 'The Likely Lads' **21** 'The Six Million Dollar Man' **22** 'Man About the House' **23** 'Dynasty' **24** 'Inspector Morse' **25** 'Casualty' **26** 'Beverly Hills 90210' **27** 'Doctor Who' **28** 'Hercules: The Legendary Journeys' **29** 'The Crocodile Hunter' **30** 'Dallas'

Quiz 133

1 56 **2** The Seven Deadly Sins **3** Aries **4** 13 **5** Algebra **6** 12
7 20 **8** Glasgow & Edinburgh **9** 1 **10** 65 **11** 5 **12** The number 13
13 2 **14** Coins, cups, batons & swords **15** 81 **16** 7 **17** 15 **18** 2
19 The Invisible Woman **20** 52 **21** 6 **22** 10 **23** 13 **24** 2000 **25** 4
26 Envy, Gluttony, Greed, Lust, Wrath (or Anger), Pride, Sloth
27 San Francisco **28** Cardinal directions **29** Seven Corporal Works of
Mercy **30** One hundred

Quiz 134

1 'A Hard Day's Night' **2** 'Moon River' **3** 'As Time Goes By'
4 'Anyone Can Fall In Love' **5** Howard Shore **6** 'Pat Garrett and Billy
the Kid' **7** 'Hair' **8** 'GI Blues' **9** 'Johnny Todd' **10** Eric Idle **11** Aled
Jones **12** 'MASH' **13** Marilyn Monroe **14** Bud Flanagan **15** 'The Per-
suaders!' **16** 'Deliverance' **17** Tim Rice & Andrew Lloyd-Webber
18 'Calamity Jane' **19** 'Handbags & Gladrags' **20** Alabama 3
21 'Captain Pugwash' **22** 'Top Hat' **23** 'Raindrops Keep Fallin' on My
Head' **24** Ronnie Hazlehurst **25** 'I Could Be So Good for You'
26 Mike Batt **27** Mike Post **28** Divine Comedy **29** 'Inspector Morse'
30 Danny Elfman

Quiz 135

1 'Casablanca' **2** 'The Usual Suspects' **3** 'The Diary of Anne Frank'

4 'The Empire Strikes Back' **5** Jurassic Park' **6** 'Love Story'

7 'Titanic' **8** 'It's a Wonderful Life' **9** 'In Which We Serve'

10 'Butch Cassidy & The Sundance Kid' **11** 'The Princess Bride'

12 'The Magnificent Seven' **13** 'Raging Bull' **14** 'The Godfather'

15 'Gone with the Wind' **16** 'Some Like It Hot' **17** 'Ghostbusters'

18 'Jaws' **19** 'Psycho' **20** 'My Fair Lady' **21** 'The Searchers'

22 'Apollo 13' **23** 'The Incredible Shrinking Man' **24** 'The Wizard of
Oz' **25** 'White Christmas' **26** 'Tron' **27** 'Ben-Hur' **28** 'Back to the
Future' **29** 'The Blues Brothers' **30** 'Pirates of the Caribbean: Curse of
the Black Pearl'